VALENCIA

Also in the Series

Buenos Aires by Jason Wilson
Oxford by David Horan
Mexico City by Nick Caistor
Rome by Jonathan Boardman
Madrid by Elizabeth Nash
Venice by Martin Garrett
Lisbon by Paul Buck
Havana by Claudia Lightfoot
New York City by Eric Homberger
Brussels by André de Vries
Prague by Richard Burton
Calcutta by Krishna Dutta
Helsinki by Neil Kent
Edinburgh by Donald Campbell
San Francisco by Mick Sinclair
Cambridge by Martin Garrett
Kingston by David Howard
Athens by Michael Llewellyn Smith
Istanbul by Peter Clark
Hamburg by Matthew Jefferies
Lagos by Kaye Whiteman
Miami by Anthony P. Maingot
Sicily by Joseph Farrell
The Scottish Highlands by Andrew Beattie
Brittany by Wendy Mewes
Bali by Arthur Cotterell

VALENCIA

A Cultural History

MICHAEL EAUDE

Interlink Books

An imprint of Interlink Publishing Group, Inc.
Northampton, Massachusetts

First published in 2020 by

Interlink Books
An imprint of Interlink Publishing Group, Inc.
46 Crosby Street, Northampton, MA 01060
www.interlinkbooks.com

Published simultaneously in the UK by Signal Books Limited

Library of Congress Cataloging-in-Publication Data
Names: Eaude, Michael, author.
Title: Valencia: a cultural history / Michael Eaude.
Other titles: Valencia, a cultural history
Description: Northampton: Interlink Books, 2019. | Includes
    bibliographical references and index.
Identifiers: LCCN 2019032407 | ISBN 9781623719319 (paperback)
Subjects: LCSH: Valencia (Spain)—Civilization. | Valencia (Spain)—
    Description and travel.
Classification: LCC DP402.V19 E28 2019 | DDC 946.7/63—dc23
LC record available at https://lccn.loc.gov/2019032407

Typesetting: Tora Kelly
Cover Image: Helena G H/Shutterstock
Photographs: Marisa Asensio

Printed and bound in the United States of America

Dedication

For Marisa, with love

Contents

Introduction xi
    A Note on Language (xiv)
    Acknowledgments (xvi)

Part One: Moors, Jews, and Popes 1

1: No One Left to Massacre 3
    Industrial Port (10)
    She Never Touched a Penny (13)

2: A Kingdom Won and Lost 21
    My Sweet Lord (23)
    Moorish Legacy: Water, Oranges, Silk (25)
    Two Languages (28)
    Expulsion (33)
    The New Order Decree (35)
    Why Don't You Write in English? (39)

3: Valencia's Golden Age 43
    Wild Heart (43)
    Martorell: Psychology and Bawdiness (51)
    The Abbess and the Doctor (58)

4: The Dukes of Gandia 63
    The Family: the Borja Popes (64)
    The Saint (73)
    Grau de Gandia (78)
    Tourist Gandia (81)

5. Anti-Pope and Tiger: Peníscola and Morella 87
    The Anti-Pope (90)
    Virgin Hills and Golden Harbor (93)
    After the King, Cabrera (98)

Part Two: Cities..107

6: Benidorm: Blowsy, Beautiful, and Corrupt.............................109
    Coastal Towns (110)
    Sparkling Dream Town (115)
    Bikini (118)
    The Island of Benidorm (125)
    Legendary Land (129)

7. Valencia 1: The Friendly Labyrinth 135
    Insults (136)
    Enter By Train (138)
    Silk (144)
    Fascism (147)
    Sistine Chapel (150)
    Silk Exchange (151)

8: Valencia 2: Three Statues 155
    Falles (156)
    Cathedral (160)
    Strangling Thought (167)
    Russafa (175)

9: Valencia 3: Along the Dry River..177
    Seawards (184)
    Our Guggenheim (188)
    Calatrava: Flown in from Outer Space (192)

10: The Party's Never Over 199
    Anti-Catalanism (200)
    The Pope, Racing Cars, and Yachts (204)
    We Are the Best (207)
    Corruption (211)

11: Alacant: Luminous and the Place of the Tragedy.................221
    Mission Impossible (227)
    Commercial City (230)
    Anarchist Alcoi (233)
    What a Brutal Life! (240)

12: Elx: Umbrellas of the Desert 243
    Dates (244)
    The Iberian Lady (248)
    Dishonest Beaches (250)
    Very Stressful (253)

Part Three: Twentieth-Century Blues 255

13: The Spanish Zola and the Light-filled Barbarian.................. 257
    The Cabin (262)
    The Frightful Chalet (265)
    Light (270)

14: Defeat of Revolutionary Hope... 275
    The Map of Horror (275)
    Social Revolution (281)
    Iron Column (286)
    The Propaganda War (290)
    Dead in Custody (292)
    The Rearguard (295)

15: No One Gets Out of Here, Even in Dreams........................ 299
    The Wanderer (299)
    Crow Manuscript (302)
    Watching the Anarchists (304)
    Daily Life in the Revolution (307)
    "I await death while singing" (311)

16: Empty Beauty.. 319
    Bare Rock (320)
    Land of Emigration (325)
    No Young Women (330)
    Harsh Beauty (335)

17: Valencia's Market Garden and Great Lake 339
    Horta and Central Market (339)
    Paella (344)
    Venetian Mirror (347)
    Rice (350)
    White Blossom (351)
    Mercadona (355)
    One Great Orange Garden (357)
    The Friar's Kitchen (362)

Bibliography... 365

Glossary 370

Index of Places and People... 373

Introduction

This book is not a guidebook, though a lot of places are described; not a history book, though it summarizes many past events; not a political book, although it discusses identity, war, corruption, and modern politics; nor is it literary criticism, though several writers (and some painters) are discussed. A hybrid. What else could a book about so diverse and complex a country be?

The book seeks to celebrate and explain Valencia, not just the capital city but what is today known as the Valencian Community, comprising the Spanish provinces of Castelló, València, and Alacant, the *país valencià*, Valencian land. Its geography is privileged, with a warm climate and hundreds of kilometers of beaches, along with forested mountains and ancient towns of Moorish origin. Its history is complex and fascinating, with an Arab legacy, a strong Spanish state pushing at its inland backdoor, and a coast open to trade, pirates, and Mediterranean winds. Its politics are conflictual, with radically opposed definitions of Valencia's identity.

The journalist Enric Juliana explains:

> The *país valencià* is the most delicate and inexact territory in the Hispanic mosaic. Strategic, complex, and inclined to tensions. Frontier between North and South. Between Madrid and Barcelona. Between the Castilian [Spanish] and Catalan languages. Between the old trading spirit and new speculative temptations. Between factories and manna from tourism. Frontier between vitality and empty ostentation. Frontier

between city and countryside. Frontier between
Moors and Christians. A land of festivals, because
only partying can civilize so many contradictions.[1]

This book has no overarching theme. Complexities of identity
make up one thread that runs through the book. A second
is corruption, from Pope Callixtus III to modern Valencian
presidents, Eduardo Zaplana and Francisco Camps.
The Partido Popular (PP) that governed the Valencian
Community from 1995 to 2015 is sunk in an unprecedented
mire of trials and imprisonment for corruption. Wars, most of
them lost, provide another recurring theme. Tourism, the big
money-earner from the 1960s on, is a fourth thread. The long
Valencian coastline has been ravaged by mass tourism's hotels
and apartment blocks. This is true, but needs to be nuanced:
much of the coast has been victim of cement and brutalist
architecture, but (a fifth thread), despite everything, a parallel
world of marshes (both sinister and beautiful, these places
that are neither land nor sea), empty beaches and orange
groves still exists. As do the remote, depopulated mountains
of inland Valencia.

The book is divided into three parts. The first five
chapters deal with history, though not exclusively. I have tried
to weave history around geography. Thus, Chapter 1 discusses
the Romans and Jews in the context of Sagunt; Chapter 4
looks at the Borja (Borgia) family through Gandia; and
Chapter 5 recalls the schismatic pope, Papa Luna, at Península
and explains the Carlist Wars through the charismatic
Ramon Cabrera, Count of Morella. Chapter 2 is different: it
summarizes the thirteenth-century conquest of Valencia by
Jaume I of Catalonia through to the loss of its *furs* (Charter)
in 1707. And Chapter 3 is one of three literary interludes

---

1   Maceda, p.11.

throughout the book: it discusses the flowering of Valencia's Golden fifteenth Century, particularly the major poet Ausiàs March, as tormented and contradictory as his country.

Part Two covers cities: Benidorm, Valencia, Alacant, and Elx. Of the three parts, this is the most geographical. Chapter 6 discusses mass tourism and the glorious (or horrific) success of Benidorm, the resort that has become a household name in Britain. Chapters 7, 8, and 9 focus on the city of Valencia: its Golden Century's buildings, its river converted to a long, winding park and its new architecture. Chapter 10 explains politics today: the PP's project to put Valencia on the map with big events and buildings and its failure, bankrupting the country. Chapter 11 goes south to Alacant, a commercial city, and Alcoi, center of working-class revolt. Chapter 12 looks still further south, to Elx, Oriola, and the British residents of the coast.

Part Three discusses the 1936–39 Civil War and its continuing impact (Chapter 14) and two writers of the Civil War, the poet Miguel Hernández and novelist Max Aub (Chapter 15). Chapter 13 is half-literary, dealing with the novels and politics of the torrential and internationally-renowned Vicente Blasco Ibáñez, and half-painterly, discussing Blasco Ibáñez's contemporary, Joaquín Sorolla. Chapter 16 looks at a mountain enclave to highlight its stark beauty and the sad depopulation of rural Spain. Chapter 17 discusses what we eat: paella, rice dishes, almonds, and the oranges for which Valencia is famous.

This is a beautiful land damaged by ugly high-rise, speculation, and corruption. It is riven by conflict. Yet, despite everything, it remains full of the light that shines from the paintings of Sorolla, the energy of Blasco Ibáñez, the joy and excess of its ceramics, architecture, food, and festivals. The *país valencià* is hard to understand, but easy to like.

A Note on Language

I have opted to use Valencian for place names, though at times it may sound strange. Few in English say Alacant (Alicante) or Elx (Elche). I have preferred to use Valencian names, both because it is a minority language, under pressure from a world language, and also for a political reason: Spanish centralist nationalism is hostile to the state's minority languages.

Language is a hot potato in Valencia. Some people strongly identify with the idea of Greater Catalonia and the *països catalans* (Catalan-speaking Lands) that include the whole Catalan-speaking area (Catalonia, the Balearics, Valencia, and Andorra). Others identify equally fiercely with Spain and treat Valencian/Catalan as a lesser, regional language. The PP and the right in general have built their recent power on a ferocious anti-Catalanism that conceals subservience to Spain. They insist that Catalan and Valencian are different languages. They are, but only in the sense that British and American English are different languages. As the British and Americans sometimes say of English, Valencia and Catalonia are separated by a common language.

Though I have opted for terms and names in Valencian, at times I use the Spanish word instead of the Valencian/Catalan one, for example, in Chapter 16, on the Spanish-speaking Rincón de Ademuz. And when discussing Blasco Ibáñez's novels, I put *huerta* for the great market-garden around Valencia city instead of *horta*. Why? Because the author used the Spanish word. No full consistency is possible, which is as it should be, for Valencians will use phrases all the time from the other language that is not their mother tongue.

Sometimes I have anglicized the names. For example, Valencia is written with an accent in Valencian, València, but the name is so familiar without an accent to English-language readers that I have omitted it. However, I have written Castelló and Xàbia, even though in English these towns are usually referred to as Castellón and Jávea, since English maps and guidebooks tend to follow the Spanish, not the Valencian.

A further language difficulty is whether to call the language Valencian or Catalan. I move between the two names, as I believe along with the majority of Valencians that the two languages are the same (though there are many different words and forms). I agree with the singer Ovidi Montllor's elegant, eloquent, and polemical formulation: "I speak Catalan in the style of Valencia."

ACKNOWLEDGMENTS

I am particularly indebted to Marisa Asensio and David C. Hall, who read parts of the book and helped me reduce repetitions and errors. The many mistakes and stupid remarks that remain are mine.

I am grateful to the following who assisted me so generously with their time and knowledge:

Esther Abellán, Brian Anglo, the late Paco Camarasa, Isa Compte, Santi Donaire, Andy Durgan, Anthony Eaude, Raúl Eslava, Vicky Hayward, Mariado Hinojosa, Angela Jackson, Víctor Maceda, Herlinda Murciano, Teresa Navès, Josep Maria Garcia i Cunillera, Josep Maria Núñez, Javier Parra, Xavi Robles, Ingrid Roddis, Miles Roddis, José Luis Rodilla, the late Lluïsa Roig, Antonio Sánchez Hernández, Mariano Sánchez Soler, Empar Sanchis, Christopher Snook, Concha Tormo, Jason Webster, and Sid Williamson.

PART ONE:
Moors, Jews, and Popes

Thoughtful? Scornful? Carving by the main
door of Valencia's *llotja*

The gate into the Jewish quarter, Sagunt

1: No One Left to Massacre

"I have been the cause of great disaster"

Queen Isabel I of Castile

History gets moving in what is today the *país valencià* with Hannibal's attack on Saguntum, which started the Second Punic War in 219 BCE. It is not clear why this most famous of Carthaginian generals chose to break a peace treaty with Rome and attack Rome's prosperous ally, Saguntum, then the first big town on the coast south of the Ebro. According to Livy, reliable historian but Roman propagandist, it was Hannibal's ambition and warlike nature that led him to deliberately provoke the eighteen-year-long war. Even the Carthaginian senate, back in North Africa, was dubious of the enterprise, but saw little choice but to support its general.

The siege of Saguntum lasted some eight months. Hannibal himself was severely wounded in the thigh by a javelin. On finally breaching the walls of the starving town, Hannibal (recovered) offered the Iberians their lives on condition that, in Livy's words, they were "willing to depart from Saguntum, unarmed, each with two garments." The town elders' noble, or foolish, reply was to light a fire, stoke it with possessions of value, and then themselves jump into the flames. Every surviving adult was put to death.

During the siege, cannibalism was rumored. Surrender was not contemplated. Spanish nationalists exalt this resistance to Africans, like the defense of Numantia (near

3

Soria) against the Romans in the following century, as the precursor of the heroic Spanish character. Even today, Sagunt's large and glossy tourist leaflet declares: "The city wrote a glorious page in the history of Spain due to the courage and heroism with which it confronted the invader." Spain? But Spain did not then exist. History is often the appropriation of the past to the glory of today's rulers.

After Hannibal's final defeat by Scipio Africanus' armies in 201 BCE, the town followed the destiny of most of the Iberian Peninsula, living for six more centuries under Roman rule until the fall of the Roman Empire, then Visigothic rule, then Moorish rule from the eighth century until Jaume I's troops drove the Moors out of the Valencia area in the 1230s (see Chapter 2). Remains of all these periods can be seen in the city of Sagunto in Spanish, Sagunt in Catalan or Morvedre (perhaps from *muri veteres*, old walls) as it was known for about a thousand years until 1877. The county surrounding Sagunt is still called the *Camp de Morvedre*.

Throughout Spain, throughout Europe, castles in various stages of ruin squat on top of strategic hills. There are Roman ruins all over, too. Few, though, are as huge or as strategic as Sagunt's. The novelist Rose Macaulay, in her 1949 travel book *Fabled Shore*, found "that splendid, breath-taking, castled Roman-Iberian-Moorish pile of walls and houses on its steep rocky hill."[2] The castle, the walled top of the hill, is 800 meters long and was the site of the Celtiberian, pre-Roman town, called (unfortunately, in our language) Arse.

From its foundation in about 500 BCE right up to the mid-twentieth century, the top of the hill was a military encampment. Miles Roddis catches the place's desolation and its long history: "Here up high, rambling through the

---

2   Macaulay, p.86.

tangle of cacti and chaos of shaped stones, you can sense the loneliness of soldiers over centuries, drafted to this lonely eyrie to watch over the plain below."[3]

Once the prize for Hannibal, the hill later became the main defense of Valencia, the city twenty miles south that was not even dreamed of when Hannibal attacked Arse/Saguntum, but which became the area's principal city after the Christian conquests of the thirteenth century. More recently, in the French invasion of Spain at the start of the nineteenth century (known in English as the Peninsular War), Napoleon's Marshal Suchet took and sacked Sagunt and its castle as the prelude to occupying Valencia.

Arse was a prosperous Celitiberian town that traded across the Western Mediterranean and minted its own coinage. It was confident in its alliance with Rome. Livy laments the vacillations of the Roman Senate in failing to come to its rescue when attacked by Hannibal. Like Valencia itself, later, and many Mediterranean towns, the Iberian trading town was not actually on the coast, but a few miles inland, as protection from invaders and, later, pirates. Nonetheless, the fate of the Iberians reminds us that no castle is impregnable. Today the steep climb is rewarded by long views of the coast and the rich plain covered by oranges. It is still as Rose Macaulay found it:

> The walls, towers and gates are mostly Moorish and mediaeval, with Roman or Iberian foundations; there are remains of a Roman temple, sculptures, fragments, capitals, inscriptions, tessellated pavement; an Arab cistern, a mediaeval mill. A fascinating jumble of ages ...[4]

---

3   Roddis, p.120.
4   Macaulay, p.87.

There are many castles better conserved. Sagunt's are little more than half-fallen walls and heaps of fallen stone among the cacti. Bits of Roman pillar lie around. It looks as if Suchet had only just left.

Halfway up the twisting road to the castle, you come to what looks like an enormous warehouse wall with loading docks at varying heights. The wall is the back of the Roman theater, restored in 1992–94 and at first sight looking as abominable as its detractors proclaim. The original eroded Roman seating, carved into the brown rock, was covered in pale marble in the restoration.

The socialists were in power in the Valencian Community until 1995. The conservative PP (Partido Popular—People's Party) in opposition took the restoration

Restored Roman Theater with castle behind

of the theater to court, alleging that the theater should be returned to its original state. A national monument should not be defiled. Ruins should remain ruins. The courts agreed and, as recently as 2008, Spain's Supreme Court ordered the demolition of the 1994 restoration within eighteen months. Then, in 2009, at the *request* of the PP, who were now in government, the Valencian Supreme Court ruled that this demolition was impossible. So the reform remains. It is what we see today.

Enter the theater itself and speak (no need to shout) across the new seats of marble toward the huge stage and you realize the quality of the acoustics of this open-air theater. Walk through the entrance corridors beneath the seating. Look at the crumbling, ancient seats on both sides of the theater, left as a memento of how things were. Maybe the theater could have been restored better, but surely it is positive that, after millennia of abandon, it has been rescued. Now the summer festival of theater is held here. Old pictures show the stage area completely destroyed, by time, by Suchet's army (Rose Macaulay: "Suchet's for-ever-damned soldiers did their worst against it, as against all monuments of the past"), and by builders: many of the theater's Roman stones now form part of the town's houses. Richard Ford, the cantankerous Tory who described 1830s Spain with maximum prejudice against French and Catholics and with subtle discernment on other questions, says that Suchet used the theater stones to rebuild the castle's fortifications. And "mayors and monks have converted the shattered marbles to their base purposes." Old ruins are free quarries.

A restoration like this theater's, where you can see clearly what is original and what is new, is refreshing. At Tarragona, 200 kilometers up the coast, the Roman theater is more beautiful, but it is hard to know what is new and what is old. Similarly here, in 2017, workmen were repairing the Sagunt castle battlements. When you look up from the theater, it looks like a "real" castle, the battlements etched brown against the sky, but they are an unacknowledged contemporary restoration. Despite the white, bare modernity of the seating, it is still a great, open-air Roman theater. From its upper rows the spectator can enjoy nature and art simultaneously: the sweep of the coast behind the dense green of the plain's trees and crops, and the performance on the stage below.

Sagunt's ancient theater has been an ideological battleground as much as the castle has been a literal one. The theater was declared a National Monument (the first in Spain) in 1896. On one of the passages into the seating (on the far side, same level as entrance), a plaque commemorates a 1947 performance, in the ruins of the theater, of a version of Cervantes' novel *Don Quijote*. It was the 400th anniversary of Cervantes' birth. The plaque makes clear how the Franco dictatorship (1939–77) was using Spain's greatest author to celebrate a Spanish-nationalist view of history. In truth, there is no great Iberian root, or Roman stolidity, or Visigothic Christianity underlying modern Spain. Like nearly all countries, Spain is a mixture of invasions and migrations, as the castle's successive occupants make clear. Unfortunately, many of its modern rulers, whether the dictatorship or the contemporary PP, deny this diversity.

There is a lot else to see at Sagunt. The fine History Museum is in the old Exchange (*llotja*), a fourteenth-century house on the street leading up to the castle and theater. Its great round-arched stone doors are characteristic of this old quarter and of the *jueria*, the Jewish quarter of narrow, winding, steep alleys, on the right of this street (more below).

Sagunt can boast too a head of Diana, the only vestige in the town from pre-Hannibal times. Allegedly, Hannibal spared it for religious reasons. There is a Roman street underneath a square near the railway station. And coming down the hill, in the main square beside the town hall and in front of his birthplace, there is a bust to Sagunt's most famous modern son, the blind composer Joaquín Rodrigo (1903-99), known internationally for his *Concierto de Aranjuez* (1939). There have been thousands of versions by artists ranging from Demis Roussos to Led Zeppelin of this Civil War lament for guitar and orchestra. The use of a guitar playing with and against a classical orchestra, without it being drowned by all the instruments, was highly original. Miles Davis adapted the *adagio*, the second movement, in his *Sketches of Spain* (1960) and said enticingly, "That melody is so strong that the softer you play it, the stronger it gets, and the stronger you play it, the weaker it gets."[5]

The melody's power lies in its constant beat, expressing melancholy and despair, finally resolved in Rodrigo's acceptance of pain. Music like this transmits powerful, basic feeling. Miles Davis set the piece on its path to international renown, but it was flamenco maestro Paco de Lucía's 1991 version that Rodrigo himself praised as the best he had ever heard.

Entrance to all Sagunt's monuments is free, unusual at contemporary tourist attractions. This reflects the strangeness of the city. It is a great, historic site that one expects to be flooded by tourists. Yet there are few restaurants and no classy hotels in the town. Indeed, for any hotels at all you have to walk a mile from the central square, nestling under the castle, to the railway station. The pick of the several cheap hotels here is the Azahar, the Orange-Blossom Hotel. It is the only one recommended in this book, for its proprietors in 2017 were the happiest and most friendly hoteliers.

---

5   Miles Davis, CD case.

Industrial Port

The whole Valencian coastline was little exploited by tourism till the 1960s boom. This passed Sagunt by, as there are two Sagunts, the monumental town five kilometers inland described above, and Port de Sagunt, on the shore. This brief journey represents a leap from Roman monuments to a Europe ravaged by the loss of its heavy industry. For Port de Sagunt is an ex-industrial town. Its industry meant it never became a beach resort for foreign visitors. Today it is a low-rise, working-class resort, specializing in "internal tourism," i.e. from the rest of Spain.

Port de Sagunt was founded only in 1900. To export iron ore, a special railway running 160 kilometers from the Ojos Negros mines, in the mountains of Teruel, to the newly built Sagunt harbor, was constructed. Spain's neutrality in World War I then brought prosperity to the export industry. In 1917 the Sagunt steel works was built, meaning that iron ore was not just exported but converted to steel in Spain. The plant's success brought waves of migration from the Spanish countryside and the working-class Spanish-speaking beach town developed, so that now Port de Sagunt is larger than the original Sagunt.

The Civil War brought disaster. Used for armaments manufacturing for the Republic, the steel plant was bombed. Post-war, the Basque firm Altos Hornos de Vizcaya rebuilt the blast furnace and the plant continued to operate until 1984, when the "restructuring" and "modernization" of Spanish industry closed it. It had become cheaper to import steel. The railway to Ojos Negros is now a cycle track through spectacular country.

The years 1983–84 saw extensive workers' struggles in Sagunt, involving the whole town. There had been a long history of collective action, including a six-month strike under the dictatorship in 1971, by which the 3,000 workers more than doubled their wage from 300 pesetas a week to nearly 3,000 a month. In 1983 Felipe González, leader of a new Socialist government to which a majority of Spaniards had entrusted their hopes for a post-dictatorship future, announced the *reconversión* of heavy industry. Spain's inefficient iron and steel industry was to be closed down. González, in some ways the Margaret Thatcher of Spain, said: "I don't know why people are protesting. We are talking of reconversion, replacing one type of work with another." Needless to say, no other work was forthcoming.

From the announcement of closure to the actual closure, there were nine general strikes in Sagunt, numerous strikes and demonstrations, including eleven marches in Valencia and seven in Madrid in coordination with the other steel plants in Asturias and the Basque Country (44,000 jobs were lost in steel closures in all of Spain). The struggle was fierce, but the people of Port de Sagunt had eventually to submit to Felipe González as the people of Arse had submitted to Hannibal.

Poverty has stalked the town since then, though the port itself is active and lively, connected to the AP7, the coastal highway from France to Murcia, and the highway inland to Teruel and Saragossa. Several factories remain around the port. There is a project to celebrate Port de Sagunt's industrial heritage, but the museum and visitors' center are still to be completed. The only advantage of the town's industrial past is that the tourist boom has not destroyed it.

Commemoration of industrial heritage is sadder than of Roman heritage, for it is recent. We can read of mass slaughter of Celtiberians 2,000 years ago with equanimity, but on a visit to Port de Sagunt you can still see the devastation of mass unemployment. The year

Port de Sagunt: what's left
of the steel plant

1984 meant sudden poverty for some 4000 families in Sagunt. What stands in commemoration is Furnace Number 2, a tall, shining tower near the port. Nearby, a classic brick factory from the early years of the twentieth century has been conserved. Between the two, bare lots of rubble and the road bearing the heavy trucks out of the port.

She Never Touched a Penny

I want to return to the Jewish quarter, in the monumental Sagunt below the Roman theater. It is particularly well conserved. From opposite the *llotja*—now the beautiful History Museum—the Portalet de la sangre (Gate of Blood), built in 1321, leads off the castle road into a steep area of a few narrow, irregular streets, cul-de-sacs, and tiny squares. No synagogue survives, but there is a small *mikveh* (ritual bathhouse).

Everyone knows the tragedy of the expulsion of the Jews from Spain. The old story can be picked out in detail in Sagunt. The unification of Spain under Ferdinand (Ferran) of Aragon and Isabella of Castile in 1492 coincided with the order of conversion or expulsion of the Jews. In Isabel's concept of a united, Christian Spain, there was no room for Jews, Moors, or democrats. For the three centuries following, the Inquisition busied itself in investigating whether converted Jews had really converted or continued to practice Judaism in secret. Chapter 8 touches again this theme, explaining the tragedy of Joan Lluís Vives' family.

The Inquisition's religious fanaticism was intertwined with less holy desires to accumulate property for the Church and with the political need to keep the masses cowed with fear of torture and wowed with spectacular burnings of heretics. Isabel herself fiercely denied any base, financial motive. Cees Nooteboom quotes her letter to the Spanish Ambassador to the Vatican:

> I have been the cause of great disaster and the depopulation of cities, regions, provinces and kingdoms, but my actions were inspired by the love of Christ and His Holy Mother. Those who say I did these things out of greed are liars and slanderers, for not once have I touched a *maravedí* of the goods confiscated from the Jews.[6]

It is a remarkable passage, where the queen's frankness about the harm done would seem to support her fierce affirmation that her motives were pure. Jews were allowed to take with them to exile more than the sorry two items of clothing that Hannibal permitted the Iberians, though they could not take capital. Some rich Jews with overseas contacts would have secured money abroad, but most Jewish money flowed into the coffers of Church and state. Queen Isabel is engaging in semantic self-deceit. She believed that she was not greedy. Probably she never actually *touched* a *maravedí*.

Many Jews left Spain, for Salonika (where the Nazis were to reduce the Sephardic population from some 50,000 in 1940 to under 2,000 in 1945), Turkey, or Morocco. In general, the Arab world was a safer destination than Christian Europe. It is said that Jewish families in these places of new exile still keep the keys to their Spanish houses. Some still speak the language of Spain 500 years ago, known now as *ladino*, as Spanish-speaking travelers occasionally find to their surprise. This loss, of a different culture, of skilled people, of an essential part of Valencian

---

6   Nooteboom, p.256.

(and Spanish) life, was a key factor in the decline of Valencia, and Spain as a whole, in later centuries. At first, the reverse seemed true, as Spanish imperialism reached its peak in the sixteenth century, following the expulsions. The new country's monarchs, convinced of the rectitude of their holy mission, became the spearheads of the Counter-Reformation against Luther and of the defeat of Islam in the Mediterranean.

After 1492, many Jews left and unknown numbers converted or appeared to convert. Benito Pérez Galdós, Spain's pre-eminent nineteenth-century novelist, was brought up in a family of secret Jews. It is easy to romanticize today, when all but militant rightists bewail past expulsions, how this secret life gave someone like Galdós the unique inside-outside view of society that feeds so many novelists. In the Inquisition's time, though, a secret Jew risked torture and death. They were routinely discovered because they washed more than Christians or found pork disgusting.

At Sagunt, Hebraic inscriptions have been dated to the second century, from the time of the first Jewish diaspora after the destruction of the temple at Jerusalem by the Romans in 70 CE. There was no impediment to Jewish emigration across the Mediterranean to other Roman territories. The Jews were suppressed because they revolted against the Empire in Palestine, not because of any racial identity as Jews. In the Moorish period, Jews were respected—or tolerated—as long as they did not interfere with Islam.

With the Christian conquest of Valencia by Jaume I in 1238 (see next Chapter), the number of Jews in the area increased. Many accompanied the king on his journey of colonization south, while others performed tasks closer to the throne, such as handling his finances or doctoring. Christian governments in the very fragmented Iberian Peninsula of the time had learned from Moorish kingdoms to employ Jews as administrators and bankers. Traditionally, the monarchs of the Crown of Aragon protected the Jews against Dominican friars and easy scapegoating. The 1492 unification of Spain, however, finally overwhelmed the traditional balances of the Crown of Aragon, whatever Ferran himself might have desired: not through sound ethics, one understands, but because the Jews had helped his kingdoms run smoothly.

In Sagunt, many Jews were silversmiths, traders, or jewelers, as well as working in the traditional professions of doctors and bankers. To focus on what the expulsions meant, the figures, though estimates, suggest that in about 1300, sixty years after the Christian conquest of the *país valencià*, some 50,000 Jews lived there. There were only about the same number of Christians. The majority of the population were Muslims (some 140,000). The figures, however rough they are, vary with sources: these are from John Payne's sober book.[7] They show that the expulsion of the Jews removed a large part of the population, with a disproportionately high skilled layer.

The Jews were essential to the dawn of capitalism in Europe, as Christians were forbidden to handle loans. The anti-semitic legends about the Jews' attachment to money stem from this medieval Christian edict. They were the only people permitted to lend out money at interest, which was needed by the monarchs who wanted to raise armies or the traders, nascent capitalists, who wished to build a boat or warehouse. No one saved up money before buying a ship any more than no one today buys a house cash down.

Sagunt's *jueria* was not sacked and burnt, as most others were. The Valencian Dominican friar Vicent Ferrer (1350–1419), many of whose daily sermons have survived, as

---

7   Payne, p.71.

his fervent followers transcribed them, preached throughout Europe against the Jews. Famous for his intellect and oratory, Ferrer could talk for hours, often improvising. Local Jews and Muslims were obliged to attend his sermons, during which they were both insulted and urged to convert, a sensible decision when surrounded by an inflamed crowd.

Despite the monarch's protection of the Jews, Ferrer and his acolytes were able to whip up popular opinion, climaxing in the infamous burning of Jewish quarters in many cities of Iberia in 1391. The Black Death had unhinged minds. People afflicted by poverty, ignorance, and disease were easily persuaded to find scapegoats for their suffering.

In 1391, the Sagunt Jews were protected by the local council. Many survivors of other burnings and massacres, especially from Valencia city, then fled to Sagunt. This meant that a hundred years later, when on March 31, 1492, the Catholic monarchs issued their edict that Jews should convert or leave Spanish territory by July 31, in those four months some 700 Jews left Sagunt. This was about one-third of the town's total population.

Vicent Ferrer was canonized by Callixtus III, the first Borgia pope, in 1456. He is the patron saint of the Valencian Community, with a public holiday on the first Monday after Easter Monday (Valencians have many days off in April). He is still revered. On his feast day, twelve altars are set up in the street in different areas of Valencia city, where children reenact his eighty miracles. The main altar is at his birthplace, the Pouet de Sant Vicent, near the Torres dels Serrans.

History is not just a record of the past. We should look too at why some bits of history stand out and others are dulled. St. Vicent Ferrer has been chosen as Valencia's great medieval religious figure. He was also a central player in his age's politics. He was Anti-Pope Benedict XIII's confessor. He played a major role in the selection of the Castilian dynasty, the Trastámara, to rule the Crown of Aragon in 1412.

Recent biographies of this erudite fanatic tend to play down Ferrer's role in attacking Jews. Their argument is that anti-semitism was the atmosphere of the times and Ferrer has to be seen in his historical context. That is true. Ferrer was not the only militant anti-Jewish priest. The times were tough, with many predicting the end of the world: the Black Death killed one in three or four and the papacy was divided. Yet there is no getting around the fact that Valencia's honored patron saint today was a man who took advantage of fear and suffering to demonize Jews and have them killed.

Representatives of the Spanish state and press, along with millions of people on the ground, like to say that "we are not racists." It is the case that there is little prejudice or violence against Jews. How could there be, when there are almost none left? Yet racial cleansing cannot itself be cleaned away overnight. Racism remains, latent or active, unless it is tackled openly.

This curious, often willful, ignorance of the country's history is expressed too in many phrases, embedded in the language. Dirty people are often referred to as *marranos*, meaning pigs, but originally meaning Jews. A *judiada* is a dirty trick, but it means, literally, typical Jewish behavior ... and so on. The Valencian novelist Vicente Blasco Ibáñez's *Entre naranjos* (*Among Orange Trees*, published in 1900) describes a usurer as *ladino*, meaning sly and crafty, but it derives from a name for a Jew. His books are full of criticisms of Jewish landlords in racist terms.

Indignation about historical crimes is all too easy and leads only to one's own bad health. Understanding, though, how these crimes are ignored or downplayed today, as in Valencia's continuing celebration of St. Vicent Ferrer's greatness, tells a lot about what underlies a place or people. Jimmy Burns quotes a 1907 book on Toledo by one Albert Calvert:

> Visiting the city in 1391 he [Vicent Ferrer] so inflamed the devout populace with apostolic zeal that they burst into the larger of two Juderias or Ghettos, put practically the whole of its inhabitants...to the sword, sacked the quarter from end to end, and demolished most of the synagogues. The saintly Ferrer reappeared at Toledo twenty years later, but there were nominally no Jews left to massacre. The Hebrews that remained had been "converted."[8]

Sagunt's buildings escaped the fires, but there were no Jews left to massacre.

---

8   Burns, p.112.

Thursday at Noon: the Water Tribunal in Session
(UNESCO/Wikimedia Commons)

2: A Kingdom Won and Lost

"la pus bela terra del món ... the most beautiful land
in the world"

Book of King Jaume's Deeds

Sagunt is one of the most dramatic showcases of the different civilizations that have inhabited what is now the *país valencià*: the Iberian, Roman, Visigothic, Moorish, Jewish, and Christian (and not forgetting dissidents and atheists). The modern history of the region can be dated to the 1230s and the conquest by Jaume I, the Christian King of Aragon and Catalonia.

The Moorish rulers and proprietors were defeated and expelled. "The bell drowned out the muezzin's voice," in the words of an anonymous Arab poet. Their irrigated lands in the already famously fertile market-garden around Valencia city were shared out among Jaume I's nobles and colonists, while the Moors who survived the invasion were pushed to lands further south or remained as cheap or slave labor for another 350 years.

When the Moors had arrived, in the eighth century, the area was known as Sharq al-Andalus, or Eastern Andalusia. Then, in the eleventh century, as Arab Andalusia splintered into small, warring states, the *taifa* (kingdom) of Valencia was founded. This consisted only of the city and its agricultural hinterland. There were various other small kingdoms in the area we now know as the *país valencià*, such as that at Dènia, which had a renowned school of medicine.

Poets in Arabic mourned their expulsion from this rich market-garden. Ibn-al-Abbar, minister of the last Moorish King of Valencia, wept from Tunisian exile:

> All has been lost
> The Bridge and the Russafa are lost
> Mislata and Massana are lost
> All has been lost
> Where are those meadows with rivers
> and green poplar groves?[9]

And 650 years later, Vicente Blasco Ibáñez put into the mouth of Rafael, the protagonist of his *Entre naranjos*, an imaginative lament for "the tragedy of the Reconquest." Rafael identifies with the Moors' "elegance unequalled by any other knights":

> He saw the court of Valencia, with its poetic gardens of Ruzafa, where the poets sang melancholy lines on the decadence of Valencia's Moors, heard by beautiful women hiding behind the tall rose bushes. And then catastrophe struck. Like a torrent of iron rough men poured down from Aragon's arid mountains, pushed to the plain by hunger; the *almogàveres* [Catalan mountain warriors], naked, dreadful and wild as savages; ignorant, warlike, implacable people, who distinguished themselves from the Saracens by never washing.[10]

---

9   *Valencia, History of the City*, p.17.
10   Blasco Ibáñez, *Entre naranjos*, p.63.

It is a strange evocation of a lost civilization by a writer not normally associated with pro-Arab empathy, an anti-imperialist passage quite contrary to official celebrations of the Christian Reconquest.

My Sweet Lord

Before this expansion south by the Crown of Aragon, based in Barcelona and Saragossa, there had been a spectacular, though brief, conquest of the *taifa* of Valencia by the soldier of fortune, Rodrigo Díaz "El Cid," best-known in the guise of Charlton Heston in the 1961 three-hour epic film, with Sophia Loren as his wife Jimena. The film pretends to no accuracy at all, but rather transfers a Hollywood Western to medieval Iberia.

El Cid (the name comes from the Arabic *sidi*, Lord) is a legendary figure, a hero for Spanish nationalists of what is known as the "Reconquest," i.e., the expulsion of the Moors and their religion from Iberia. The *Cantar del mio Cid* (Song of My Lord) is a ballad from around 1200, the earliest surviving in Spanish literature. The long anonymous poem is based on eye-witnesses or recent oral history. Cees Nooteboom, a perceptive modern commentator on Spanish history, celebrates the ballad's

> ...style which is brisk, descriptive, realistic, Spanish, not exalted and mystical like the *Chanson de Roland*, not a high-minded crusade, but the story of a warlord, an hidalgo who is not a member of the class of *ricoshombres* (landowners who could muster a private army), who has earned rather than inherited his wealth and status, a soldier of fortune who loves money and power...[11]

---

11   Nooteboom, p.267.

In the *Cantar*, El Cid emerges as a much more sober and prudent warrior than legend would have it. The poem established the legend, but then the legend overtook the poem. The film with Charlton Heston helped the Franco dictatorship exploit El Cid in its political ideology of exalting the Christian unity of Spain.

In fact, Rodrigo Diaz was a soldier from a village near Burgos who made his living by conquest and rapine: "that enterprising, ferocious and perfidious mercenary, the Cid," in Rose Macaulay's polite adjectives. No Christian hero, he served Arab kingdoms as well as Christian ones, always acting independently, in his own interest. His final and most famous feat was the conquest of Valencia in 1094. There he established an independent fiefdom until his death aged about fifty in 1099. His wife Jimena maintained control until 1102, when the Moors took back the city. We learn from the *Song of My Lord* of Valencia's wealth: "there were untold quantities of gold and silver. All who took part became rich."[12]

Cees Nooteboom concludes that El Cid should be interpreted as the symbol of divided Spain, rather than as a founding legend of the unity of the "nation":

> Rodrigo Díaz de Vivar, the mercenary who sold himself to both sides and who would carve a dominion for himself out of Muslim Valencia, El Cid, Campeador, Sidi the warrior, champion of alternating alliances and consequently the symbol, so to speak, of those confusing centuries during which the quarrelsome Christian lords moved steadily towards the Moorish south.[13]

---

12   Payne, p.75.
13   Nooteboom, p.264.

This brief interlude of Christian rule of Valencia has left no trace apart from a grimy statue on the city's Plaça d'Espanya, which is little more than a multiple road intersection rather than a square, and the noisy, wide Avinguda del Cid. The rest is legend. It was not till 130 years later that Jaume I conquered the area.

MOORISH LEGACY: WATER, ORANGES, SILK

The Arabs have left their mark on Valencia in a way only comparable in Iberia with Andalusia, making the area's history quite different from that of Catalonia, Aragon, and Northern Spain, occupied by the Arabs only briefly or not at all. They lived for five centuries in the Valencia area. The Arab legacy is most visible in the place-names on the maps and signposts, which distinguish the *país valencià* from anywhere else in the Spanish state, Andalusia included: all the "Benis" (property of/children of)—Benicàssim, Benicarló, Beniarjó, Benidorm, Benissa, Benifairó, etc.—then all the "al-s": Algemesí, Almussafes (site of the Ford factory), Alboraia, Albaida, Alcoi, Alcira, Alacant (Alicante). Al- as a prefix is the Arab article.

More profoundly, Arab skills molded the landscape. The famous system of irrigation channels, using water-wheels and lock-gates, has sustained Valencia to this day as a great agricultural producer. Ted Walker understood the love of water of the Arabs and Berbers who came from dry lands:

> It was the Moors' genius for bringing water to where no water was, their quest to slake deserts and to introduce verdure and colour to the parched earth that created these lovely cool corners…you may easily comprehend the very obsession that led

to the irrigation of the great *huertas* of Valencia producing their several crops of fruit or vegetables a year.[14]

Water was important for aesthetic reasons, too. The Arabs loved gardens, seen most famously in the Generalife in Granada. Colorful mosaics, gushing fountains, and orange trees were the essential elements of a Moorish garden. In Valencia city, unlike Granada, none survive. *Russafa* means garden in Arabic, but in the city neighborhood of that name (see Chapter 8) no greenery remains.

The complex administration of water is ritualized in an imposing ceremony that takes place every Thursday at twelve noon by the Gate of the Apostles, one of the three doors to Valencia city's cathedral. The Tribunal for the Waters of the Valencia *horta* dates back to Arab times. The Tribunal members are not professional judges, but eight male farmers, elected by their peers. They represent the eight main water channels taking water off the Túria into the *horta*. Wearing black smocks and white espadrilles, the Tribunal members used to sit on a long sofa, separated by a low fence from the public. Now their footwear is more conventional and they sit on hard chairs with arm rests that can be seen in the permanent Water Tribunal exhibition in the Carles Ros library just opposite the Door of the Apostles.

The Tribunal hears evidence on water disputes, confers briefly, and dictates sentence. There is no appeal; no business is postponed for a week; no records are written. "No paperwork, as paper's only purpose is to ensnare honorable men," as Blasco

---

14   Walker, *In Spain*, p.170. The British poet Ted Walker (1934-2004) died suddenly at his home in Alcalalí village in Alacant province. Like Chester Himes (see Chapter 12), he is buried in Benissa.

Ibáñez put it.[15] More practically, a water dispute cannot be put off, for the land concerned could dry up.

The most remarkable thing is that, even today, in an age of predatory lawyers, these decisions on irrigation are respected. Experienced and just the eight men may be, but not every sentence will be fair or generally considered fair. Yet the decisions are accepted because it is a closed society of farmers who elect their representatives and desire no outside interference—with the expense of lawyers and procedural delays that the regular courts would involve.

In Chapter 4 of *La barraca* (*The Cabin*), Blasco Ibáñez's protagonist Batiste is falsely taken before the Water Tribunal by his scurrilous rival Pimentó. Batiste is unfairly fined, on Pimentó's word alone. With a certain scorn for tradition, Blasco Ibáñez underscores the injustice of Batiste being unable to appeal and having to pay what he cannot afford, when the only evidence is an enemy's lie. As Pimentó controls the water in that area and Batiste is a newcomer, the Tribunal appears bigoted by tradition.

The irrigation of the *horta* also led to the variety of vegetables we now associate with Mediterranean cuisine: pumpkins, zucchinis, eggplants, peppers, or green beans. The basis of this cuisine was the use of olive oil, because Moors and Jews would not use pig fat, i.e., lard, for cooking. The Moors also introduced rice to the marshy coastal areas. They started the ceramics industry at Manises and Paterna, where the clay was found. This was both basic production of plates and pots and the sophisticated production of glazed, colorful ceramics and tiles, such as those which shine in the Borja Palace at Gandia and adorn the blue domes of Valencian churches. Ceramics became an art, exported all over the Mediterranean.

---

15   Blasco Ibáñez, *La barraca*, p.102.

Oranges, too, though mass production did not arrive till the nineteenth century, were introduced from Asia by the Arabs. The Xàtiva paper industry was one of the first in Europe, developed in the eleventh century. The Valencian silk industry also dates from Moorish times. Let Rose Macaulay's romantic riff sum up what was lost in the Conquest and what has remained:

> One can eat as many [oranges] as one has a mind for, thanking the Moors for their intelligent irrigation. Moorish engineering, Moorish castles, Moorish-looking minarets and domes, Moorish faces and songs, memories of Moorish battles against the armies of Jaime the Conqueror, who fought them all down this coast and hinterland and finally beat them and took their kingdom, but still they stayed on the land, and their Moorish-Iberian descendants now darkly and beautifully ride their donkeys about the roads, and walk gracefully from the water troughs with their tall Moorish pitchers on their heads.[16]

No donkeys or pitchers now, but one gets the idea.

Two Languages

If you stand back from the main door of the Valencia city hall and look up, you will see the sculpture of a large black bat flying out of the wall. The bat, a mammal called beautifully *murciélago* in Spanish and *rat-penat* in Catalan/Valencian, is

---

16　Macaulay, p.85.

the heraldic symbol of the city. The city's Arabs already held the bat in high regard, for its flashing flights at dawn and dusk devoured the mosquitoes of the Albufera lagoon. The army of King Jaume I of Aragon and Catalonia was camped before the walls of the Moorish city in early October 1238, awaiting the final attack. A bat nested at the top of the king's tent. The prescient king ordered that it should not be removed. One night, the sleeping soldiers were woken by the beating of a drum. Alerted, the king realized that the Arabs were about to launch a surprise attack. In the battle that followed, the Arabs were driven back and the next day the victorious Catalan army entered the city.

Jaume I's bat on Valencia Town Hall

But who had aroused the sleeping army? No one stepped forward and it was established that it was the *rat-penat* that had beaten the drum with its wings. As the eagle is the emblem of the United States and the bear is the symbol of Russia, the bat was honored as the emblem of Valencia. Bats are believed to bring good luck throughout the Catalan lands, as its adoption as a symbol by the rum company founded in Cuba in 1862 by the Catalans Facundo and Amàlia Bacardí shows.

Modern historians have established that Jaume I was not even present at the final battle. The myth of conquest required that he be there, though. Jaume I is Valencia's founding father. Other Valencian kings have faded into history's morass of forgotten glories, but Jaume I is the wise king who granted Valencia its *furs* (Charter), the valiant warrior who defeated the Muslim infidel, and the protector who moved the rice fields away from the city to prevent malaria. Jaume I even wrote, or had written under his name, the *Llibre dels feyts del rei en Jaume* (Book of King Jaume's Deeds), to make sure his version of history endured.

Jaume's troops became the colonists who took over the lands of Moors. The Christian Kingdom of Valencia was founded. The 1238 conquest of Valencia (October 9 is the day it is still celebrated) was not as final or straightforward as later accounts make out. Under al-Azraq (the Blue-eyed One) the Moors revolted in 1247. Their resistance was not reduced until 1276. It is this final Christian victory that inspired the famous three-day festival of *moros y cristianos* (Moors and Christians), enacted around St George's Day (April 23) in several towns in the south of the *país valencià*, especially Alcoi.

Jaume I's army was polyglot, with Navarrese, English, Italian, and even Hungarian soldiers (Jaume's wife Violant was Hungarian). Most soldiers, and then colonists, were from Aragon and Catalonia, the two kingdoms over which he ruled. The origins of these settlers explain the original coexistence of two languages in the Kingdom of Valencia. After victory, Jaume assigned different towns and areas to his nobles and their soldiers. Valencia city had a Barcelona quarter, with 500 houses; a Terol (Teruel) quarter, with 400; and Montpelier, with 150.[17] The names indicate that the quarters' nobles and colonists were from Catalonia, Aragon, and Occitania, respectively. Power, though, was exercised in Catalan. The predominance of *castellano* (Spanish) today is not due to natural origins at the time of founding, nor just to migration for work from the rest of Spain, but to policies of introduction and imposition.

The first entry of Spanish as the language of power into Valencia can be dated to 1410, when Jaume I's descendants, the line of Catalan kings, died out. Martí "the Humane" died with no heir and in 1412 a Castilian-speaking monarch, Ferran of the Trastámara dynasty, gained the throne. After the formal unification of Spain in 1492, the sustained centuries-long assault on Catalan for political reasons commenced.

As power now spoke in Castilian, bureaucrats and courtiers also used the language. With statesmanlike criterion, needing to govern three kingdoms, Jaume I had introduced the *furs*, which for nearly five centuries granted to the Kingdom of Valencia a degree of self-government and rights within the Kingdom of Aragon. Castilian dominance, including language, was accelerated when the *furs* were abolished in 1707 after the centralizing conquest of Valencia by Felipe V, the first of the Bourbon dynasty that still rules Spain today in the form of Felipe VI.

---

17   Furió, p.39.

Felipe V: the man who burnt Xàtiva hung upside down

Today Felipe V's portrait hangs upside down in the Museum of Xàtiva, the city he burnt in the name of the unity of Spain under the Bourbons. The Spanish state's history has always understood unity as the suppression of diversity, never as unity by choice, negotiation, or agreement. Suppression does not always work: it has been and is key in keeping alive the spirit of resistance in the Catalan-speaking lands.

In 1836 the Castilian-speaking county of Villena was added to Alacant and in 1851 new Castilian-speaking areas (around Requena and Utiel) were attached to the province of Valencia. The administrative changes served to strengthen the weight of Castilian within the *país valencià*. It is a long story, culminating in Franco's post-1939 attempt to eliminate the language altogether, and there is a lesson. Languages change. Languages die out. But where for five centuries, the mass of people refuse to change their language, it is feasible to think that languages cannot be suppressed when they are tied so closely to people's identities.

Most tourists in Benidorm or Valencia city will not know there is more than one language spoken, though they may be confused by the two names of streets and towns. A visitor may not hear Valencian spoken at all. This, though, is misleading: it would not be spoken to tourists or foreigners who, it is correctly assumed, would not understand it. But indoors, on the fishing boats, on the farm, in local bars of the towns and villages along the coast, it is spoken as a matter of course.

EXPULSION

The treatment of the Jews in Spain was discussed in Chapter 1. The expulsion of the Moors is equally part of Spain's dark history and did even more damage to Valencia's economy. As seen above, the Moors left their marks on many of the buildings, culture, agriculture, and industry of the *país valencià*. In 1492, all Moorish rulers had been expelled from Spain with the conquest of Granada. Yet, especially in Valencia, where they made up about a third of the total population, they remained as key agricultural labor. For this reason, Valencia's nobles and artisans turned something of a blind eye to the central monarchy and the Inquisition's demands to enforce strictly the Moors' conversion. Throughout the sixteenth century, though, the Moors' position deteriorated.

In 1519–23, there was a major revolt of the *Germanies* (guilds) against the centralizing power of the Crown. This was a general revolt throughout the Spanish state of an over-taxed artisan class and nascent bourgeoise in the cities against abuses of nobles. It was exacerbated in Valencia because the king had granted its inhabitants permission to carry arms against the threat of Berber pirates. Nobles were killed, houses burned. Unfortunately, this democratic movement also targeted the Moors, seen as allies of the nobles because, as serfs of nobles, they were mobilized to fight the guild movement. After the bloody suppression of the *Germanies'* revolt, the Crown took advantage with a 1525 edict to oblige all Muslims to convert to Christianity. As John Payne puts it: "As had happened to the Jews, it was forced conversion that opened the way to the Inquisition (were the conversions sincere?) and eventual expulsion."[18]

The Moors were seen increasingly through the sixteenth century as "the enemy within." The Muslim Turks were fighting the Spanish for control of the Mediterranean: Valencia's Muslims were suspected (probably correctly) of supporting the Turks. North African pirates often raided the coast: the Muslims might well give them succor. Finally, in 1609 arrived the mass expulsion. The effect was catastrophic. It left Valencia short-handed in industry and agriculture, in grave crisis. The population of the Kingdom fell from about 400,000 to 275,000.

One example: the town of Bunyol had, by conquest, purchase, or negotiation, seven different "owners" between 1238 and 1609, when the newly created Count of Bunyol, one Gaspar, complained to the king that his town was practically empty and called for new settlers. Through all the changes of ownership, reflecting political deals and shifts in power, the anonymous inhabitants were the Moorish farm laborers. Without them, production dropped dramatically. Gaspar might well have become a count, but suddenly he had no subjects or workers.

Some commentators argue that Valencia has never recovered its Golden Age due to the loss of its Jews and Moors, between one-third and one-half of the total population. With 1609, at the cost of Valencia's economy,

---

18   Payne, p.27.

the Spanish Crown had taken a decisive step further on its road to one united Spain dominated by one Church.

THE NEW ORDER DECREE

Decline was not palliated by peace. A hundred years later, in the War of Spanish Succession, the final nail was driven into the coffin of Valencian independence.

In a restaurant on Torrent d'en Vidalet in the Barcelona neighborhood of Gràcia, a portrait of Felipe V, King of Spain from 1700 to 1746, hangs upside down. The restaurant is the Arrosseria Xàtiva (Xàtiva Rice House) and the portrait is a reproduction of the famous portrait in Xàtiva's Municipal Museum. What infamy did this long-reigning king, originally Philippe d'Anjou, victor of the War of the Spanish Succession (1701–14), commit to be remembered as if he were the Anti-Christ?

Xàtiva, "a fortress amid a paradise of flowers and fruit,"[19] is a city of about 30,000 inhabitants fifty-five kilometers inland from Gandia and about eighty kilometers south of Valencia city. Its old quarter on a hillside is attractive: churches, a heavy, dark-stoned cathedral, small squares, and narrow, cobbled streets where the occasional car announces itself with a disagreeable rattle. I noted that Xàtiva's doors often had blinds that reached right to the ground, perhaps because Xàtiva regularly records the highest temperatures in the Valencian Community. The city is steeped in history. It was the earliest producer of paper in Europe, dating from 1056, when the Moors established a factory using the abundant water and flax grown locally.

In 1244, Jaume I negotiated Xàtiva's surrender from the Arabs, apparently through diplomacy and without bloodshed,

---

19   Havelock Ellis, p.121.

when it was the second city of the Kingdom of Valencia. The blood would be shed later. From Xàtiva the Borja (Borgia) family emerged from obscurity: Pope Alexander VI's birthplace can be seen. Later, the *país valencià's* finest painter Josep Ribera *Il Spagnoletto* was born here. Both Alexander VI and Ribera ended their days in Italy. The town is pretty and monumental, like other Valencian hill-towns such as Oriola, Morella, Cofrentes, Villena, or Jérica. Known as the "city of a thousand fountains," its water and architecture give it an Italian air. Its glory is the castle overlooking the town. It is two castles really, with long well-conserved walls and impressive dungeons, which from the fifteenth century served as a state prison. Its military position dominated the approach from inland Spain.

The prosperous city's fortunes changed in the terrible events of 1707, during the War of the Spanish Succession. All the Catalan lands supported the Archduke of Austria against the French Bourbon, Felipe V, already on the Spanish throne. The British took the side of the archduke and swore to protect the lands of the old Crown of Aragon. Later they changed sides and abandoned Valencia and Catalonia to their fates. Perfidious Albion.

At the Battle of Almansa on April 25, 1707, the Duke of Berwick commanding the Bourbon forces routed the archduke's army. Almansa lies sixty-five kilometers inland from Xàtiva in the present-day province of Albacete. The victory opened the whole of Valencia to the Bourbon army. The defensive walls of Oliva and other towns were demolished. A properly united Spain, thought Berwick and Felipe V, had no need for one part of the state to defend itself with walls against other parts.

That same summer Felipe V enacted the New Order Decree, which abolished the *furs* granted by Jaume I nearly five centuries earlier and definitively integrated the Kingdom of Valencia into the Spanish state. While October

9, which celebrates Jaume I's triumphant entry (after the bat incident) into Valencia city, is now the official Day of the Valencian Community, April 25 is a day when modern Valencian nationalism, remembering the defeat at Almansa, recalls the *país valencià*'s lost liberties.

The War of the Spanish Succession was fought all over Europe, as England and France maneuvered for possessions and trade. Though hardly any Spanish soldiers fought at Almansa, the battle's outcome had profound consequences for the *països catalans*. Valencia was by no means united in its response to Felipe, but the repression after Almansa did unite the country.

To some degree the war was one between absolutism and nascent parliamentarism (intrinsic to the *furs*). This may seem an exaggerated comment, when the opponent of Felipe V was the Hapsburg Emperor, i.e., two absolutist kings. Yet the abolition of the Catalan, Aragonese, and Valencian *furs* should be seen as a key step in a centuries-long fight to form a centralized, Catholic, totalitarian state. Spain expelled its Jews and Moors, conquered and enslaved most of the Americas, burned or exiled its dissidents, and fought hard to defeat Protestantism. The *furs* of the Crown of Aragon were obstacles. Felipe V was clear everything had to be under his absolute control. Berwick proclaimed of Valencia:

> This kingdom has rebelled against His Majesty and has been conquered after committing grave treachery against His Majesty. So it now has no more privileges or charters than those that His Majesty might wish to grant in the future.[20]

Xàtiva suffered the worst of Felipe's vengeance. Berwick swept on from Almansa, laying waste to the country. Xàtiva

---

20 Quoted in Furió, p.373.

resisted a siege until June 12. When it fell, hundreds were massacred, much of the city was burnt and many of its inhabitants were deported to Castilian lands. To this day, the people of Xàtiva are known as *socarrats*, the scorched. This is why the portrait of Felipe V hangs upside down in the city's Municipal Museum and in the Arrosseria Xàtiva in Barcelona. Some 800 soldiers, mostly English, took refuge in the castle, but were eventually starved out. Xàtiva lost its position as the second city of Valencia. It even lost its name for a hundred years: it was re-named Nueva Colonia de San Felipe (New Colony of St. Philip). When Suchet occupied the castle in 1812, a century later, French chroniclers observed that there were still whole streets destroyed in the fire and not rebuilt. Nevertheless, not all the city was burned: there are still a great many buildings from previous epochs, such as the birthplace of Roderic Borja.

The castle of Xàtiva

Here is the only Royal gossip paragraph in this book. The ruthless Duke of Berwick was son of Arabella Churchill (ancestor of both Princess Diana Spencer and Spain's largest landowner, the Duke of Alba) and James II of England. Arabella was, too, sister of John, who became the first Duke of Marlborough, victor at Blenheim in the same Europe-wide war. Berwick's presence at the head of Felipe V's army underlines the international nature of Europe's ruling class. Indeed, anecdotally, Almansa is the only battle in history where the French army was led by an Englishman and the English army (English and Portuguese made up most of the Archduke's soldiers) was led by a Frenchman, the Marquis de Rouvigny. End of Royal passage.

Royals are famous and infamous. Some 5,000 anonymous men in Rouvigny's army died at Almansa in the afternoon of April 25, 1707.

Why Don't You Write in English?

> At school they stole your memory,
> they turned the present into a lie.
> Life waited at the door
> while we went in as young corpses.
> …
> Who will compensate me for years
> of disinformation and lost memory?
> Raimon, "Al meu país la pluja"
> (In my Country, Rain (1983))

In modern times, Xàtiva's best-known figures have been Alfonso Rus, mayor from 1995 to 2015, and the singer-songwriter Raimon. The former represented the PP's corruption and clientelism (see Chapter 10). He also boycotted any invitation to Raimon to perform in his home town.

Raimon is a mighty cultural figure. Born in December 1940 in the Carrer Blanc (White Street; before Franco's victory Carrer de la Llibertat, Freedom Street) to an anarcho-syndicalist cabinet-maker father and socialist mother, he became the main Valencian singer-songwriter of his generation. He learned early to play the flute and guitar, read music, and sing. This was not uncommon for children in the *país valencià*, which is a land of music, with bands and choral societies in every town. Most of his extended family played in Xàtiva's working-class band. There was another band for the dictatorship's supporters. He also learned politics early, which side he was on, for his father was in and out of jail for his opinions. At home he spoke Valencian; at school, Castilian Spanish by obligation.

Carrying Xàtiva with him in his heart, Raimon left the *país valencià* for Barcelona in the early 1960s and became a leading figure of the *Nova Cançó* (New Song), a mass cultural movement in Catalan that articulated opposition to the dictatorship in the 1960s and 1970s. Despite censorship and hardly any radio or TV time, Raimon and other *Nova Cançó* singers regularly packed out venues and stadiums when they were allowed to play.

They sang against fear:

An immense fear
That has made us so silent;
An immense fear
That still keeps us silent.

Singing about fear gave people the courage to fight. Raimon's roots were in Xàtiva in the poverty-stricken years after the defeat in the Civil War of 1936–39. There he learned what informed his life and songs: that there was no difference between the fight against Spanish centralism and the social struggle against the dictatorship. To win, the national and social struggles had to be interlinked.

Raimon has a raw, powerful voice (often called *un crit cantat*, "a sung shout") and a thrumming guitar that suits the short, harsh Catalan words. His songs explain the Valencian "difference," that the *països catalans* is a nation, one of fire and music different from the rest of Spain:

> *T'adones, company*
> *Que fa ja molts anys*
> *Que ens amaguen la historia*
> *I ens diuen que no en tenim:*
> *Que la nostra és la d'ells*
> *T'adones, amic.*

"Do you see, friend/ that for many long years/ they've been hiding our history/ and telling us we have none:/ that ours is their history,/ you see, friend?"

Raimon often recalls that the great Valencian poet Ausiàs March (see next chapter) was never even mentioned, let alone taught, in his literature classes in Franco times. His own Valencian history was hidden. If a people's true history and culture (the collective memory) is stolen, its very identity as a people is crushed.

When asked by the Uruguayan socialist Eduardo Galeano why he didn't sing in Spanish to reach a wider audience, Raimon responded, "Why don't you write in English?" He went on to explain that, touring in South America, singing in Catalan made him explain the songs beforehand and allowed him to show audiences the difference between state and nation. A nation's language does not often coincide with a state's boundaries. Raimon's power came from his language and that he felt his language as the expression of an oppressed people.

In April 2016, the Generalitat Valenciana sponsored the seventy-five-year-old Raimon's farewell fifteen-concert tour of the *país valencià* with tickets priced cheap, between ten and fifteen euros. The socialist Ximo Puig, president of the new coalition government, saw the tour, bringing Raimon's art and message to a new generation, as an act of reparation for the twenty-year boycott by the PP. Raimon's generation had been ignorant of Valencia's history, but the new generation should not remain ignorant of those such as Raimon and the fight against the dictatorship.

3: Valencia's Golden Century

"[Tirant lo Blanc's] prodigiously conserved world of bustling life"

Mario Vargas Llosa

Gerald Brenan, in *The Literature of the Spanish People* (1951), the best, though idiosyncratic, survey of Spanish literature in English, affirms with a fine appreciation and real modesty that he cannot review Catalan literature because he does not know enough Catalan. Then he writes five pages about Ausiàs March. That is how important Ausiàs March is.

WILD HEART

It is customary to describe March (pronounced Mark) as Europe's greatest poet of the fifteenth century. As scholar and translator Robert Archer argues, this is to damn March with faint praise. It is loose thinking, too, for who has read all the other poets of the age to know that March is the best? Archer makes a more realistic and also higher claim: that March, a difficult and original poet, is still accessible to us today. Like other medieval poets whose names have come down through the centuries, such as Dante, Chaucer, Villon, or Petrarch, March deserves to be read. That he is less known today is, in great part, due to the low status of the language he wrote in.

Beside a new platform built as a viewing-point over the River Serpis in the centre of Gandia, the opening four lines of March's *Veles e vents* (*Sails and Winds*), a poem on love, death and the treacherous sea, are inscribed on a whole wall in huge black letters:

> *Veles e vents han mos desigs complir...*

> "Let wind conspire with sail to give me what I long for,/carrying me across the sea's perilous highways!/Even now I can see the winds from the West and North-West gathering hostile forces:/ the Sirocco and the South-Western must hold them back..."[21]

Neither the sea nor feelings are calm in Ausiàs March. He is not a poet observing a still world. Like a boat, he is buffeted by conflicting winds. Here are the first lines of the second stanza of *Veles e vents*, not on the wall in Gandia, but illustrating the concreteness of March's "somber and disturbing" imagery and "the dangers of the elements, particularly of his great symbol of turbulent moods and feelings, the sea" (both quotes from Arthur Terry):

> The sea will boil like a pot in the oven,
> changing its colour and natural state...[22]

I asked in the town's tourist office if they had any leaflet on the poet or if his house and estate in Beniarjó, now incorporated into Gandia, existed still. There was no leaflet. No one knew

---

21   Robert Archer, *Ausiàs March, A Key Anthology*, pp.60-61. Poem XLVI.
22   Terry, p.59.

about the house. Gandia is committed to the fourth Duke of Gandia, Pope Alexander VI's great-grandson, St. Francis Borja. Gandia's pope and poet are acknowledged, but placed on a lower rung on the ladder of tourist attraction than the saint.

The prominent verse on the wall owes a lot to Raimon, who put seventeen of March's poems to music, including this one. The medieval poet was resurrected by a singer-songwriter engaged lifelong in the dual task of affirming Valencia's national identity as part of the *països catalans* and of dragging his country out of the oppression and self-hatred of the Franco years.

Ausiàs March was born in about 1397–1400 and died in 1459. Of a minor noble family, he was at the court of Alfonso "the Magnanimous" in Valencia in his teens and fought various campaigns overseas, in 1420 in Sardinia and Corsica, and in 1424 against the Moors at the island of Djerba. Around about 1425 he retired from his military career and spent the rest of his life between Gandia and Valencia. One of the king's falconers, head falconer in 1427 and 1428, he hunted on the Albufera lagoon, just south of Valencia city, and in the *marjals* (marshes) along the coast of Gandia.

He married twice. His first wife Isabel Martorell died in 1439 after just one year of marriage. In 1443 he married Joana Escorna, who died ten years later. The marriages gave March no children, though he had several children with both free women and Muslim slaves. Male, and racial, privilege runs deep through the centuries. The conquered Muslims were laborers without rights on the land.

King Alfonso left Catalonia in 1432 and during the twenty-six remaining years of his long reign never returned. He abandoned his devout wife Maria, who became Regent of the Kingdom of Aragon in his absence. She was responsible for befriending and encouraging Sor (Sister) Isabel de Villena (see page 58), another of the great writers of Valencia's Golden

45

Century. Alfonso the Magnanimous established in Naples one of the most renowned courts of Renaissance Italy. He attracted poets and painters with sumptuous fees, though his love of luxury and generosity led him into debt, which in turn made him tax the Jews heavily to keep him out of bankruptcy. Not so magnanimous.

Ausiàs March, though, never traveled to Naples. His poetry became well-known in his time—well-known, that is, among a literate upper class, the narrow sector of the population that could read and the even narrower that did. Some 10,000 lines in 128 poems, mostly on love, have survived. Yet the king's falconer's work never, apparently, attracted Alfonso's attention. The king preferred sung poems and his court business was conducted in Italian and Castilian, not in Catalan.

Ausiàs March was an original. He was trained in the courtly style of troubadours singing of their unrequited love for noble and virtuous ladies. Jordi de Sant Jordi (c.1400–c.1424) wrote exquisitely within this Provençal tradition, but March went further. Here are the opening two lines of XXIII:

> I don't need to write like the troubadours,
> all so inflamed that truth's soon left behind.[23]

His two giant steps forward were that he broke with the formal Provençal language, using a vernacular Catalan, and he went beyond the traditional themes of courtly love. Brenan wrote that "he is a poet who should particularly appeal to us today because he is a psychological poet whose subject is *Angst*."[24]

---

23   Archer, *Verse Translations*…, p.93.
24   Brenan, p.112.

March is introspective, describing feelings and analyzing the conflicts between spiritual and physical love. He uses simile and analogy extensively, allowing him to present abstract, philosophical arguments in concrete terms. At times he is hard to understand—and not only because I do not easily read medieval Catalan, but because of his "stark and concentrated style" (Brenan). March is never writing conventional, pretty pieces to his beloved, but composes searing, self-questioning verse. Though March's frame of reference is religious and misogynistic, normal in his times, his voice speaks to us because it is individual and struggles with real conflict. He explores the constant tension between instincts and spirituality: March craved pure love, yet his and his lady's natures drew them to sex. His verse is (Brenan again) "psychological, introspective, perversely tormented— so that one finds it hard to believe that it was written in the Middle Ages."[25]

Raimon explained, in the Galeano interview:

> March is a poet in constant struggle between the very strict rules of the Church and his own temperament...Constant tension...There's a line that goes: *Catòlic sóc, mes la fe no m'escalfa*, I'm Catholic, but faith doesn't make me hot...At that time, to write a line like that, he really had some guts. I mean, he's saying, yes, this God stuff, that's OK, but what he's interested in is something else...all the religious norms and he sees that his entire instinct and his entire life is against these rules.[26]

---

25 *Ibid*, p.113.
26 Galeano, p.35.

His six poems known as the *Cants de mort* (Poems on Death) are one of the peaks of poetry. Here he expresses his grief over the death of a woman, most probably his second wife, Joana. In the "courtly love" convention, the pure woman, who in life was the object of the writer's unrequited yearning, when dead is praised in laments and is always assumed to be in Heaven. March, however, fears his beloved might be damned and thinks he might be responsible and that he too could be damned. He is talking about a real woman, not an idealized icon. March and she have felt animal passion; now she is dead, he wonders if love can be spiritual, too. He posits a mixed love, both carnal and spiritual. He expresses several stages of bereavement: his anguish and longing or his feeling of guilt at his own survival, all part of modern understanding of bereavement processes.

His other peak is the anguished *Cant espiritual* (Spiritual Poem), addressed to God. Robert Archer summarizes:

> Here in twenty-eight stanzas of unrhymed verse March achieves and maintains an emotional pitch quite unmatched [by any contemporary] ... The poem swings dramatically between the extremes of despair and hope.[27]

March flays himself and his *cor salvatge*, his wild heart. He admits he does not love God, but only fears him: "My fear of you is greater than my Love." He is afraid of death because he may go to Hell, but wishes to die before committing further sins. Life is painful, but he fears the eternal pain of damnation. He wrestles with the conundrum, still central to Christian debates today, of

---

27   Archer, *Verse Translations* ..., pp.18-19.

predestination and free will: why does God, if he knows everything, allow humans to sin, so hurting others and condemning themselves?

Surprisingly, Gerald Brenan jumps across cultures and centuries to compare Ausiàs March with the nineteenth-century French poet Baudelaire. He cites four points in common: March and Baudelaire's sense of the tragedy of human experience; their use of their own erotic experiences as examples; their redemption in suffering and poverty; and common "images and turns of phrase." I am not familiar with Baudelaire's work, but the bold analogy may well open a path for readers into March.

The Valencia where March lived much of his adult life was a city of some 70,000 people, making it the equal of any European city of the time. By the fifteenth century it was bigger and wealthier than Barcelona, because of civil conflict in the latter and the Black Death, which had affected Valencia less. The King of the Crown of Aragon was the most powerful Christian ruler in the Mediterranean. When Ausiàs March wrote in Catalan, he was writing in the language of a major power, not in the minor language smothered by Spanish centralism that it was destined to become. And yet, as the king's main court flourished at Naples, March was also on the fringes of the world of culture. In addition, though the Kingdom of Valencia was an equal part of the Crown of Aragon, real political power was exercised from Barcelona, not Valencia city. The latter was more a center of commerce and industry, an emporium in Joan Fuster's word.

The fifteenth century was Valencia's age of maximum wealth and glory, in which Catalan trade, protected by its warships, dominated the Mediterranean. It was the time of many of the great monuments in Valencia city that we see today—the Torres dels Serrans, the Llotja dels Mercaders,

Sant Domènec monastery, the Miquelet tower, the Palau de la Generalitat…The century saw, too, the flowering of Ausiàs March's poetry. Joanot Martorell's novel, *Tirant lo Blanc*, was published in 1490; Sor Isabel's *Vita Christi*, in 1497. The first printing press in all of Spain was set up in Valencia in 1474.

Yet this epoch of glory was deceptive. Already the power of the Crown of Aragon had started to slip and clouds were gathering on the horizon for the Catalan language. No one would have perceived this at the time that Ausiàs March was writing. The future imperial capital Madrid was a windswept inland town on a bare hill. Yet rapidly the Spanish Empire was to grow, with Madrid becoming the capital of the Counter-Reformation. The conquest of America shifted wealth and power west from the Mediterranean, Catalonia, and Valencia to the Atlantic and Seville.

For centuries, the absolutist Spanish Crown would attempt to break the power of the nations on the Mediterranean coast. Why was it unable to do so? It had more money and the bigger army. A well-known anecdote, told in the *Chronicle* of King Pere "the Ceremonious" about his predecessor, illustrates the reason. Eleanor of Castile, the wife of Alfons "the Benign" (reigned 1327–36), wanted to give their several children lands and titles to compensate them for not reaching the throne. Many of the royal dominions in the Kingdom of Valencia were to be ceded to these princes. This meant that these extensive lands, from Castelló to Oriola, would fall under feudal dominion. They would no longer be protected by Valencian *furs*, the Charter granted by Jaume I to Valencia in 1261. The city of Valencia rose up against the dictate. The magistrates averred that they were prepared to die before agreeing to these "donations." And if they died, the embassy dispatched to the court explained, the people would revolt. "Ah, my Queen, did you want to hear this?" Alfons said. Enraged, Eleanor replied: "Lord, King Alfonso of Castile our brother would not agree to anything less than cutting all of their throats." And the Benign replied: "My dear Queen! Our people is free and not subjugated like the people of Castile. For they have Us as their Lord and we have them as good vassals and companions." The donations of land were revoked.

Though a medieval story, it is used right down to today to underline the differences between the absolute, feudal power of the King of Castile and the relationship of the Crown of Aragon with its subjects, based on accords between the monarch and various social classes codified in the *furs*. Fractures run long and deep.

The story has to do with money, too. If the king ceded large tracts of the kingdom to the princes, then more taxes would have to be levied from the city's merchants and landowners. This is why the merchants of the city were prepared to defend the *furs* so fiercely.

The story also shows another side of the coin: the vulnerability of Valencia to central power. The partial independence of the prosperous mercantile classes, protected by the *furs*, could be overturned by the diktat of centralized, feudal power, as did occur centuries later in the War of the Spanish Succession. Spanish was becoming a world language and Catalan was a marginalized and stateless language, only sustained through the following centuries by the extraordinary stubbornness of its people in continuing to speak it. With rare exception and few writers of quality, it was no longer the language of culture.

MARTORELL: PSYCHOLOGY AND BAWDINESS

There were other fine poets of Valencia's fifteenth century whose names have lasted in the history books, but none to equal March. There was another writer of the time, though, and of similar status who needs to be mentioned, Joanot Martorell. *Needs to be mentioned* both because he illustrates Valencia's Golden Century and because, like March's verse, Martorell's novel *Tirant lo Blanc* is part of world literature.

In newly-unified Spain under the Hapsburgs, what is called the *Siglo de Oro* dates from the early sixteenth century, when gold and silver began to pour back from the Indies and Spain was Europe's dominant nation, to the mid-seventeenth, when defeat in Flanders ushered in centuries of decline. This was a period of literary marvels: novels like *La Celestina* (from 1500, precursor of the Golden Age) and Cervantes' *Don Quijote*, the poets Garcilaso de la Vega, Quevedo, and Góngora, dramatists like Lope de Vega, Calderón, and Tirso de Molina, painters like Velázquez. As this Golden Age was beginning, Valencia's was over. Its Golden Century was the previous one, which illustrates how the different nations that make up the Spanish state do not march in consonance. Yet they are not separate, for Madrid and Seville's full tide was Valencia and Barcelona's ebbing.

Joanot Martorell (c.1410–68) was also from Gandia and was the brother of Ausiàs March's first wife, Isabel, i.e., March's brother-in-law. It shows the narrowness of the upper class that wrote. Like March, Martorell went to wars on behalf of the Magnanimous. He appears to have been a belligerent knight, engaged in lawsuits and duels, traveling to Naples, Portugal, and England. "Quarrelsome, boastful, and tough-talking," concludes his translator, David Rosenthal. He was an unlikely character for such literary sensibility: in surviving letters of his concerning arrangements for a duel, "man of letters" is used as an insult. He hated lawyers, too, having them hanged by the feet then quartered in *Tirant lo Blanc* (XLI) for their crime of endless disputation.

Gerald Brenan, so flowing on March, restricted his comment on *Tirant* to one line: "*Tirant* pleases by its mingling of adventures with realistic descriptions of contemporary life."[28] The description is accurate, but its insulting brevity reflects perfectly the book's marginalization over the centuries. Fortunately, Spain's most famous author, Cervantes, paid tribute to *Tirant lo Blanc* in *Don Quijote*. He put into the mouth of an enthusiastic priest:

> "Here's Tirant Lo Blanc!...I promise you I've found a wealth of pleasure and a gold mine of enjoyment in it...I swear to you, my friend, that it's the best book of its kind in the world. The knights in it eat, sleep, die in their beds, dictate wills before they go, and many other things you cannot find in other works of this sort...The author deserved to have it kept in print all his life. Take it home and read it, and you'll see everything I've said is true."[29]

Cervantes is praising the realism of this novel that includes ordinary events, like eating and sleeping. However, it is still a work "of this sort," i.e., a book in the knightly tradition of medieval manners. It is something of a transitional book. Some will claim it as the first European novel, though others favor the picaresque *La Celestina*, dealing with the lower classes, published in 1500, just a decade after *Tirant*. Both owed their distribution to the new printing press. No longer did literature have to be painstakingly copied by hand, as had happened only a few decades earlier with Ausiàs March's poetry.

---

28 Brenan, p.162.
29 Quoted by Rosenthal, Introduction to *Tirant*, p.vii.

In realism lies *Tirant*'s historical originality. It breaks with the formulaic, moralizing prose works that preceded it. Mario Vargas Llosa, Nobel Prize winner and one of the novel's great paladins, goes further. He sees Martorell's realism as attempting, like the greatest novelists, the impossible task of grasping total reality: "...a novel of chivalry, of fantasy, historical, military, social, erotic, psychological: all these at the same time and not solely any of them, no more nor less than Reality."[30]

Both *Tirant* and *La Celestina* feature prominently a procuress, though in *Tirant* Plaerdemavida (Pleasure-of-my-life) smuggles Tirant into a princess' bed, while La Celestina lives by selling sexual services at all levels of society, including at the very bottom.

There is a magnificent translation into English of *Tirant lo Blanc* by David H. Rosenthal (1945-92), lover and tireless promoter of Catalan literature. It is written in modern language, without artificial archaisms and without the slangy phrases that date rapidly. Extraordinarily, Rosenthal's translation is, I believe, the very first into English. 500 years late. Rosenthal saw it as an "underground classic," as it is so greatly appreciated by the happy few and so little read. Generations of Catalan schoolchildren have to study it now, though this is not perhaps the best way of persuading people to love a book.

Rosenthal wrote:

> For its wit and vivid realism, Tirant deserves to be placed in an entirely different group of works: those medieval and Renaissance masterpieces like *The Decameron*, *The Canterbury Tales*, *Gargantua*

---

30   Mario Vargas Llosa, *Carta de batalla por Tirant lo Blanc*, Seix Barral, Barcelona 1991.

and Pantagruel, and *Don Quixote* itself that remain both "great books" in the academic sense and very enjoyable reading for anyone who happens to pick them up.[31]

Tirant starts as a novel about the education of a knight in the rites and responsibilities of chivalry. To become a knight, a man had to learn and practice an essential set of Christian values and code of behavior. The young Tirant goes from Brittany to England for his education in chivalry. There he falls asleep on a horse and ends up at the cave of a hermit, William of Warwick. William had gone on a crusade to the Holy Land and had the news spread that he had been killed. He returned secretly to live in a cave and lead a life of contemplation. Summoned by the King of England to repel a Saracen invasion, William successfully did so before returning to his holy cave.

The events summarized in the preceding paragraph occupy just forty pages of this 620-page book. Martorell has taken from other sources the story of William of Warwick, the paragon of a great warrior and Christian. "Plagiarism" was not then the crime it is now: like Shakespeare, Martorell happily used and adapted whatever stories he fancied. Tirant's falling asleep on his horse, which leads him to the hermit, is a "magic" episode, but it is described completely realistically. In *Tirant lo Blanc*, there are no supernatural events. All is explained in realistic terms.

William spells out to Tirant the laws of chivalry and Tirant then learns them in practice, winning the tournament of the knights of all England. Famous now, Tirant goes to fight in Sicily, Rhodes, the Byzantine Empire, and North

---

31   Introduction to *Tirant*, p.vii.

Africa. Over half the book has Tirant as a general, saving Constantinople from the Turks. This was a highly topical fiction of wish-fulfilment, as in reality Constantinople had fallen to the Turks in 1453.

As well as the battles, the novel contains numerous comic passages and erotic descriptions. It glides in and out of public and private lives. It reveals, as novels can do better than history, the behavior of kings, queens, princesses, and knights when they are not in their public robes and roles. It shows them changing clothes rapidly, rushing along corridors, or worrying about what people will think. And it conveys too the formal public language of the Byzantine court (assumed by all commentators to be a portrait of the Valencian court) and its private language, the direct, colloquial Valencian.

The empress lusts after a page-boy; the procuress (herself chaste) Pleasure-of-my-life helps Tirant into the Princess Carmesina's bedroom; several lesser characters are engaged in complex liaisons. There is no moralizing: another key difference with previous medieval stories. It is what turns *Tirant* into a novel, not a tract. There is no sermonizing, but difference between reality and appearance is drawn out with narrative skill. Martorell takes us behind formal scenes of ritual speeches, the great emperor on a golden throne to psychology, direct dialogue ,and bawdiness.

Chapter 120 is a good example. Pleasure-of-my-life lures the emperor to the lady-in-waiting Stephanie's door on her wedding night, by telling him that Stephanie had been screaming, which made her fear murder. It is early morning and all is silent. "Could you not utter that delightful 'Aaah' once more, for truly, nothing is sweeter than a maiden's cries?" Pleasure-of-my-life asks Stephanie through the door. Stephanie complies. The emperor laughs at Pleasure-of-my-life's "spicy jests." He exclaims that she's so exciting that if he wasn't married, he'd propose to her. The empress now appears. Like Pleasure-of-my-life and her husband, she is in her night-clothes. "Die quickly, my lady," Pleasure-of-my-life tells her, "for my lord the emperor has sworn that were he unmarried he would propose to me." The empress "turned to the emperor and said: '…idiot, what do you want another wife for? Your weapon is better for slapping than stabbing…' Laughing and joking, they all returned to their rooms."

Martorell is a vigorous narrator. Events are swiftly and economically reported; and then, changing pace, he enters a scene with full slowness. He shifts scene rapidly, too: immediately after the royal family's low-life badinage above, we move to the preacher's sermon at High Mass. In Martorell, sex is pleasurable and normal. There is no contradiction with being religious. The self-torturing guilt about damnation that haunts Ausiàs March is absent in his brother-in-law Martorell.

As well as his brilliant bedroom scenes, Martorell brings military scenes to life: sieges, a soldier's discipline, the best strategies, and ruses of war. Tirant is a general who studies war just as he had studied chivalry.

All this praise should not hide the many long-winded passages, especially those about chivalry and, toward the end, those of the verbose Martí Joan de Gualba, who completed the novel after Martorell's death. Yet, all in all, it is hard to disagree with Dámaso Alonso, one of Spain's most eminent twentieth-century critics:

> I don't understand why I don't see this Joanot Martorell as someone far away in the deepest medieval obscurity. I see him very close, as a contemporary. He has that world-weary attitude

of someone without illusions, only tireless in his sensuality, melancholy and mocking at the same time. A European of our time.[32]

Tirant is much easier to read and more entertaining than Ausiàs March. Vargas Llosa found the novel "forgotten in its unjust tomb…waiting for its readers to at long last enter its prodigiously conserved world of bustling life." And he went on to describe Martorell as "the first of that lineage of God-supplanters—Fielding, Balzac, Dickens, Tolstoy, Joyce, Faulkner—who try to create in their novels an 'all-encompassing reality.'"[33]

High claims. It's worth following Cervantes' advice: "Take it home and read it" and see if all the praise is true. There are copies of Rosenthal's translation into English floating around the internet (or rather lying in dusty boxes in the back rooms of second-hand bookshops), though I imagine few potential readers would be as lucky as I was, finding an immaculate copy in dust-jacket for 75p in a charity shop in Wincanton, Somerset.

THE ABBESS AND THE DOCTOR

The very first woman to be published in Valencian was a nun. Sor Isabel de Villena (c.1430–90) was baptized Elionor, the illegitimate daughter of a nobleman. Aged four, she was taken into the court by Queen Maria, who was based in Valencia and effectively the sole ruler of the Crown of Aragon in Alfonso the Magnaminous' absence in Naples. The childless queen regent was Elionor's protector and friend.

---

32   Alonso, "Tirant lo Blanc, novela moderna," *Revista valenciana de filología*, 1951.
33   Quoted by Rosenthal, *Tirant*, p.vii.

Elionor became Sor Isabel when she entered the Convent of the Poor Clares in Valencia at the age of fifteen when it was founded by Queen Maria. She became abbess in 1463. Possibilities for women were so slight in those days that a convent was a real option for women who wanted to study and develop their intellect and avoid the dependence that marriage involved.

Sor Isabel became one of those powerful abbesses of medieval Europe. St. Teresa of Ávila is the template, equally at home as a spiritual leader of her nuns and as a practical manager of a convent. Sor Isabel's huge stone convent is still there, in central Valencia, just across the dry river from the Parliament building, reached by the Pont de fusta, and still home to Poor Clares.

Sor Isabel's only surviving book is the astounding *Vita Christi*, published seven years after her death from plague. The

The Trinitat Convent of the Poor Clares, where Sor Isabel lived

book does not so much recount the life of Christ as discuss the women in his life. It opens and concludes with the birth and death of the Virgin Mary. Written to explain the life of Christ to her fellow nuns, it does not rely only on the Bible, but uses local stories. The *Vita Christi* can be considered a very early feminist work, in that its focus on women is a response to the general misogyny of medieval society, and, in particular, the literature of Jaume Roig (c.1400-78), Valencian poet and doctor. I use "feminist" and "misogyny," though these are words unknown in the Middle Ages. There was, though, a centuries-long debate (among men) on whether women were the source of sin or to be placed on a pedestal and revered (whores or virgins). Roig and Sor Isabel's writings are part of this argument. She earns the anachronism "feminist" because she shifts the debate toward more real women who are neither evil nor super-virtuous.

Roig shares the satirical vein of Joanot Martorell. His *Lo spill* (The Mirror) consists of 16,000 four- or five-syllable lines of rhyming couplets, an original form. Arthur Terry summarizes:

> ...the whole book...consists of a virulent and exhaustive denunciation of women, interspersed with an enormous variety of anecdotes...unremittingly pessimistic...[34]

Conventionally, but extremely, Roig considered women the source of sin. *Lo spill* tells how several disastrous marriages prevent the (male) first-person narrator from settling down in respectability and comfort. Though apparently Roig was an amiable man, his poem shows a morbid and vicious imagination. Here is a sample:

---

34   Terry, p.46.

una en penjaren,
viva escorxaren,
gran fetillera
e metzinera …

This is Arthur Terry's translation of these four and then the next eight lines:

> They hanged one of them/and flayed her alive,/a great witch/and poisoner./She used to come at night/unaccompanied,/and would climb up alone/ and tear out/the teeth and molars/of hanged men/ on their tall/gallows.[35]

Literary historians believe that the language and abuse are so grotesque that they would have brought a smile to the lips of his contemporary readers. This is to say that, though sincere in his diatribe, Roig borders on satire. His mirror was deliberately distorted.

Roig is buried in the Sant Vicent Ferrer chapel in the St. Nicholas Church. Suitably, for one can see in the violence of his imagery a likeness to Vicent Ferrer's disgust at humanity and delight in recounting the crimes of the Jews. Remarkably, Roig was the doctor for Sor Isabel's convent. God knows what the discussions of the abbess and the doctor were like! In her clearly written work, Sor Isabel reverses stereotypes: her women are firm-minded and men are unreliably effusive. Where women are often associated with the devil, Sor Isabel creates honest women. She has Jesus himself prefer women's minds and disavow prejudice.

---

35 *Ibid*, p.59.

After its Golden fifteenth Century, Valencia produced no writer of note until Vicente Blasco Ibáñez, on the cusp of the nineteenth to twentieth centuries (see Chapter 13). These were 400 years of decline from the city's golden age of commerce and wealth, exacerbated by the suppression of Valencia's *furs* in 1707.

4: The Dukes of Gandia

"O Dio, la Chiesa Romana in mani dei catalani!"
*("Oh my God, the Roman Church in the hands of
the Catalans!")*

Pietro Bembo

Between Valencia and Alacant, the coast bulges out into
the Mediterranean toward the island of Ibiza (Eivissa).
On the north-east-facing side of this promontory, which
reaches its furthest east just south of Xàbia (or Jávea) at Cap
(Cape) de la Nao, the land faces Italy. The climate here is
damper and favorable to oranges and the rice grown around
the Albufera lagoon and Sueca. To the south of the cape,
toward Alacant and beyond, the land faces Algeria. Here
the air is drier and palms and olives predominate in a sub-
tropical climate.

Gandia, on the orange side of this divide, is a coastal
town of some 60,000 people, about an hour's drive
south of Valencia city. It is divided into three. Similar to
Sagunt, the main, prosperous town with elegant shops and
pedestrianized streets lies some five kilometers inland. Then,
a small working-class town of drab blocks and tattered villas
stands on the coast between the harbor and the mouth of
the River Serpis, one of the many rivers that race swollen
to the coast in the rainy season and trickle in summer.
Third, on the other side of the deep-water harbor, a ribbon
development runs north for two kilometers along a wide,
flat beach of fine sand—a ribbon some five blocks deep of
vacation rentals and hotels.

THE FAMILY: THE BORJA POPES

Gandia's principal claim to fame is the Palace of the Borja family. In 1485, Roderic Borja bought the Duchy of Gandia, which included this palace, from the King of Aragon and future king of a newly unified Spain in 1492, Ferran or Fernando (or Ferdinand in English).

Though Santiago Calatrava or Blasco Ibáñez might like to dispute it, Roderic, born in 1431 in Xàtiva, is the most famous Valencian. He became a cardinal at the age of twenty-five. This was a prime example of nepotism, the promotion of *nipoti* or nephews, for his uncle was Pope Callixtus III. In 1492, Roderic, by then Archbishop of Valencia, was crowned Pope Alexander VI, the second pope in the family. Among the pope's children were Cèsar and Lucrècia. If you hadn't guessed, the Valencian Borja family were the notorious Borgias, such an emblem of simony, incest, nepotism, and murder that Pope Francis, referring to a contemporary Vatican sexual scandal, exclaimed as a matter of course: "I just thank God that there's no Lucrezia Borgia."[36]

In 1992, the fifth centenary of the "discovery" of the Americas by Columbus was celebrated in a blaze of Spanish nationalism, glorified by the Sevilla World Fair and the Barcelona Olympics. The commemoration that same year of the accession to the papal throne of the most famous of the four Spanish popes was muted. Little surprise: Alexander VI has long been painted as the Anti-Christ (Savonarola's term), who made a pact with the Devil to gain the papacy; his daughter Lucrècia, the "pope's tart," is supposed to have poisoned more people than Agatha Christie; and his son Cèsar is believed to have murdered his brother. Mario Puzo, renowned author of *The Godfather*, wrote his novel *The*

---

36   *Telegraph*, December 1, 2015.

Family about the Borgias and called them "the first great crime family, the original Mafia family." Their reputation for evil has never faltered.

The dark legend started with Papal Master of Ceremonies Johann Burchard, who wrote damningly in his diary during Roderic's reign:

> There is no longer any crime or shameful act that does not take place in public in Rome and in the home of the Pontiff. Who could fail to be horrified by the … terrible, monstrous acts of lechery that are committed openly in his home, with no respect for God or man? Rapes and acts of incest are countless … [and] great throngs of courtesans frequent St. Peter's Palace; pimps, brothels, and whorehouses are to be found everywhere![37]

A comparison springs to mind between then and now. Valencia bred corruption in the form of the Borja family in its Golden Century, and 500 years later, in the massive overspending on prestige projects over the twenty years up to 2015, it showed itself equally corrupt. Too facile a comparison, though. In recent decades, the black legend of the Borgias has been reviewed and toned down.

There are several points to be made. First, the family's behavior differed little from that of other Renaissance families or that of previous and subsequent popes, though you wouldn't want to meet Cèsar Borja down a dark alley. Nepotism was standard practice. For instance, of the twenty-seven cardinals of the College who elected Roderic in that sweltering August 1492, ten were cardinal-nephews of previous popes. The fifteenth century saw a change from

---

37   *Historia*, June 2004, p.14.

a College of Cardinals with a majority of career churchmen to a College dominated by families of popes wanting to perpetuate their influence after their particular pope's death. The College of Cardinals was overwhelmingly a political forum, not a religious one. The simony—selling of Church positions—of which Alexander VI was accused was common practice: most cardinals had either bought their positions by donations to the Church/pope or had been preferred as a part of political alliances and promises.

Second, the Borgias' ambition, amorality, and ruthlessness were exaggerated by their rivals because they were foreigners, "stealing" the papal throne from the half-dozen Italian families who believed it theirs by right (if not divine right, the practical right that they had the armies to defend it). Roderic brought some 800 Valencians with him: they were "those filthy Catalan pigs" for the Italian families. Burchard's diaries, quoted from on the previous page, may be true, but are just as likely to reflect his inflamed, sexually repressed imagination and shocked xenophobia. Núria Cadenes imagines him listening at key-holes and only half-understanding. Third, as foreigners, the Borja were especially tight-knit, unusual among Italian aristocratic/ecclesiastic families. This closeness gave credit to the stories that Roderic and Cèsar slept with Lucrècia. When Burchard saw the adolescent Lucrècia sitting on Roderic's knee, he could not grasp any other but a sexual motive.

The close family. We should step back to look at its roots. On April 8, 1455, Alfons Borja, born in Canals or Xàtiva in 1378, swore his oath as pope in Catalan. You have to imagine what it meant for a man from a small town in a non-Italian country to reach the throne: intelligence, ambition, diplomatic gifts, and hard work. Alfons liked to spread the story that Vicent Ferrer (later canonized by Alfons) prophesied that Alfons would be pope when Alfons was still a student at the University of Lleida.

Alfons entered the service of his namesake, King Alfonso the Magnanimous. He became a councillor of the king and organized the government in Naples. He may well have sailed in the same fleet as the great poets Jordi de Sant Jordi and Ausiàs March. Alfons Borja is also credited with solving a particularly tricky problem: healing the Schism of the West, dealt with in Chapter 5. King Alfonso had supported Papa Luna, the Anti-Pope exiled in Peníscola, which made his relations with Rome delicate. After Papa Luna's death, Alfons de Borja's diplomatic skills persuaded Papa Luna's successor to renounce his papacy claims in 1429. He was rewarded by becoming Bishop of Valencia that year (politics, not religion made churchmen) and cardinal in 1444.

Cardinal Alfons Borja summoned his nephew Roderic to Rome in 1449. Roderic was an eighteen-year-old minor noble. As second son, he was destined to the clergy. In 1457, Alfons, now Pope Callixtus III, named Roderic vice-chancellor, the Pope's second-in-command, responsible for all the paperwork, in charge of the papal army, and head of the ecclesiastical high court. For thirty-five years, until his own accession to the papacy, Roderic was the power behind the throne. Popes may have hated him (the Borgias were called "the Catalans" with disdain, for they spoke among themselves in a language Italians and Spaniards did not understand), but found him indispensable. In the four elections to the papacy between Callixtus III and his own victory, the votes that Roderic controlled were decisive. The Vatican was a state like Milan, Venice, Florence, or Naples, but one where it was easier for a man of talent to enter and rise, for power in the Vatican did not depend on inheritance.

Roderic was not only a skilled administrator and able and ruthless (Machiavellian before Machiavelli) politician, but also an attractive man. Here is one Gaspar of Verona:

> He is a beautiful man with laughter in his face
> and a vivacious nature. His voice is agreeable
> and cultured. He delights distinguished ladies
> wherever he encounters them and he exerts a
> power of attraction over them stronger than the
> power of a magnet on iron.[38]

Doubtless Gaspar was seeking advancement through flattery, but other reports, even from his enemies, attest to Roderic's physical beauty and power of attraction.

He had many lovers, not uncommon (though not universal) among churchmen of the time. The Church was a career, not necessarily a vocation. In the late 1460s he met Vanozza Catanei, who became a permanent companion (she would outlive him and all their children) and mother to four of his children, including Cèsar and Lucrècia.

Lucrècia is particularly hard done by. The dark legend of the Borgias tells that she poisoned her enemies, slept with her father, and loved orgies. She might have done all these things, and there is no evidence against it, which is the nature of calumnies. What is known of her is that, in three arranged marriages, she served the interests of her family. She spent time in a convent, bore eight children, and died of puerperal fever at the age of thirty-nine. Not exactly the portrait of an evil monster.

In truth, Lucrècia Borja, (Lucrezia Borgia), is a victim of prurient misogyny. People love to hear tales of sexual misconduct, repeat them, and condemn them. A clever woman of power and beauty was an easy target for her ambitious family's rivals. The whole Borgia family has been painted as evil, but Lucrècia more so. She is one of history's outstanding examples of how women with power

---

38   *Ibid.*, p.15.

are attacked—an attack that served its use at the time and has been embroidered down the centuries. The old warning to women: know your place and don't step out of line.

Even if the stories of incest were true, it was hardly Lucrècia's fault for she would have been victim of her father's and brother's dominance, just as she was a pawn to political alliances through marriage to men she'd never met. The calumnies (or true stories) that have sealed her reputation stem from her second husband, Giovanni Sforza, rival and enemy of her father. Sforza married Lucrècia in 1493, so sealing an alliance between the Vatican and Milan. Two years later, though, Roderic no longer needed the alliance. A plot was hatched to kill Sforza, but he escaped. A messy divorce followed, in which Sforza refused to accept an annulment. He was challenged to have sex with Lucrècia before witnesses to prove his virility. Not unnaturally, he refused. Finally, in 1497, his family obliged him to sign a document declaring his "impotence" that allowed the marriage's annulment. During this drawn-out divorce, Sforza alleged that both Roderic and Cèsar were Lucrècia's lovers and sought to eliminate him out of jealousy. The calumny, true or not, has resounded down the centuries. Gossip and slander became the standard history; it was too good a story to let die. Victor Hugo gave it a new impulse with his successful 1833 play, *Lucrezia Borgia*, basis for Donizetti's opera of the same name.

After her third arranged marriage, with Alfonso d'Este in 1501, Lucrècia made the court of Ferrara a center of Renaissance culture. She had seven children with him before her death in 1519. Lucrècia never returned to Rome. One could speculate that she created a space for herself at Ferrara, away from the forced marriages and murders swirling through the corridors of the Vatican. In this age of attempts to rectify the calumnies or ignorance of standard male-written history, Lucrècia's reputation is at last beginning to change. Here is Marion Johnson: "The people of Ferrara praised her for pious works, for founding convents and hospitals; she had become 'the good duchess.'"[39] The latest Borgia novel has traveled a long way from Victor Hugo's play: Sarah Dunant's 2017 bestseller *In the Name of the Family* reflects a revised view of Lucrècia. For Dunant she is a woman of "sweetness and modesty." Someone should tell Pope Francis.

The Catalan Manuel Vázquez Montalbán, Spain's outstanding intellectual of the fourth quarter of the twentieth century, put into Lucrècia's mouth the following lament in his 1998 novel *O César o Nada* (Caesar or Nothing): "They let me study Latin, read the classics, debate philosophy, but I can't choose a husband and they don't even let me keep those they foist on me." Vázquez Montalbán's novel is a fascinating meditation on the family's ambition and power. His title refers to Cèsar's megalomaniac emblem, *Aut Cèsar aut nihil*. In his short life (1474–1507), Cèsar became the leading diplomat and general at his father's court. Created cardinal at the age of twenty, he is one of few and one of the youngest to voluntarily resign his cardinalship, three years later. After the murder of his brother Joan, he had to take on the mantle of the family's military leadership. Anyway, he was a man of action, not a churchman. One could argue that he was more honest than most princes of the Church, with their fine foods, carpeted palaces, and concubines despite their vows of chastity. Cèsar was also, like his father and sister, a person of culture. He was a friend of both Leonardo da Vinci and Machiavelli: the alliance of warrior, artist, and philosopher. He is usually pictured wearing gloves, supposedly to hide his syphilitic lesions.

---

39   Marion Johnson, p.206.

In Vázquez Montalbán's novel, Machiavelli advises César in the basics of modern statecraft. The philosopher sees in César the modern man, the prince who will do away with feudal kingdoms. Deceit in diplomacy and war were necessary to win: "The end justifies the means." The end was a strong state, a united Italy. Violence is necessary to construct this state that will control disordered society: "You apply it or they apply it to you." Terror must be used in conquest, but it should never be gratuitous or useless. It must be applied for a purpose. Machiavelli saw the Borgia family not as more wicked than other families, but better than others, because the Borgias applied violence usefully, for a purpose.[40]

Cèsar was indeed the modern prince, breaking with feudalism, but he was also the hinge between past and future. The objective conditions had not ripened for a united Italy, which could exclude the French and Spanish armies that repeatedly ran riot through the peninsula. Cèsar was still the feudal lord, murdering his opponents ("kill or be killed"), taking any woman he wanted, acting himself as prosecutor and judge, allowing his soldiers license to rape and loot and accumulating wealth robbed. He was also the germ of the future: he wanted a standing army, not dependent on mercenaries, and a united country. A standing army requires taxes from the growing merchant class, which in turn needs trade and a semblance of peace. The capitalist revolution was in the air, but it blossomed not in Machiavelli's Florence, but a few decades later in London and Amsterdam.

---

40   Montalbán's novel was presented in the Ducal Palace at Gandia by Manuel Vicent, who commented brilliantly: "All states are founded with a murder and the myth involves sealing the murder hermetically in a box…Alexander VI converted the box into the famous Reason of State that Machiavelli then wrote up." (*El País*, May 19, 1998).

Cèsar's star was extinguished on Roderic's death in 1503. This is another reason the Borgias could be slandered: after their pope's death they were weak. They had risen like rockets, but were not so well established as the Italian noble families once the boss—the pope—died. Cèsar was handed over to Isabel, Queen of Spain, who wanted to try him for treason because of the alliances he had formed with the French king. He was also accused by his brother Joan's widow, mother of the third Duke of Gandia, of murdering Joan. This murder, plausible and possible, is unproven: another of the stories about Cèsar on which scholars are divided.

Roderic had assisted the new unity of the Spanish state by backing Ferdinand and Isabel. Isabel had benefited from Roderic's most lasting decision as pope—the 1493 division of the Americas after Columbus' landings, so that Portugal only retained Brazil and Spain held the remaining territories of Central and South America and the Caribbean. Roderic also conferred on Ferdinand and Isabel the title still used to describe them, *los reyes católicos*, the Catholic Monarchs.

In this world of shifting alliances, these favors counted for nothing once the pope was dead. Isabel was intent on centralizing Spain with one state, one language, and one power. There was no room in this project for other nations with other languages. Her persecution of Catalan language and power set the standard for the struggle, latent or in eruption, against separatism that has lasted right down the centuries to Franco and beyond.

Cèsar escaped from prison after Isabel's death in 1504 and fled to Pamplona, where he was appointed general of the army of the King of Navarre, Juan d'Albret, his brother-in-law. He died on March 12, 1507, at Viana near Pamplona, galloping alone into twenty troops of the noble, Luis de Beaumont, who represented the French king.

Cèsar Borja's end was unlike him, for he was a follower of Machiavelli, a shrewd and able general, not at all given to sudden impulse. Perhaps he was persuaded by his own legend. Or perhaps his syphilitic lesions affected his judgment. It is tempting to share Vázquez Montalbán's suggestion: Cèsar saw that all was probably lost and the shrewdest option was to prefer one last gamble. If he alone could defeat a squadron of twenty horsemen, this could be the springboard for his comeback. *Caesar or Nothing* was his shield. At Viana, Cèsar became Nothing. God? Cèsar was the prototype of the modern tyrant. God does not enter the simple equation of Me or Nothing.

THE SAINT

The Ducal Palace in Gandia is not ostentatious. It stands at a curve of the river, dominating views up and downstream. From the street, it looks like the military fort it also was. Its simple, brown wall with high and few windows belies the wealth within. Wealth but not luxury. It is cold in winter with its stone floors, tiled walls and floors, and high windows, but winter is only a brief irritant here. To be cool in summer is the key quality of a Valencian coastal palace.

The main Borgia featured at the palace is the fourth Duke of Gandia, Francesc (1510-72), who in 1671 was canonized as Sant Francesc de Borja (St. Francis Borja). Francesc was the great-grandson of Roderic on his father's side and of Ferdinand "the Catholic" on his mother's. Francesc's story is something of a whitewash of dark legend. It is safer to boast of a saintly duke descended from royalty than of "the first Mafia family." Indeed, in 2010, the 500th anniversary of his birth saw the town's authorities fling themselves into celebration. Among the processions and exhibitions, there was even a cruise ship excursion to Rome and back.

The Borja Palace

Apart from any ambivalence about evil Roderic and his children, it is logical, too, that Francesc is the main Borja commemorated in Gandia, for the palace was his birthplace and home, as it never was, or was only fleetingly, of the more famous Borgias, based in Italy. There is even a mock-up of his bedroom, cot and blanket included. The guidebook says that the bloodstains from his self-scourging, atonement for his family's sins, can still be seen on the wall. We didn't spot them. The story recalls the reddish tinge in the pitted limestone at the point where Thomas Becket was struck down in Canterbury Cathedral, also said to be blood.

The palace is built around a large, square inner courtyard, where hundreds of armed men could assemble. The shield of the Crown of Aragon is still visible on the cast-iron bolt of the entrance gate, to remind visitors that the palace belonged to the royal family before Roderic de Borja bought it. As well as soldiers, Ausiàs March and Joanot Martorell knew this palace. These two writers were also knights and bore arms in this courtyard, as well as stepping upstairs to the noble rooms.

Today the palace displays a variety of styles, from its reforms over the centuries. When Roderic bought it, the Crown Room was yet to display the fourth duke's remodeling, mainly in praise of himself, with the double crown of the Borgias, ceramic wainscoting, and painted wooden ceilings converting it into a magnificent reception room.

The glory of the palace today is the later, long Golden Gallery, of five open-doored rooms decorated in the Baroque style, which the tenth Borja duke constructed to celebrate the canonization of Sant Francesc de Borja in 1671. These rooms culminate in the allegorical tiled floor in the final room, the Sky and Earth Hall, where fire, air, water, and land are represented in concentric circles. The Earth had recently been established as circular. Birds and dragon-flies, ships and fish, animals and people, are all conserved in fine detail and color. Ceramic tiles are an art form brought to a peak in Valencia. The domes of its churches are tiled blue. Where in more northern climates, tapestry or painted imagery covered the wealthy's walls, in Valencia cooler, adorned tiling is the normal decoration.

Francesc is the good Borgia. Born three years after Cèsar's death and nine years before Lucrècia's, he grew up in Gandia. Pious as a child, wanting to be a monk, he was sent in the 1520s out into the great world: to the court of Carlos V, where he fought in several campaigns and rose to be an intimate of the emperor, who married him to Leonor, lady-in-waiting to his wife. More noble titles followed and Francesc became Viceroy of Catalonia. In 1539, the Empress Isabel, reputed to be one of the most beautiful women of her age, died in childbirth (as Lucrècia had done twenty years earlier) at the age of thirty-six and it was her principal knight Francesc, Duke of Gandia, who accompanied her on her final journey to be buried in Granada.

The story goes that when the monks at Granada received the coffin, they opened it to check it was indeed the empress. The corpse was so decomposed after the long journey that they could not recognize her. They asked Francesc to vouch it was her. He replied: "I've brought the corpse of Her Majesty under rigorous guard from Toledo to Granada, but I hardly dare swear that this is her whose beauty I admired so greatly…I do swear it, but I swear too never to serve again a mortal master." It is a good story to explain his illumination on the road to Damascus. He renounced his dukedom in favor of his son and was ordained a Jesuit priest. He rose to become the Society's third superior general. Under Francesc's generalship the Jesuits spread rapidly to South America and Asia. Clearly Francesc shared with Roderic administrative ability and personal charisma. And like Cèsar, he was a man of action. He founded in Gandia in 1549 the world's first Jesuit university, whose aim was to convert the Moors of the area to Christianity, a sinister aim as we have seen, for conversion was not conducted by verbal argument. It was closed in 1772 after the expulsion of the Society from Spain.

Francesc's University building is still there, serving now as a private secondary school run by the Escolapian Order. In the square in front of the University, statues of the five famous Borjas stand: Callixtus III, Alexander VI, Cèsar, Francesc, and Lucrècia. Lucrècia has one bare breast, a common portrayal of her to confirm her reputation as a scarlet woman. She is represented like this in a painting of her time by Bartolomeo Veneto, repeated on the wall of the *Corts valencianes*, the Valencian Parliament. In 500 years

Lucrezia Borgia has not been able to escape the calumnies of her second husband. Perhaps the tales were true—many scholars think so—but Giovanni Sforza did not know whether they were true or not. And nor do we. It is time to cover Lucrècia's bare breast.

The story of the great noble, confidant of the emperor and empress, who renounced all worldly titles and goods to live humbly and lead the Jesuits, is a powerful and romantic story. The future St. Francis Borja died in an aura of sanctity. The story of Francesc's conversion on the road to Granada is not original, but is highly effective. It is given a further twist because of the evil reputation of Alexander VI and his children. Francesc was doing penance for the sins of his family. The great, cruel warrior identified himself with Julius Caesar under the emblem, *Caesar or Nothing*. For the great Christian warrior Francesc, this would be converted to God or Nothing.

Cèsar Borja, Machiavelli's Prince. Statue in Gandia by Manuel Boix

The fuller story is not so holy. The Jesuits, Church within the Church, in their missions in the Americas and the Philippines, acted as the educational wing of Spain and Portugal's conquering imperial armies. After the defeats of Peru's indigenous peoples, it was the Jesuits who came to educate them in the true faith. The Society of Jesus supplied the intellectual and religious cover to conquest and forced conversion.

When the eleventh duke died without heir in the mid-eighteenth century, the Ducal Palace changed hands several times and was abandoned for a century before the Jesuits, in honor of Sant Francesc, bought it in 1890. Today five Jesuits still live in the private rooms and run a school.

GRAU DE GANDIA

The working-class town of Gandia is known as the Grau, the Valencian word for port or harbor: Castelló and Valencia city also have their *graus*. Towns in medieval times were often not built right on the coast, because land there is often unhealthily marshy and through fear of pirates. Even in the early twentieth century, in a town like Dènia, it was the poor fishing families and sailors who lived on the shore, where a storm could flood or wash away their shacks. The bourgeois vacationers of 100 years ago built their villas discreetly inland, away from malaria, poverty, and sea incursions.

Nowadays there is little movement through Gandia's harbor. Many years ago, before and just after the Civil War, it was the *país valencià's* main orange-exporting port, but now few oranges travel by boat, as most ride north by lorry along the Mediterranean Highway, the AP7, to France and Northern Europe. Here is Rafael Chirbes writing in *En la orilla* (*On the Edge*) of his fictional Misent (based on Dènia):

The bombardments of the war left the port in ruins for decades and Misent became a dead city. Ships that unloaded wood or cement and loaded raisins and figs, oranges, grapefruit and pomegranates, wood packing painted in striking colors within which the pieces of fruit were wrapped in delicate tissue paper, these ships no longer arrived.[41]

Gandia was little different. Today, there are few exports through Grau de Gandia. Many of the big harbor's quays are empty. The only visible signs of commercial activity are enormous brown rolls of newsprint stacked high in warehouses, imported for the Spanish newspaper industry. There is still a fishing fleet and men (no women) fish off the long harbor wall.

The *grau*, the wide protected harbor, is not old. It was constructed in the 1880s and in 1892 was taken over by the Alcoi-Gandia Railway and Harbour Company Ltd. This London-based firm constructed a railway from the inland industrial town of Alcoi to Gandia to import coal (lack of coal was a brake on Spain's industrial development) and export the products of Alcoi, an important industrial city of paper, engineering, and textiles (see Chapter 11). The line is still there, running across a traffic roundabout into the port, but was closed to trains in 1969. One of its locomotives stands, a toy or a ghost, in front of Gandia's railway station.

The British connection led to a curious anecdote many years later. In March 1939, at the end of the Spanish Civil War, Franco's victorious troops rapidly occupied the *país valencià*, the last part of the state to remain in Republican hands. Desperate bureaucrats and soldiers flooded the ports of Alacant and Grau de Gandia, hoping against hope for a ship to carry them to safety.

---

41   Chirbes, *En la orilla*, p.100.

Gavin Henderson, the second Lord Faringdon, a socialist fully committed to the Republican cause, had lent his 1915 Rolls-Royce as an ambulance in the Civil War. It returned home with bullet-holes in the chassis. He himself had volunteered as a stretcher-bearer. He opened Buscot Park, his stately home in Oxfordshire, to Basque refugee children.

At the end of the Civil War, Henderson was active again. The National Joint Committee for Spanish Relief hired a ship in Marseille. Henderson and others used the ship to take about 400 people from Alacant to Oran. They then returned to Gandia to pick up more refugees. Moored in Gandia harbor, the ship and HMS *Galatea* had no time to leave as Franco's troops moved into the *grau*. Faringdon and crew members hoisted a Union Jack and closed the harbor gates, telling the fascist soldiers they could not enter as the port was British property. Their bravado purchased a valuable few hours and the boats got away. *Si non è vero, è ben trovato*. Among the *Galatea*'s passengers was Colonel Casado, leader of the anti-communist coup in Madrid a few weeks earlier that hastened the end of the war.

Between the harbor and the mouth of the River Serpis lies the town of Grau de Gandia. One part is fairly poor, with narrow streets and blocks of apartments blistered by the salt and sun that assail seaside buildings. It looks like a working-class area of a large city and it cuts against preconceptions to find it here on the Costa Blanca. Beside it the neighborhood of Venècia (Venice), with ordinary villas toward the beach, has the touch of rococo fantasy that is characteristic of Valencian housing. You can call it imaginative, you can call it vulgar, but throughout the *país valencià* you see bright colors: a red, green, or yellow house, a fancy iron balustrade, or a curving marble stairway on a tatty suburban house.

TOURIST GANDIA

To the north of the *grau* stretches the third town of Gandia: *Gandia platja*, Gandia Beach, the strip of hotels and apartment blocks, high-rise with bars, restaurants, beachwear shops, trinket stalls, and estate agents on the ground floor, running northwards along the magnificent wide beach with its occasional imported palm and flimsy lifeguard stands on four white stilts. On the front, a few nondescript villas, with a woman's name ("Mari", "Nieves"…), a palm and orange tree in their gardens, recall the first vacationers to build by the beach fifty or sixty years ago.

In winter, this is a ghost town, block after block of empty apartments and hotel rooms. Sometimes at night you see a light in a high apartment: a few people do live in these hollow, tall shells. A family in crisis may have sold their city apartment and end up living more cheaply by the beach. Maybe someone thrown out of work hoped to sell their beach apartment, but too many people had the same idea. The multitude of tattered For Sale notices testify to the difficulty of selling a small flat in poorly-built blocks.

In summer Gandia's population of some 60,000 swells to 300,000. This is the classic high-rise beach resort, which has changed the entire Valencian coast in the last fifty years more than at any other time in human history. There is work, precarious and ill-paid, but work it is, in the summer, but for a visitor to Gandia platja, the mild winter is the best time.

There are three fine walks. The first runs from a beach hotel south into Grau de Gandia, past the harbor, through Venècia and up on the walkway along the River Serpis, a trickle in summer, but a surging torrent carrying soil and torn trees after autumn storms. Here you will see herons and ducks if you're lucky and a wild tangle of bamboo and reeds.

The second is north along the beach. After the hotels come the apartment blocks. The high-rises end quite abruptly. Suddenly the beach runs between the sea and marshy land full of tall reeds and water-birds for some two kilometers to the next town, Xeraco. Always, the low line of mountains behind the coast: "the bare mountains: stony, bluish slopes on which an occasional copse of pines grows; lower down, the terraces dotted with olive trees and the stain of a carob."[42] Colors vary, according to season, weather and the light changing through the day. Where Chirbes saw bluish slopes, Gerald Brenan described Gandia as "a landscape of orange trees and date palms, with the blue Mediterranean beating close by on a flat beach and the rose and violet mountains cutting the horizon in the distance."[43]

---

42   *Ibid*, p.95.
43   Brenan, p.112.

Beachcombing, Gandia, 2017

In winter the hills seemed bare and gray. We walked after a storm and all the junk of modern life, mainly twists and red bobs of plastic, was scattered across the sand, along with some of the little-remaining weed and small shells from the Mediterranean. We met an elderly man with three ancient horses, who was beachcombing. Out on the beach, you look inland: the ghostly, unoccupied near-skyscrapers are grouped to the left and, in front, an empty landscape of last year's dry, brown, and yellowish reeds poke out of the marsh's mud and water, running toward those bare hills five or six kilometers back from the shore. When you read of the coast destroyed by the tourism building boom, it is largely true, but it is not uniform tower-blocks from France to Gibraltar. Between the fishing villages converted to resorts, there are other landscapes. This beach, called L'Auir, is one of the few stretches of virgin shore left in Valencia and gives a poignant idea of what the whole coast was once like.

The Mediterranean is barely tidal: the sea rises and falls only a meter or so. This means that, all along the coast, there are marshy areas between land and water. In storms the sea sweeps into these marshes, bringing not just water, but sand forming dunes, which, when the sea is calm, separate the marsh, the *marjal*, from the sea. Then from the limestone mountains countless underground streams trickle into the marsh, bringing fresh water, "sweet water" as they say in Spanish and Catalan. The marshy land you see behind the L'Auir beach is a fascinating in-between domain, full of rotting vegetation, the detritus of the sea, the rubbish dumped by humans, tracks where fishermen find a path through the canes, tracks that change each season as the land changes with the movements of water. They say there are quicksands, mud that sucks you down. Into the *marjals* have vanished the unwary, murder victims and the corpses of dogs, cats, horses. In Rafael Chirbes' *On the Edge*, the great novel of the Spanish crisis, the muddy waters of a *marjal* become a symbol for where broken dreams and lives are dumped. There is no nature to offset corruption, rubbish, and death. The *marjal* is a shit-hole.

The third walk is inland. As you emerge behind the four or five blocks of the coastal high-rise strip, you find networks of paths leading into the orange groves, with irrigation channels running the water down from one of the numerous streams pouring off the hills. Many of these groves are on land reclaimed by draining the marshes. These are not big agricultural developments, but smallish plots, often with a house that is self-constructed and run-down. They are unpainted houses with broken fences, not wealthy housing nor weekend homes. People live here. The *país valencià* has not been a country of big estates, but relatively small exploitations, like these ones at Gandia. Nowadays, agro-industry is taking over and developing much of the country, but on this marshy land just back from the shore there is still no sign of it.

Parallel worlds: beach hotels from the orange groves

Alongside, behind or beside the tourist town, there is a parallel world where people live and work. This is probably true of most tourist resorts: people carry on their normal lives in Venice or downtown Barcelona despite the throngs of tourists. What is different here, in the Marina, on the Costa Blanca, is that there are places like these expanses of orange farms where tourists rarely tread, even though if you raise your head on the farm, you see that long line of cement and glass and even though anyone can walk away from the coast and into the groves. Few do, for it is a step through the looking-glass, into another world.

Water is a problem for the summer hotels, but not a problem for sustaining the orange groves and the small town, despite the 300-plus days of sun a year. In autumn, when the sea-wind meets these hills, as much rain falls in just a week as in the rest of the year. The faces of the hills looking out to the sea are often bare, but behind they are green and damp, with palms, pines, oaks, and carobs. The water hollows out caves in the limestone rock. In several of these, such as el Parpalló, cave paintings show that the coast was inhabited by humans some 30,000 years ago.

A paragraph of nuance, of warning not to romanticize what was. A century ago the plain between the hills and the sea was all marsh; no oranges. These *marjals* produced endemic malaria until well into the twentieth century. They were places where "reds" could be hunted and "disappeared" by Falangist patrols after the Civil War. Many were drained to give agricultural land to Franco's veterans or to build the tourist blocks. They were (and are) putrid-smelling dumping grounds for all sorts of detritus and the waste of the coast's industries.

Nor should we bend the stick too negatively: the *marjals* must have been wonderful places of early-morning mist and mystery, with flat-bottomed sculls paddled along the channels through the tall, thick reeds, quiet in the middle of the bustle. Today there are numerous small sweet-water lagoons (*ullals*) scattered among the fruit plots. They are full of wildlife: ducks of all kinds, herons, small turtles among water-lilies. On the *ullal gran* there is a bird-hide and an interpretation center, housed in the Alqueria del Duc (The Duke's Farmhouse), where the Dukes of Gandia entertained their often-royal guests with hunts through the marshes. You can imagine the king's falconer Ausiàs March with his birds on his outstretched, mail-clad forearm. And there are black horses grazing, often used to pull carts along the reed- and orange-fringed tracks of the area. Not only does a world parallel to tourism persist, but the past is present and tangible alongside the beach resort on all three walks: along the river, in the orange-filled recovered marshland, and on the long beach.

5: Anti-Pope and Tiger: Peníscola and Morella

"papa sum et XIII"

Papa Luna

Peníscola is the most beautiful village on the entire coast. A narrow isthmus, with beaches on both sides, leads to the old town on a rock. A nigh-impregnable fortress, "that tremendous castle poised on its high rock that juts out to the end of a narrow stalk of causeway"[44] in Rose Macaulay's phrase. The town is only walled on two sides, for on the other two, the guano-streaked cliffs drop vertically to the sea. It was originally an occasional island, as storms would drive water across the sandy isthmus.

I have had the luck to approach Peníscola on a sunny spring day. Some oranges were still on the trees while the new blossom was flowering alongside the fruit. The strong scent of the flowers filled the air. The tourist authorities dubbed this northern part of the *país valencià* the Costa del Azahar, the Orange-Blossom Coast. Fields of globe artichokes mingled with the lemon and orange smallholdings: the multi-leaved pale-green vegetable rose from among its long, curling, thistle-like leaves.

Ahead on this warm day, clouds covered the shoreline. As we drove into Peníscola, the day was transformed by a sea fret. The top of the great island-fortress ahead was covered in mist. The siren from the lighthouse on the mount

---

44   Macaulay, p.82.

was booming. When we got out of the car by the harbor, we watched the fishing boats emerging out of the fog, guided in by the siren.

Spain's greatest river, the Ebro, spills into the Mediterranean at the spout of its flat delta, like a horizontal volcano, only fifty kilometers to the north. The chemical nutrients carried off the fields by the river waters swell the size and numbers of fish in this part of the Mediterranean. In the *llotja*, the auction-house, the chanting auctioneer was knocking down lot after lot to Mercadona, the area's dominant supermarket chain (see Chapter 17). Outside, among the howling gulls, part too of the food chain, we began the climb to the square castle. The dimmed sun filtering through the mist cast magic over the village.

"That's a big one": unloading fish at Península

Here we are in the north of the *país valencià*, in the province of Castelló. Benicarló, connected by a ten-kilometer-long beach and high-rise strip to Península, and Vinarós are the remaining two villages before Valencia reaches Catalonia. Península was a setting for Anthony Mann's *El Cid* with Charlton Heston as the warrior. Luis García Berlanga, the fine if intemperately voluptuous Valencian director, used it in *Calabuch* (1956) and in his very last film, *París-Timbuctoo* (1999). Península is a picture-postcard town. Its cobbled, steep streets are car-free. Geraniums and aloes cascade from iron balconies on whitewashed houses. The balconies have tiles colored underneath, a Valencian feature, so that from the street you can look up at their beautiful patterns and glazing. Rose Macaulay in 1948 found these balconies "piled with ripening melons and hung with washing"[45] and felt the town was little changed from medieval times. The writer Paco Candel in 1964 thought it had a Greek air. He found people sitting on low stools by their front doors and sewing nets in the street. Early tourist consumers, Candel and his friends bought necklaces of coral and sea-shells.[46]

There is now something of an imitation of what really was a rougher, poorer place. The structures of the houses and alleys are the same; but the interiors and inhabitants have changed. Some streets are completely given over to tourist restaurants and trinket-shops run mainly by Argentinians and Andalusians. Nevertheless, you can still see the elderly in slippers with sticks staggering up and down the alleys and swearing in Catalan, *valencià*, that vernacular that has surprisingly survived centuries of Castilian-favoring centralist dominance.

---

45   *Ibid.*
46   Candel, Chapter 7.

At the top, the imposing castle. The mount was ceded by King Jaume I to the Knights Templar, who built their castle on the previous Arab fortress, modelled on those they had seen in the Holy Land during the Crusades. They completed it quickly, between 1294 and 1307, but were then expelled from Catalan lands by Jaume II (the "Just").

THE ANTI-POPE

By the castle gates, a great black two-meter-high seated statue of the most stubborn pope of all time, Papa Luna, gazes out over the town to sea, toward the Rome where he never reigned. The Borgias are not the only two Valencian popes. There were two others: Benedict XIII (Papa Luna) and, briefly, his successor, Clement VIII. Like the Borgias, their history is troubled. While Roderic de Borja was the Anti-Christ, Papa Luna was the Anti-Pope.

Born in 1328 in Illueca, Aragon, Pedro Martínez de Luna was a learned professor of canonical law at Montpellier and became a cardinal at Avignon in 1375. The papal schism was a result of a conflict between the French monarchy and the papacy. The French Clement V, narrowly elected in 1305, had refused to move to Rome, settling the papal court in Avignon in 1309. Six French popes succeeded him, until finally, in 1376, Gregory XI moved the papacy back to Rome and unity. The intransigence (dementia, perhaps) of Urban VI, Gregory XI's successor, led to a further split, known as the Western Schism. Papa Luna, who had supported the 1376 reunification, was this schism's second pope, elected in Avignon in 1394.

The French Crown soon withdrew its support for this second split and the king's armies besieged Avignon. Luna fled, first to Perpignan (or Perpinyà, then belonging to the

Crown of Aragon) and Barcelona, then to Peníscola, where he arrived in 1415 with his depleted finances and court of only four cardinals.

Despite limited support, this very old and, by most accounts, brilliant man insisted he was the true pope, resisting all attempts at conciliation. At the 1415 Council of Constance he was condemned as a heretic, but continued to issue his papal bulls from Peníscola. He died aged ninety-four in 1423 and by 1429 the papacy was reunited, in large part through the diplomacy of the young Alfons de Borja, the future Callixtus III. The papacy being reunited by a Borgia is a pleasing link between the Crown of Aragon's four popes.

Benedict XIII's notorious stubbornness probably led to the common Spanish phrase *mantenerse en sus trece* ("to hold to your thirteen"), meaning to hold firm to one's beliefs or position against all sound arguments. Luna was his family name, but it also means moon in Spanish, with the easy association of lunatic. Luna is supposed to have repeated at each challenge to his legitimacy, *papa sum et XIII*. At the crack in the rock, known as the "pope's blow-hole," where the sea on a rough day appears to boil and roars up, you can still hear Benedict XIII's cries of protest.

What are we to make of Papa Luna 600 years on? A ghostly, distant figure in a lost world, yet he is a solid, real, awkward old man, as Rose Macaulay caught in one of her brilliant evocations:

> He too paced those high ramparts, and stared across the Mediterranean towards Rome, surrounded by his bored, Rome-sick, Avignon-sick cardinals...he composed and declaimed angry bulls, that should cause the future to change, the Council of Constance to reverse its declaration of schism and summon him from this

so tedious way of life. Did the young Moors of Peñíscola stare and jeer and throw stones from the ramparts as the fallen anti-pope and his cardinals swept in and out of the ancient church, or up and down those steep streets to the little beach and back? ... Did poor Papa Luna look a proud pope, or merely a lonely, weary, schismatic, disgruntled elderly man?[47]

I doubt that anyone dared throw stones at the fallen Anti-Pope. He lived at Peníscola under the protection, fragile given his condemnation in 1415 but protection nonetheless, of King Alfons "the Magnaminous." The Avignon papacy was not without its support. From 1380 on, the famous Dominican rabble-rouser and Jew-hater, Vicent Ferrer, had preached in favor of the Avignon popes. Joan I ordered that no one should harm Ferrer, explaining with surprising liberalism "that God has given freedom of knowledge and choice, especially in questions of conscience."[48]

It was not that the Kings of Aragon were paragons of free thought, but rather that they ruled over a world that demanded complex balances. The Cathar (or Albigensian) heresy had also found support in Catalan lands. The kings found it expedient to practice "tolerance" of some religious differences. The fifteenth century in Valencia was not yet the age of the religious orthodoxy associated with the Counter-Reformation.

In April 2000 Papa Luna was back in the news. His skull was stolen in the early morning from a semi-abandoned palace in the village of Sabiñán, near Saragossa. It soon transpired that the thieves were not skilled. They wrote to

---

47   Macaulay, pp.82-3.
48   Fuster, p.187.

the Mayor of Illueca, Papa Luna's home town, demanding a ransom. They were not quite so stupid, though, as to turn up to meet the police for the agreed payment. The hand-written letter, published in the media, contained multiple spelling mistakes. In a second letter, equally riddled with errors, the author complained bitterly about public mockery of his low level of culture. A third letter weeks later stated that the skull had been sold and was being used for satanic rites.

Finally, after five months confounding the Civil Guard, a twenty-year old called Santiago was arrested. He and his underage brother had stolen the skull. The saga ended with a mild prison sentence, later converted to a fine, for the perpetrator. But Papa Luna's name had hit the headlines. The prophecy of Vicent Ferrer, when he turned against Papa Luna after the Council of Constance, was spectacularly fulfilled: "To punish Papa Luna's pride, someday children will play ball with his head." Peníscola should put up a statue to the failed Santiago, whose macabre and comical theft brought Papa Luna back from oblivion.

Virgin Hills and Golden Harbor

Peníscola's northern beaches are little different from Cullera or Gandia's, but running south nearly twenty kilometers to Alcossebre is the startling coastal range, the Serra d'Irta. These low hills, rising between highway and sea to reach 573 meters at the highest point, are the only extensive virgin coast remaining in the *país valencià*. Building is prohibited by the area's classification as a nature park. It now has well-marked routes up and down the hills, leading to numerous rocky coves. Here you can bathe, nude or clothed, alone or in chosen company, in a sort of dream abstracted from the packed beaches, fried food, and smell of sun lotion of the rest of the coast.

From Peníscola town hall, follow the signs that lead rapidly into the park. The main route is circular, so you return to your starting point. The *serra* smells of thyme, rosemary, juniper, sage, and lavender, the rough, hardy bushes that survive dry Mediterranean summers. When you brush against them, sharp scents are released.

Two routes, one high and one near sea level, lead (a half-day's walk) from Peníscola south to Alcossebre. There are isolated coves and dunes on the low path. You may come across the Torre Abadum, a Moorish watchtower, the ruins of later towers that looked out for Berber pirates and the remains of a police station that spied on smugglers till the mid-twentieth century. It can be hot, very hot. The pines are the skeletons left after forest fires and the twisted olives, dwarf palms, carobs, and holm oaks among the stone and scrub are few and stunted, providing little shade. Little shade and little noise. The silence allows you to hear a cicada whirring, a breeze stirring leaves or a wave breaking on the rocks.

South from Alcossebre, a quiet town famous for paella and hot springs on the beach, lie Benicàssim and Orpesa and a sudden change. The Marina d'Or (Golden Harbor) complex north of Orpesa is the antithesis of the Serra d'Irta. Started in the 1990s, it occupies 1.5 million square meters of former agricultural land and stretches along two kilometers of coast. This "Vacation City," a "new concept" according to the propaganda, with its 18,000 apartments, five hotels (two three-star, two four-star, and one five-star), restaurants, pools, cinemas, supermarkets, beauty salons, sports facilities, and golf courses, is aimed at children and infantilized adults. It is like a shopping mall with residences and attraction park thrown in. Marina d'Or does not respect public right-of-way along the coast as its beaches, expanded with sand dragged from the seabed, are private. It is modeled on Las Vegas as its elephant sculptures in the sea, Disney architecture, and gaudy colors suggest.

It was going to be even bigger. It was going to have several golf courses and 30,000 apartments gobbling up orange groves and wetlands. Promotion offices for the scheme were opened in Beijing and New York. In 2008 the economic crisis struck. Suddenly the credit tap dried. Fortunately, in this case, because Marina d'Or is an ecological disaster as well as an ethical and aesthetic one. There is not enough water. Even if the economic crisis had not struck, the expansion might well have been stopped, for the local council was insisting that, to go ahead, the complex would need its own sewage works and water-desalination plant.

The promoter and owner of this tourist complex is a former mattress manufacturer, Jesús Ger. When crisis struck, he skillfully separated the building part of his company, which declared bankruptcy, from the park, which continues to function. At its peak, some fifty apartments a week were being sold at 300,000 euros apiece. Now there are weeks with zero sales and the flats are on offer for 80,000. Thousands of owners are trapped. The complex loses money today, but Jesús Ger's developments in Eastern Europe have kept it afloat. Ger is now looking for investors, but it would seem they are not rushing to Castelló airport.

Just as Benidorm's lift-off had been boosted by the new airport of Alacant in 1966, so Marina d'Or would depend on Castelló's airport. "If you haven't got an airport, you don't exist," said Ger. The new airport opened officially in 2011, just before regional elections. However, there were no airlines contracted to use it and no government license for its operation. It was an airport without planes. The first commercial flight landed in September 2015. By 2017, there were five destinations: an early-morning arrival from Bristol and others to and from Eastern Europe.

Castelló airport, which cost 150 million euros, has become a symbol of corruption in the *país valencià*. It failed to reproduce fifty years later the mutually profitable relationship between Alacant airport and Benidorm. All around Spain, closed provincial airports and little-used high-speed train stations stand as monuments to the politicians who between c.1990 and 2008 had them built. Why? One, because they found a way to stay in power by exploiting their voters' feelings of local pride; two, because it seemed money grew on trees and large branches could be broken off for politicians' friends, the builders; and three, the lust for immortality that drives ambition. Leave my name in stone.

The promoter of this airport, Carlos Fabra, president of the Castelló Diputació (Provincial Council) from 1995 to 2011, certainly thought he was immune, if not immortal. Immune to mockery, he had a statue of himself placed by the airport entrance with a plane on its head. Son and grandson of presidents (the old Francoist families never die), one of no fewer than seven Fabras to become president of the Diputació since the nineteenth century, he was finally sentenced in 2014 to four years' imprisonment for tax fraud to the tune of 700,000 euros. Living way above his salary, Fabra, collector of vintage cars, fell foul of the tax authorities like Al Capone. His explanation of his wealth was that he had won the lottery several years running, which led to a popular new phrase, "as lucky as Fabra."

To underline the grotesqueness of the money spent on the empty airport, the new hospital at Llíria, a big town inland from Valencia, that cost some 20 million euros to build, was mothballed until 2015, six years after completion, because of lack of funds. Castelló airport has become a symbol of megalomania and squandering of public money at a time of austerity.

The only plane soaring
at Castelló airport

It is worth turning off the AP7 highway at Torreblanca and climbing through thickly forested hills the fifteen kilometers to the airport at Benlloch. The huge steel and copper statue, fourteen meters high and weighing 33 tons, dominates the entrance to the airport. Yet, if one can abstract oneself from the dire corruption and waste surrounding the airport, it is a fine work of art in itself: an enormous cubist head facing three ways with a plane perched on top. The rust-browned part of the trunk has made it a two-tone sculpture. One of the three faces has a finger raised in query or quandary to its lips. The sculptor Juan Ripollés says that it is an "allegory of the human brain's creative capacity." The airplane roars out of the statue's brain: a modern creation myth.

Castelló airport is the quietest I have ever seen. We saw only one person inside the terminal, a young woman jabbing at her *telefonino* in the car-hire kiosk. No cafeteria open, no security, no check-in, no departures, no arrivals. One wall is dominated by a huge advert for Marina d'Or, somewhat poignantly. Castelló airport is ghostly, a surreal witness to waste of public money.

AFTER THE KING, CABRERA

Not many novelists are bankers. Even fewer are left-wing bankers. Elena Moya employs her grasp of the economics of the crisis to explain what is happening and combines this with a keen sense of the injustice of the 1939 defeat of the Republic. Her second novel *La maestra republicana* (*The Spanish Maestra*) is set in Morella, "a labyrinth of narrow slopes and streets established on top of a hill crowned by a medieval castle."[49] The plot explains the corrupt workings of the Generalitat Valenciana, including Castelló airport

---

49   Moya, p.57.

discussed above. It is a work of fiction (the novel's Mayor of Morella has absolutely nothing to do with the real Mayor of Morella at that time, Ximo Puig) that rings true on Valencia's finances.

Morella, remote, cold, and arid, stands in the Maestrat (Maestrazgo) mountains, named originally after the presence of the Templars (Masters). At 960 meters above sea level, Morella is under an hour's drive inland from Peníscola, that other great castle on a rock. Morella's walls are intact: two and a half kilometers long, two meters thick, and ten meters high, with fourteen towers and six gates. It takes an hour to walk right around the walled town.

Morella has been a strategic point since pre-Roman times, but it is not impregnable. Nowhere is. El Cid stormed it in 1084. Espartero took it from Cabrera in 1840. Today it is one of the most exceptional towns in Europe. Inside the walls its medieval street layout is tempered by modern tourism, but not so much as one might expect, given how spectacular are both its setting and stones. This town on a rock is surrounded by a plateau cut deep with gorges, giving a rippling effect to the views.

Valencia has been a war-torn land. Not only in the thirteenth century with the conquest of Valencia by Jaume I, but in the twentieth century with the Civil War (Chapter 14), in the nineteenth with the French invasion and the Carlist Wars, and in the eighteenth, with the burning of Xàtiva and slaughter by the troops of the Bourbon king (Chapter 2).

Protestant missionary and adventurer George Borrow had this to say of the Carlist Wars:

> The Spanish armies of Don Carlos were composed entirely of thieves and assassins, chiefly Valencians and Manchegans, who, marshalled

under two cut-throats, Cabrera and Palillos, took advantage of the distracted state of the country to plunder and massacre the honest part of the community.[50]

A good political polemicist, Borrow liked to reduce the opposition to criminals.

The career of the *cut-throat* Ramon Cabrera is a fascinating one. It is the story of Carlism, that strange (to us) nineteenth-century phenomenon of a mass movement based on absolutist principles that took particular root in Catalonia, the *país valencià* and the Basque Country. Carlism had huge popular support. Karl Marx coined the phrase: "Carlism, people without ideas; Liberalism, ideas without people." Cabrera (1806–77) was Carlism's most famous general. Dubbed "The Tiger of the Maestrazgo" by his enemies, he became the pretender Don Carlos' Count of Morella.

During the reign of Spain's absolutist monarch Fernando VII in the 1820s, it was assumed that his brother would succeed him as Carlos V. Yet Carlos was outmaneuvered and, on Fernando's death in 1833, it was his daughter Isabel who became queen. Aged only three, the infant *Infanta* was controlled by Fernando's widow the Regent María Cristina. Not only was Carlos deprived of the throne, but in reaction to Fernando VII's absolutism a more liberal regime was introduced. Civil War over the succession broke out, the first of the three Carlist Wars of the nineteenth century (1833–40, 1846–49, 1872–76).

The Carlists particularly detested the government of Mendizábal, the only Jew ever to preside over the Spanish government (1835–36). A queen, a Jewish prime minister,

---

50   Borrow, *The Bible in Spain*, p.xi.

the Inquisition abolished—what was absolutist Spain coming to! It was under Mendizábal that the monasteries were disestablished, reducing though not smashing the Church's power and providing the cities with new building land.

Spain's liberal reformers of the 1830s had their bases in the big cities, whereas Carlism had no problem attracting a peasantry disaffected and impoverished by the Napoleonic Wars and the changes in society caused by nascent capitalism. Carlos promised the restoration of the traditional *furs* granting local rights, abolished in the New Order Decrees of Felipe V. Add to this that Carlism's main support was in the "periphery," the Basque nation and the area of the former Crown of Aragon, where centuries-old resentment at conquest then taxation imposed from Madrid thrived. In Catalonia and the Maestrat, too, guerrillas (or bandits) had a long history.

Carlism was a reactionary movement whose many individualist leaders and supporters were affected by liberal-romantic ideas. Byron, poet and would-be liberator of Greece, was an inspiration, as was Simón Bolívar, liberator of South America. Beethoven's Heroica Symphony was appropriated as an anthem. Later, Carlism chimed with Conservative forces in England, as we will see, and Joseph Conrad wrote a haunting romantic novel, *The Arrow of Gold* (1919), on Carlism. Conrad, whose family had fought for similar ideas in Poland, shared the romance in the ultra-conservative values of God, Fatherland, and King, the three traditionalist "ideas" of Carlism.

Ramon Cabrera was born in 1806 to a seafaring and trading family in Tortosa, a town near the mouth of the River Ebro in southern Catalonia. He was not destined to be a general, as he trained for the priesthood. Nor did he show any great affection for Carlos's cause until the uprisings in the Tortosa area in 1833 against Isabel's accession to the throne. Nevertheless, along with dozens of other young men of Tortosa, Cabrera was suspected of Carlist sympathies and was ordered into preventive exile in Barcelona by the military governor. He left, ostensibly to go to Barcelona, but traveled cross-country, now an outlaw, to join the Carlists who had seized Morella.

Morella was then rapidly retaken by the liberal forces, a disciplined army against Carlism's rag-tag volunteers. Cabrera's legend started in the following months. Filthy and hungry, with just a few companions, hunted through the Maestrat mountains by Isabel's troops, he steadily recruited to his band. In classic guerrilla style he moved with speed, harassing the more static armies. The liberal army, billeted on the local populations, was as hated as any occupying force. By the start of 1834, Cabrera was already a recognized leader. "After the King, Cabrera," was the Carlist salute during his years of glory. His adventures, slipping at times in disguise into Tortosa to see his family, or traveling incognito to see the Pretender Carlos in Navarra, have fed countless romantic novels (at least twenty!), films, and legends.

A hundred years later, the *maquis* communist guerrillas followed Cabrera's trails through the hills of the Maestrat, "tapping into a long-held Spanish tradition of bandoleros and outcasts swarming over an untamed countryside," in Jason Webster's words in his excellent *Sacred Sierra*.[51] The *maquis* fought the Franco dictatorship during the 1940s in these same mountains and was again sustained by considerable popular support. For ten years small groups of the AGLA, the Guerrilla Groups of the Levante and Aragon, with the advantage of local knowledge, kept in check the Civil Guard. The AGLA was the largest *maquis* in Spain, aided by its relative closeness to France and the

---

51   Webster, *Sacred Sierra*, p.163.

local guerrilla tradition. It integrated many anarchists, given the greater weight of anarchism in the area and the AGLA's looseness of structure. Another strange detail was that one of the AGLA's most famous members was Juana *la Pastora*, the Shepherdess, an intersex person who on finally being arrested was sent first to a women's, then to a men's prison. *La Pastora* survived seventeen years in prison after a commuted death sentence, married as a man, and died aged eighty-seven in 2004.[52]

To return to the Carlists, in 1834 Cabrera's mother, María Griñó, and three sisters were imprisoned in Tortosa. On February 16, 1836, after eighteen months in prison, his mother was shot on the orders of General Agustín Noguera. This barbarity was then matched by Cabrera, who had wives of army officials captured and executed. A cycle of reprisals led to the intervention of British envoys (as the Spanish Mediterranean coast's principal trading partners, they wanted peace for business) who urged, to little avail, their "Liberal" allies to respect the rights of prisoners.

In 1837, Cabrera led the "Royal Expedition," the march on Madrid to dethrone Isabel. The Carlist columns from Navarra and the Maestrat combined and on August 24 defeated the queen's army at Villar de los Navarros, near Daroca in Aragon, opening the road to the state capital. Carlist fervor was then at its height among British Tories. Excited journalists rode out from Madrid to meet the pretender's army. Cabrera's advance cavalry reached the wall of Madrid's Retiro Park, but the Carlists failed to occupy the capital despite the road being clear. Like Hannibal before Rome, the Pretender Don Carlos and/or Cabrera hesitated. Cabrera turned back, to "consolidate support." The Carlists did not risk all on victory and lost all by not risking. The

---

52   *Ibid*, p.164.

queen's general Espartero harried the retreating Carlist armies, turning the tables by avoiding a direct engagement and using guerrilla tactics. The Carlist rank-and-file was demoralized and felt betrayed. Eventually, in 1840 the war was lost.

After the failure of the march on Madrid, Cabrera daringly took Morella and established a mini-state in the Maestrat. His military skills resisted the queen's army, which laid siege to the town but was forced to withdraw. Nevertheless, the failure to take Madrid represented the end of any real possibility of victory for the Carlists. In 1840 Cabrera was finally forced out of Morella by Espartero and found refuge, first in France, then in London. Here, in 1850, in an improbable historical twist, the fearless ultra-Catholic general married a twenty-nine-year-old Protestant heiress, Marianne Richards. The second part of Cabrera's life could not have been more unlike the first. Marianne bought the Wentworth estate in Surrey. Cabrera lived in great wealth between Wentworth and London for the rest of his life and died at Wentworth in 1877.

The enormous Wentworth estate consists now of luxury mansions and three golf courses, much played on by the golfer from Castelló, Sergio García. Wentworth was host for forty years to the World Match Play Championships and is still headquarters of the Professional Golf Association's European Tour. Marianne and Cabrera lived in what is now the main clubhouse. There are few traces of Cabrera: a portrait in the clubhouse, which Cabrera had named Tortosa Cottage, and in the village, a Cabrera Avenue and Morella Close. I wonder what the residents make of those names.

Cabrera moved in high society in London. Despite Carlism's Catholic extremism, Marianne assisted Cabrera to raise enormous sums from Tory sympathizers of the cause.

Yet Cabrera took no part in the Third Carlist War, which started in 1872. He had distanced himself from the fanatically religious grandson of the original pretender, also Carlos.

There is a fascinating final act to Cabrera's life. In 1873, aged sixteen, the future King Alfonso XII (reigned 1874–85) was a cadet at the Sandhurst Military Academy, just five miles from Wentworth. He and his entourage initiated various contacts with Cabrera. Alfonso courted the aging general: Spain was in a lamentable state, they could agree, because of the First Republic. If he reached the throne, Alfonso maintained, he would bring stability and peace. Alfonso insisted on his commitment to traditional Catholicism, distancing himself from the "Liberalism" of his mother Queen Isabel (the three-year-old who had come to the throne in 1833 and was deposed in 1868). He would restore properties seized from the Church in 1838. There were, too, personal enticements: he would confirm Cabrera as Count of Morella and grant him a full general's pension. The future king visited Cabrera's sumptuous residence at Wentworth. One would love to have been concealed behind the thick curtains.

The deal was struck. Cabrera's support for Isabel's son fatally weakened the Carlist cause: their most famous general and greatest fundraiser had gone over to the enemy. The Tiger had been tamed. A few weeks later, in January 1874, Alfonso landed at Valencia and entered Madrid as king. Though the Carlist armies fought on, politically and soon militarily their cause was defeated.

To this day, of the remaining gaggles of Carlist sympathizers, many see Ramon Cabrera as a traitor. Rightly so: he sold out. He was also their greatest, most charismatic leader, who took them to the brink of victory in 1837.

D. RAMON CABRERA

Ramon Cabrera, the Tiger of the Maestrazgo
(Wikimedia Commons)

PART TWO:
Cities

The Banco de Valencia, pride and glory of the city's business
class, sold to CaixaBank for one euro in 2012

"Little Gibraltar": the Penyal d'Ifach, Calp

6: Benidorm: Blowsy, Beautiful, and Corrupt

*"A new Europe had sprung up along the beaches
of the Mediterranean, in effect a linear city 3000
miles long and 300 meters deep, that stretched from
Gibraltar to Glyfada beach beyond the eastern
suburbs of Athens"*

James G. Ballard[53]

The AP7 highway from the north runs past a long line of resorts. From the highway, you can read the huge sign announcing MARINA D'OR, the "Golden Harbor" leisure complex just north of Orpesa. Benicarló and Peníscola precede Orpesa; Benicàssim follows it on the Orange-Blossom Coast. South of Valencia city, after the flat rice fields of the Albufera, a hill on the shore announces CULLERA in big white letters, preceding the ribbons of apartments and hotels along the beaches of Cullera, Gandia, Dènia, Xàbia, Calp, and Benidorm, on what the tourist industry dubbed the Costa Blanca (White Coast).

For Valencians, this coast around Benidorm is the Marina, a Catalan-speaking area. Despite the intense tourist development of the past sixty years, it is still recognizable (this is why people keep coming) as what Ford saw in the 1840s:

The whole Marina is a picture: you have a beauteous sky, blue broken headlands, a still deep

---

53   Ballard, *The Kindness of Women*, p.121.

green sea, with craft built for the painter skimming over the rippling waves, and a crew dressed as if for an opera ballet; then inland are wild mountain gorges, mediaeval turrets and castles, rendered more beautiful by time and ruin.[54]

COASTAL TOWNS

Benidorm is the concentrated working-class resort *par excellence* and much of this chapter will focus on this world-famous city. First, a look at neighboring towns. I used to think they were all the same: golden beaches, high-rise buildings, and the bare hills behind, but this is not so. Go north from Benidorm just fifteen kilometers to Altea and there is no high-rise strip. Altea's buildings along the front do not exceed four or five stories. Its considerable bohemian-artistic population has the economic clout to control development. Altea's style is assisted, too, by its lack of sand: the beaches are pebbly. Steep streets ascend to the old quarter's flat hill-top square, paved with a type of modern cobble: pebbles set into cement. Its restored houses are mostly painted white. From the top of the hill, you can see the skyscrapers of Benidorm to the south and the mountainous cape separating Altea from Calp to the north.

The writer Arturo Barea went there to convalesce in 1937 during the Civil War:

> Altea is almost as old as its hill; it has been Phoenician, Greek, Roman, Arabic, and Spanish. Its flat-roofed white houses, plain walls pierced by window-holes, climb the hill in a spiral which follows the mule-

---

track with its age-polished, worn stone steps. The church has a slender tower, the minaret of a mosque, and a blue-tiled dome…Around the hill are olive and pomegranate groves, and terraces of cultivated land scooped out from the rock.[55]

Altea is extremely pretty, with great views of sea and mountain: always the hills, changing color as the time of day, the weather, or the season changes. Pretty but contrived: like Peníscola, it is now an imitation of the Mediterranean fishing village that it was in Barea's time. All the businesses on the hill are bars or restaurants: you have to clamber down and back up again with a heavy basket if you live there and want to go shopping.

Beside Altea, another of the small rivers that run off the hills every few kilometers has created a small estuary with swans, moorhens, and grebes. Here too are eels and the threatened Spanish turtle. Despite pollution, despite the unsustainable construction, the Marina maintains its private corners.

If Altea and Benidorm organize themselves differently, Cullera is slightly different again. This town lies some twenty kilometers north of Gandia (see Chapter 4). Like Gandia it is divided into a harbor and working-class quarter, an older town and a long, thick ribbon of tourist high-rise blocks. Here, though, the main town is not inland, but between the long beach and the harbor on the River Xúquer, the Valencian Community's longest river at 498 kilometers.

On the quays at the mouth of the Xúquer you can watch the ancient theater of a fishing fleet chugging in toward winter dusk. Flat trolleys with boxes of ice are wheeled out, the boxes are passed onto the boats, the fish are sorted into the boxes by men in neck-to-ankle yellow aprons and the

---

55   Barea, pp.686-7.

boxes are passed out again to the trolley. Then, the trolley is pushed into the *llotja*, the auction-house. Pulleys wind up nets on a large wheel. Other nets are stretched out on the quay and men with enormous wooden needles stitch the holes. The whole process is comfortingly labor-intensive. When the boats come in, there are two hours of hard work.

Old men watch. Tourists, like us, take pictures (though the postcards nearly always have better ones). The quay on the Xúquer has the fascination of a working port. The smell of old fish, brine, and diesel is pleasant by the river, though not a smell you would wish to take home. Locals carry fish home in buckets. Do not be lulled, though, into the romantic dream of centuries-old labor and an unchanging sea. Fish are scarce, the Mediterranean is seriously contaminated and, nestling in its beautiful valley 100 kilometers up-river, lies the threat, invisible from Cullera, of the Cofrentes nuclear power station, cooled by the Xúquer's water.

A few kilometers south of Cullera is another startling spot: L'Estany de Cullera, the Cullera Lake, a magical lagoon separated by a brief ridge of dune from the sea. It is an old mouth of the Xúquer. You can walk right around this large lake, adorned with swans, ducks, moorhens, grebes, and black, sleek-feathered cormorants, which sit in elegant alertness on mooring posts and prows of rowing boats.

In several places the mountains on this coast reach the sea: the Montgó range between Xàbia and Dènia, the cape sheltering Moraira from the northerly winds, the huge mountain between Calp and Altea, with a spectacular road through tunnels and between precipice and ravine. The Trenet de la Marina, the little train or tram that runs from Alacant to Dènia along the coast, is even more spectacular. In summer it serves to take drinkers and disco users home at all hours.

The most famous of these mountains is the Penyal d'Ifach at Calp: a 332-meter rock upended on the coast and a famous navigational aid for ancient mariners. It was a beacon for pirates, too, who so ravaged Calp that it remained uninhabited for most of the seventeenth century. The Penyal d'Ifach is known as "Little Gibraltar," as its shape, seen side-on, with a few trees straggling along the top like lone hairs on a bald head, is not dissimilar.

The Penyal today is the smallest of Valencia's nature parks, home to twenty-two plant endemisms and refuge to rare snails and lizards. Here gulls come into their own. Just flying rats chewing over fast-food droppings in the cities, they become elegant owners of the air over and around the Penyal. They are so common that we hardly notice them, but if they were rare, camera-loaded twitchers would be elbowing each other for a shot at this big bird's pure-white chest, yellow beak, and mottled tail. The soundtrack of the climb up the Penyal is their hoarse cries; or, to be anthropocentric, their mocking laughter as they caw, croak, and whistle. You can climb the Penyal, passing through a tunnel to the seaward side and a path to the peak with ropes and chains to hang onto. From the top, Ibiza (Eivissa) is visible on a clear day, it is said. You can certainly see the towers of Benidorm.

Calp has historical attractions. In its Roman baths and storage pools by the sea, fish could be kept alive until it was time to eat them. It has a substantial old town with a Catalan-speaking population and restored walls built to keep the pirates out. And it has another sensational natural attraction: the salt flats just behind the Penyal and the front. These were flooded with sea water, then drained for salt until the second half of the twentieth century, but now it is a wild lake, with flamingos who live there all year round since global warming has removed their need to migrate. From the viewing platform by the lake you can get quite close to the young, less cautious flamingos. They are white, while the adults have the pink wings of the pretty flamingo. I learned something: the pinkness comes from pigments in the crustaceans they eat. Young ones haven't yet eaten enough to stain their feathers.

Some years ago, before visiting this coast, I imagined it totally covered in concrete, as James G. Ballard's quote that heads the chapter suggests. It is not quite like that: first because the mountains and cliffs prevent building, but also because the parallel Valencian world stubbornly persists alongside the tourist one. There is another feature, though, that took me by surprise. I'd seen enough photos of Calp and Benidorm to know what to expect of the high-rise seafront. What I hadn't bargained for was the extent of villas covering every possible nook and cranny, perching under cliffs, climbing steep hillsides. These are mostly second homes, not two-week tourism lodgings, but villas where retired pink-faced foreigners (Spaniards, too) winter like migrating flamingos.

The foreign residents and long-term visitors have created another parallel world. Few desire to learn Spanish or Catalan. They live in ghettoes, with their own bars, their own discos, their own lawyers, their own churches, their own supermarkets. In the small village of Moraira I counted eight estate agents (one grocery store). Near Altea there is a huge gold-domed Russian Orthodox church. Everywhere you stumble over German supermarkets or English bars. Read the *Costa Blanca News* and you can hire English-speaking plumbers or dog groomers, lawyers, massagists, or car dealers.

Two anecdotes. An *alacantina* told me this one. She enters a bar in L'Alfàs del Pi, orders a beer and, seeing all the posters and signs in English, asks the English guy serving, "Do you get a lot of foreigners 'round here, then?" "No, no, hardly any. Just occasionally, a Spaniard like you."

The other anecdote occurred at a point at the northern end of Calp, where there is a beautiful side-on view of the Penyal d'Ifach. We entered a bar, to have a coffee and savor the view. In Chapter 1, I praise the Hotel Azahar at Sagunt; here I mention the Bar Flamenco. Just as the hotel is the only hotel, this is the only bar in the book.

We asked a middle-aged woman for two coffees with a dash of milk (*cortado* or *tallat*, Spanish/Catalan), one of them weak in coffee. We spoke in Spanish. She came back with a *cortado* and a long black coffee. "No," we said, "two *cortados*, but one weak in coffee." Marisa tried to explain. The woman's face closed: "No, we haven't any." She was hostile; she did not try to understand. She stormed off. We left too. Please avoid the Bar Flamenco in Calp. Only later, in another bar where the young Valencian women, seeing my foreign features, amiably attempted to speak in English, did I realize that Flamenco means in Spanish both Flamingo and Flemish. It will have been a Flemish bar.

How can someone run a bar in a Valencian village without speaking any Spanish at all? It's common, because of this other parallel world, where Germans hang out in German bars and the British drink pints in union-jack pubs. It is hard to describe the strangeness of a town like Calp, a mini-Benidorm with its hotels and apartment blocks all along its two main beaches, then the great untamable rock and, right behind the line of hotels, the lake, with ploughed fields around it. And flamingos. And the Bar Flamenco. Various parallel worlds.

Sparkling Dream Town

One might think Benidorm's name had Latin roots and meant "Sleep Well." No. Like many a Valencian town, its name is Arabic, Beni-darhim, property of the Darhim family.

The poets Sylvia Plath and Ted Hughes spent several weeks in Benidorm on their honeymoon in the summer of 1956. Sylvia was on a high, in the happiest and most optimistic period of her short life. A radiant letter to her mother ("Our life is incredibly wonderful"[56]) gives her first impression of the village:

> After an hour of driving through the red sand desert hills, dusty olive orchards, and scrub grass that is so typical around here, and then saw the blaze of blue sea, clean curve of beach, immaculate white houses and streets, like a small, sparkling dream town, I felt instinctively with Ted that this was our place.[57]

They rented a room from a woman they'd met on the bus, right on the front, "with a palm and pine tree growing in the front yard, a back and side garden full of red geraniums, white daisies, roses, a fig tree...a backdrop of purple mountainous hills, incredibly lovely."

For the sake of verity, it should be recorded that Sylvia's highs were part of sharp mood swings. In her diary she contradicts the letters to her mother. The racist from a privileged background pops out. She records the "bad dirty bathroom, ant-infested kitchen...to be shared with...the piggy Spaniards."[58] Both were true: the beauty and the beastly.

Sylvia Plath was in Benidorm right at the start of the development of the village:

> ...while Benidorm is just being discovered by tourists, except for the hotels, it is utterly uncommercial, built along a mile curve of perfect beach, with glassy, clear waves breaking on shore, a large rock island out in the bay, and the most

---

56   Plath, p.263.
57   *Ibid*, p.262.
58   Anne Stevenson, p.93.

incredible azure sea, prussian blue toward the horizon and brilliant aqua nearer shore.[59]

Sylvia was living in an exultant, inner paradise and she had found a place to reflect her excitement and joy. Rose Macaulay, passing through a few years earlier, corroborates her vision:

> Benidorm...whose sandy bay is like a crescent moon, stands crowded very beautifully round its domed and tiled church on a rocky peninsula.[60]

So what is the story of Benidorm in the sixty years since? A fall from paradise to the ugly high-rise city of today, as Rafael Chirbes narrates? Toward the end of his life, Chirbes wrote two books on the destruction of the Valencian coast, *Crematorio* and *En la orilla* (*On the Edge*). They are harsh, bitter novels that leave no character intact or, as they say in Spanish, leave no puppet with its head. They explain the ubiquity of brothels and casinos, the dominance of crime, and the intricacies of property speculation. More grandly, they evoke the fall:

> Juan says: The recent history of Misent is a parodic, inverted journey: it starts in Paradise and goes on downhill until it hits the bottom...the Misent of his childhood, with almost deserted beaches where the sea left shells, starfish, dry sponges, and that smelled of Posidonia rotting, of sea-weed drying in the sun, of putrid fish; smell of iodine, of saltpeter; textures sliding between solid and liquid...this Misent does not exist; it's

---

59   Plath, p.262.
60   Macaulay, p.107.

been replaced by all these houses being built, the booms of the cranes crossing the sky, the half-asphalted streets.[61]

BIKINI

Or perhaps the story is more nuanced. Plath talks of "clean, colorful poverty." Despite her happiness, she could see the poverty of a fishing village even while she prettified it. This was a village of defeated people in a fascist dictatorship. After the poverty of the 1940s, many would have benefited from the jobs brought by the tourism that was just about to take off. Notwithstanding, as the story below explains, the main beneficiaries of the tourist industry were not fishing families, but the very same exploiters who had won the Civil War.

For tourists, Benidorm could be an ambivalent place, too. It became by the 1960s the archetypical package-vacation destination for the British, a great place for two weeks of sun, sea, and cheap alcohol. It meant working-class people could leave the British Isles, which previously had only been possible for the upper class—or for the working class if they were sent to die or be wounded in wars.

Yet the downside is that many of these hotels were not good. Even in democratic cheap-vacation Benidorm, some hotels have gardens on the seafront and others are several blocks from the front, across traffic-clogged avenues, with the return uphill from the beach in the baking sun. For Benidorm is not flat. And the cheaper hotels, up the hill, may very well have thin walls, so you can hear people talking or having sex, let alone shouting drunkenly, or vomiting cheap wine and pizza after a night out.

---

61   Chirbes, *Crematorio*, pp.91-2. My translation.

No town in Spain grew so fast as Benidorm did in the 1960s. A fishing village of 1,500 inhabitants in 1950 expanded to become a city of 70,000 today, whose population soars to 300,000 in August. The take-off was not entirely accidental. It had a lot to do with the ambition and foresight of Pedro Zaragoza Orts, born in 1922 and Mayor of Benidorm from 1950 to 1967.

Pedro Zaragoza was a Falangist who became mayor when Benidorm had just a few hotels and villas for wealthy people from Madrid. He had to be a Falangist to reach such a post in the one-party dictatorship, but was not just a time-server and had a vision for his impoverished village. Pedro Zaragoza's administration was the first in Spain to draw up a General Town Plan, in 1956. Normally, the rich just built where they wanted. Benidorm locals were amazed to see wide avenues and access roads. Many of these avenues still exist and help ease the summer traffic jams. The other key feature was to remove any restriction on height, yet to insist that the tall buildings should have land around them.

Toward the end of his life, in the early 2000s, Zaragoza was interviewed by Giles Tremlett:

> "The building volume could be used like this," he said, laying the book flat. "Or it could be used like this, or this," he said, placing the book first on its spine and then, holding it upright, as if sitting on a bookshelf. "And if they did it that last way, there was space for gardens, for swimming pools, for tennis courts, or for car parking." The match-stick high-rise was born.[62]

---

62   Tremlett, p.107.

This means that the archetypical cheap-vacation resort Benidorm has a much better layout and more green space than most tourist towns, which grew chaotically as speculators dumped hotels beside the villas of the previous generation or the shacks of the generation before that. Zaragoza's vertical vision seemed perfect: make ourselves rich by packing in vacationers on a narrow stretch of land beside fabulous beaches. Not so much agricultural land was gobbled up and, like rare animals, tourists could be confined to their reserve.

Nevertheless, Zaragoza's dreamed city is not sustainable, for water is a permanent problem in most of the southern half of Spain. It will get worse. Climate change will convert much of it to desert (no exaggeration: read the 2015 report on the Mediterranean from France's National Centre for Scientific Research). Water can be a particular issue for tourist resorts, with sudden summer spikes in population. For instance, Sitges, south of Barcelona, had only salt water in the old town's pipes for many decades. If you wanted to drink water you had to buy a bottle. Benidorm, like most of the *país valencià*'s coastal areas, had Moorish irrigation channels bringing water from the hills for agriculture, but no piped drinking water. "Drinking water was sold by a man with a mule that dragged a huge cask on wheels," as Tremlett puts it.[63] Development destroyed the ancient channels. Water was then piped to Benidorm's new taps from Polop fifteen kilometers in the hills behind. Someone in a high-rise hotel or apartment uses between forty and eighty liters of water a day, a lot of water though half what a visitor to the villas climbing every mountain consumes.

---

63 *Ibid*, p.106.

When Plath and Hughes spent their honeymoon there in 1956, the town had not yet taken off. Priests with lanterns and Civil Guards with batons patrolled the beaches at night. Even local couples holding hands could be chased off. The full-scale sex one may stumble across on the sand on a summer night in liberal Benidorm in recent decades could only be fantasized.

In fascist Spain, bikinis were completely off limits. But when tourists began to appear in them at the end of the 1950s, Zaragoza defied the norms by refusing to ban them. He even had a bylaw passed that fined anyone who insulted a woman wearing a bikini. This was too much for the police, who fined the tourist bikini-wearers, not the insulters. Bishops preached that the morals of Catholic Spain were being undermined. The Archbishop of Valencia, Marcelino Olaechea, threatened Zaragoza with excommunication if he did not outlaw the bikini. Two government ministers backed the archbishop. In Franco's Spain, this was no joke: few would dare employ you if you were excommunicated.

Undaunted, Zaragoza put a newspaper under his shirt to protect him from the cold, mounted his Vespa scooter, and drove the 400 miles to Madrid (nine hours: no highways then). He sought and was granted an audience with Franco. Amazingly, the dictator was persuaded of the benefits of allowing foreign women to wear bikinis and Zaragoza got on with the task of putting his village on the map. The Civil Guard and archbishop quickly saw which way the Marina's sea-breeze was blowing and backed down.

Bikinis made Benidorm. Zaragoza became friendly with the Franco family and the dictator's wife Carmen Polo, never one to turn down a free dinner, spent several vacations as his personal guest. This was in 1959, when a World Bank report told the Spanish state it was two months from bankruptcy. For the two decades since the end of the Civil War in 1939 Franco had pursued a policy of "autarky," self-sufficiency in economic policy, with Spain isolated from the rest of Europe. Faced by financial collapse, though to the dismay of traditionalists and fascists, Spain was forced to open itself to foreign investment, which led to the economic boom of the 1960s. Foreign capitalists could not believe their luck. For a decade there was a 10 percent growth rate: it was like China in the 1990s. Investors revelled in few planning restrictions, low wages, and a working class kept in place by the police.

The economic liberalization led to political change. A mass movement would defeat the dictatorship in the 1970s. And it led to social change. More visitors began to visit Spain. The Mediterranean coastline was developing its tourist potential. Pedro Zaragoza and his Benidorm had everything in place to take advantage of the northerners looking for guaranteed sun, cheap drink and beautiful beaches. The following is a quote from the late sociologist José Miguel Iribas that defines this change. The quote is long, but precise:

> Benidorm is the extreme case of industrial concentration and efficiency, which has made it the most enjoyable space for mass tourism... Its success lies in its being an absolutely clear product. Benidorm is like a litre of Coca-Cola. Everyone knows what they're buying. What Benidorm promises, it delivers...It offers the young European working class a non-stop San Fermín and thus fulfills an anthropological function. The industrialized North of Europe has seen the disappearance of its peasant festivals, which supposed a moment of rupture in a

working life…in which people subverted the established world through a bacchanal, to then return to daily routine. This bacchanal consisted of three elements: alcohol, dance and furtive sex. Industrialization, with its monotonous continuous calendar, broke this festival, which has had no replacement until Benidorm and other similar destinations offered precisely alcohol, dance, and furtive sex.[64]

I don't know about "furtive." Sex is open enough in Benidorm. Furtive though, in the sense that it is out of sight of the neighbors in one's daily life. When you're in Benidorm on vacation, you assume another personality. It is like Carnival for the British. As Sherrie Hewson, actor in the long-running but unlikely sitcom *Benidorm*, says: "At home, I wear a lot of black so I change into sunny colors when I arrive: bright orange, pink, and yellow."[65]

Carnival. The world turned upside down. I wrote "unlikely" about the sitcom because its stereotyped characters seem to belong to a 1970s Carry-on-type comedy world: Hattie Jacques and Kenneth Williams would fit in fine. Benidorm is both very up-to-date and stuck in a recent past.

Tourism brought the money Spain needed. Tourism defined the direction this relatively poor country would take to develop. It still brings in the cash. Today it accounts for about 11.5 percent of Spain's GDP; 53 million foreign visitors in 2005 had swollen to some 82 million by 2017. It is not sustainable, but the bubble has not yet burst. Benidorm accounts for 5 percent of all these

---

64 *El País*, August 6, 2001. My translation.
65 *Sunday Telegraph*, June 29, 2014.

foreign visitors to Spain. Pedro Zaragoza's Vespa journey to Madrid encapsulates the moment of change, when the dictatorship understood it had to open the country's frontiers. If this meant smaller bathing costumes like the bikini, it was a small price to pay.

Later, Pedro Zaragoza was instrumental in the building of Alicante airport, not far from Benidorm. This opened in 1966, at the perfect moment to promote the package vacation boom. In the decades since, Benidorm has maintained its position as Spain's beach-tourism leader. It is the skyscraper capital of southern Europe, with some 350 high-rise buildings. At 186 meters, the Gran Hotel Bali is the tallest hotel in Europe.

The "Sun, Sea, Sand, Sex, and Sangria" image of the 1960s and 1970s still exists, and massively. On the Llevant beach front, look at the Penelope Beach Club, opened in 1968. On its Thursday Women's Night, women are given a free drink and are entertained by a male striptease. Its cocktails include "Virgin of Vice," "Erotic Foam," and "Sex on the Beach." There is an area (around Carrer Mallorca) on and behind the Llevant beach that is known as the Britzone: pubs, clubs, chip-shops, pizza parlors, and live sex shows. The Sex, Junk Food, and Drink vacation thrives.

But now too, like Lloret in Catalonia, Benidorm is open all year 'round. Pensioners from the North fill the hotels in the winter. Some 80 percent of the city's 50,000 hotel rooms are occupied in February. And it is not just elderly foreigners escaping the cold. Benidorm is full of Spanish pensioners: it is as reputed in winter as a good place for older people to find a sex partner, as it is in summer for the young. The town does not rest on its laurels. The care of pensioners taken by the city includes free afternoon dances, free fitness sessions on the beach, and pioneering free accompaniment for blind and disabled bathers.

Ponent beach with skyscrapers

Benidorm has two magnificent crescent beaches, curling away from the old town that sits on a headland: the Ponent (western), more residential, and Llevant (eastern). On the Ponent there is a new kilometer-long swirling beach promenade, sensual curling waves of concrete in twenty-four colors. Nowhere else is there anything like this "huge park, a hinge between the Mediterranean and the city," as its architect Carlos Ferrater enthused. "We've transformed the conventional idea of the promenade as a barrier between land and sea."

THE ISLAND OF BENIDORM

The bay of Benidorm has a triangular island outlined at dusk against the sky. Legend has it that Roland, the warrior nephew of Charlemagne and hero of the *Chanson de Roland*, cleft the twin-peaked Puig Campana mountain with his mighty sword when he was trying to kill a Moor and the chunk of rock was hurled into the sea to form the island. The mountain is only five miles behind the coast, yet rises to 1,406 meters.

The Beautiful Island, Benidorm

Behind Puig Campana are intensively cultivated valleys of fruit trees. If you take one of the roads up to Callosa d'en Sarrià, you pass lemons and oranges, then, climbing a bit, olives, almonds, and especially medlars, grown under thick mesh. This plastic protects against birds and occasional frost and brings on the medlars earlier. There is always more cash in the early crop. The medlar is a medium-sized tree with long ribbed deep-green leaves and a yellowy-orange fruit with brown patches (not unlike the vacation clothes of Sherrie Hewson). Tourism affects these valleys too, but does not overrun them: Polop and La Núcia are quieter and cooler than the coast and their villas enjoy long views of the sea.

Higher up, at 585 meters, the ancient village of Guadalest has been turned into a tourist center. You wonder how the coaches can get around the mountain bends. Its castle, bell tower and cemetery perch on seemingly inaccessible hills. Final access to them is on foot only. This village of 200 people has nine museums: vintage motor-bikes and cars (on the road up), salt and pepper cellars, nativity cribs, micro-giant (the Kremlin painted on a shell), micro-miniatures (where a sculptured camel passes through the eye of a needle), torture, and capital punishment (!), the municipal museum, a magic garden, an ethnological museum. It is tourism reduced to the ridiculous. Why so many museums? I asked in the tourist office (there is one of these, too). Her reply was tautological: "Because there are a lot of visitors." The only museum worth visiting is the municipal one, which takes you through a seventeenth-century Spanish mansion to the castle on top of the rock. The rest is mere exploitation: the museums have no connection to the village's history or life. The torture museum ought to be closed down. The shops sell trinkets. The cafés over-charge. To park you have to pay. Oh dear! Guadalest, home is best.

Guadalest is only the *reductio ad absurdum* of modern museumism. Every small town in the area has a museum now. Ibi produces toys: it has a toy museum. Xixona has a *turró* (nougat) museum. At Onil they make dolls: there's a doll museum. Elda has a shoe museum. La Vila Joiosa has two chocolate museums. And so on...but at least these museums are associated with local activity.

There are, of course, other stories to Benidorm. Four others: exploitation, crime, pollution, and corruption. The first is covered elsewhere: for cheap vacations, you need systematic exploitation of staff. This was exacerbated by the 2008 economic crisis and the 2012 Labor Law Reform, meaning that *kellys* (room-cleaners), waiters, street cleaners, kitchen-staff, and everyone else who makes Benidorm work are kept on low wages, short-term contracts, etc. If you're in Benidorm, you can see this graphically by walking up one of the wide avenues planned by Pedro Zaragoza, the Avinguda Rei Jaume I, climbing the hill from the Ponent beach. Two minutes from the golden sands, you're in a street of cheap shops and a permanent market (great for buying knickers at one euro each), which runs through very basic non-tourist unpainted blocks of balconyless flats. The streets are packed with local people, the migrants from other parts of Spain who came in the 1960s boom and their descendants. These are the poor who service the tourism industry and they stay poor, unlike Pedro Zaragoza and his friends.

Inevitably, and this is the second story, a place like Benidorm with a mobile population out to have a good time attracts thieves, card-sharps, the Pea-Men (*trileros*), and all kinds of opportunists. In November 2015 British residents demonstrated in protest. It was a turn-around from the 1980s when British "lager louts" smashing up urban furniture were the criminals. A Spanish Home Office report confirmed the British residents' complaints: Benidorm's petty crime rates were the highest in the state.

The third story is one of ecological spoliation. A restaurant was opened on the beautiful island in 1968. Like most beach restaurants at the time, it operated with no legal papers or environmental inspections. Ever since, the restaurant has been emptying its fecal and kitchen waste into the bay. A 2017 report by the Nature Protection Service, SEPRONA, explained that the restaurant has no permit or insurance, employs workers without papers, occupies public space, has introduced exotic fauna and flora, and has discharged fecal waters directly into the sea "with grave danger to health."

Counter-attacking, the Cervera family hired biologists. Their report exonerating the family, three months after the SEPRONA report was delivered to the Prosecution Service, dates from February 17, 2017. However, one small detail was overlooked: the restaurant is closed from October to March, so it is not surprising that the waters are crystal clear by February!

At the end of 2017 the state insisted on its ownership of the island, underlining that this was part of the Serra Gelada Nature Park. It looks like this long, illegal, tax-free occupation of the island, with the City Council turning a blind eye, is coming to an end. Whether this case will lead to the closure of the restaurant or whether it will be another episode lost in a labyrinthine court case or cut short by Cervera's political allies is not to be known yet. But it is known that the Cervera family are related to Eduardo Zaplana.

After Pedro Zaragoza Orts, Eduardo Zaplana, Mayor of Benidorm from 1991 to 1995, is the most important person in Benidorm's history. And this leads to the fourth story: corruption. Zaplana (born 1955) had a meteoric career. Representing the PP (Partido Popular), he became Mayor of Benidorm in 1991, president of the Generalitat Valenciana from 1995 to 2002 and minister of labor in the Spanish government of José María Aznar from 2002 to 2004.

LEGENDARY LAND

Eduardo Zaplana's political career almost stopped before it started. In 1989 the PP treasurer Rosendo Naseiro and others were put on trial for financing their party by charging commissions to builders in exchange for contracts. Various telephone taps provided ample evidence. However, the prosecution case collapsed dramatically in 1990 when defense lawyers persuaded the judge that the phone taps were illegal and, therefore, evidence from them was inadmissible. Everyone was acquitted, but not before several of the recorded conversations had been leaked. In one of them Zaplana, then the young PP president in Alacant province, said: "I have to get rich, because I'm broke." And in another, concerning the purchaser of a site that could be reclassified for building: "You ask [him] for a commission and we share it out under the table."[66] His career would never have taken off if the Naseiro

---

66   Castillo Prats, pp.110-11.

prosecution had not been abandoned on a technicality.

Zaplana loved to boast that he was clean, the only major Valencian PP politician of the last thirty years who had never been charged with corruption. And so it seemed: family members, close friends, his political appointees all fell, but he strode arrogantly and miraculously unscathed. Then, on May 22, 2018, Zaplana's world collapsed. He was arrested for bribery, tax fraud, and concealing at least ten million euros from illegal commissions in tax havens during his time as president. (Justice is slow in Spain.)

Zaplana became Mayor of Benidorm in 1991, when a councillor was persuaded to switch from the Socialist benches to the PP. Ambitious but with slim majorities, both he and the new Mayor of Valencia city Rita Barberá understood that the PP, to become hegemonic, needed a clear political project. They had the political instinct to grasp that restoration of pride in being Valencian was the key. The year 1992 saw the Barcelona Olympic Games and the World Fair in Sevilla. The Valencian PP's political project was to promote such major events to attract business and overcome any inferiority complex of being second- or third-best. "We are," boasted Barberá deliriously, "ready to assume the 'pole position' of the world's great capital cities."[67]

The City of Arts and Sciences in Valencia, the City of Light film studios in Alacant, and Terra Mítica (Legendary Land) in Benidorm were the main 1990s projects. Journalist Sergio Castillo Prats wrote:

> The Terra Mítica theme park was the star project of Eduardo Zaplana and the PP to relaunch

---

67   Maceda, p.77.

tourism in Benidorm and on the Costa Blanca. If Catalonia could enjoy its Port Aventura and Dragon Khan, we Valencians were not going to lag behind.[68]

Terra Mítica is located behind Benidorm, between the highway and the mountains. The 1,100-hectare site was protected forest that could not be built on. However, after a forest fire in 1992, the land was sold off cheaply. A number of friends and associates of Zaplana, including his mother-in-law, acquired plots. When the burnt forest was reclassified for building the park, the land tripled in value.

Terra Mítica is, according to its web page, "a marvelous mix of spectacular shows and heart pounding rides…The magic of Rome, Greece, Egypt, the Islands, and Iberia awaits you in Terra Mitica."[69] It opened in 2000. It never came near the three million visitors a year needed to break even. It never exceeded two million. In its last two years before being sold off to private enterprise, it received 535,000 (2010) and 680,000 (2011) visitors. The park limps on, open now only in the summer months: Benidorm's elderly winter tourists are not avid customers of giant roller-coaster rides.

It has been a total disaster, running over budget, with multiple criminal investigations, and bankruptcy because not enough people went through the turnstiles. The initial construction budget of 240 million euros ended up at 376 million. In 2012 it was sold for 67 million. Enormous sums of public money had been poured into the park.

---

68   *Ibid*, p.234.
69   (Consulted February 15, 2018) http://www.benidorm-spotlight.com/themeparks/terra-mitica.html

The criminal trials for payments of false invoices in 2000/2001, tax evasion, and kick-backs show that a lot of the cash ended up in private pockets. The American John Fitzgerald, director of the park from 2001 to 2009, said in 2006 that there were "forty million euros in building works that do not correspond to any contract." The public prosecutor alleged in 2009 that much of the money was in tax havens such as Switzerland and Andorra. In March 2015, two managers of the park and eighteen contractors were finally given prison sentences.

One of these was Vicente Conesa, a businessman who had received, when Zaplana was mayor, the contract for Benidorm's "green map." Scandal had swirled around this appointment, as the money paid to Conesa was double the market price. Conesa was sentenced in 2016 to twenty-three years in prison for coordinating false invoices to the value of over six million euros during the construction of Terra Mítica. All in all, the twenty people found guilty were sentenced to a total of 305 years in jail and seventy-one million euros in fines. Despite these severe sentences, most commentators believe, like John Fitzgerald, that there is a lot more money unaccounted for and many more who got off.

Zaplana, instigator as Mayor of Benidorm and enabler as president of the Generalitat, was never put on trial. There was a moment when two businessmen were recorded saying that Zaplana received money from false invoices, but later the two denied this and the recording was not admitted as evidence. Zaplana's brother-in-law and retired lieutenant-colonel, Justo Valverde, the park's general services and contracts manager, was sentenced to four years.

Benidorm provides an honest vacation, for it gives visitors what it offers. Yet it is dishonest: a hidden, long story of dishonesty: exploitation, crime, pollution, and corruption. The "honest" Benidorm is the caricature of a vacation resort, with its bars with British names, UK soaps, draught bitter. It can be seen as a good idea, allowing working-class foreigners to let down their hair in the sun. Or an abhorrence, representing cheap, standardized consumerism and ruining the beautiful coast.

Benidorm is blowsy. And it is beautiful. Those two crescent beaches of fine sand, with the triangular island in the bay, the hills cuddling around the city to keep it warm, pigeons white as gulls and, as Sylvia Plath wrote, "the most incredible azure sea, prussian blue toward the horizon and brilliant aqua nearer shore."

Such happy British tourists

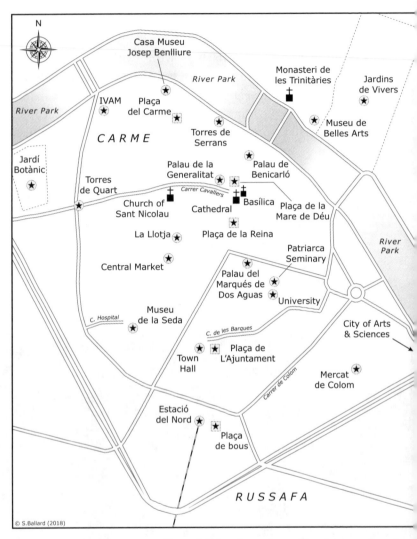

Central Valencia, embraced by the waterless river

7: Valencia 1: The Friendly Labyrinth

"[Valencia] … a strange place, hard to get to know—
but it has an undeniable and not at all unpleasant
baroque flamboyance overall"

Colman Andrews, *Catalan Cuisine*

Now the third city of the Spanish state in population, behind Madrid and Barcelona, in the fifteenth century Valencia was the largest city on the western Mediterranean. Here is Joanot Martorell extolling it, in Chapter 330 of *Tirant lo Blanc*:

> …a most blessed and noble Spanish port endowed with valiant knights and abundant in everything but spices. This city, which exports more merchandise than any other, is inhabited by virtuous, peaceful, and well-spoken men. Though its women are not very fair, they are wittier than elsewhere and captivate men's fancies with their charming ways and sweet discourse.

Despite witty women and virtuous men, Valencia declined from its Golden fifteenth Century and one of the keys to understanding the modern city is that in the late twentieth and early twenty-first centuries, its authorities, supported strongly for two decades by the majority of voters, were rushing to catch up with what was lost five hundred years before. Or rather to catch up with their particular interpretation of the Golden Century.

Insults

This chapter and the following two discuss Valencia city. Its images in Spain today are not always positive: soberer Spaniards from the high, central plain may see its people as hedonistic, idle, too much in love with fire, fireworks, and food, lacking the austere seriousness of the Castilians who built a mighty Empire, yet—the Spanish state's Achilles' heel, even today—were unable to construct a united nation.

Many visitors have been unenamored of the city. Casanova, yes THE Casanova, wrote in 1767, in *Spanish Passions*, the sixth volume of his memoirs:

> [In Valencia] One is ill lodged and ill fed, there is no good wine and no good company, there is not even any intellectual provision, for though there is a university, lettered men are absolutely unknown. As for the bridges, churches, the arsenal, the exchange, the town hall, the twelve town gates, and the rest, I could not take pleasure in a town where the streets are not paved, and where a public promenade is conspicuous by its absence. Outside the town the country is delightful, especially on the side towards the sea; but the outside is not the inside...[70]

Broke, jaded, in his forties, and feeling old by the time he wrote of Valencia, nevertheless Casanova's view does reflect decline from the city's glory and the provincial lethargy in which it lolled.

Richard Ford, whose 1845 three-volume *Handbook for Spain* is always good value if you want lively insults, characterized Valencians as "vindictive, sullen, fickle, and

---

70   Burns, p.11.

treacherous...nowhere is assassination more common; they smile and murder while they smile."[71] In a page-long tirade, Ford buys into the myth of the Borgias, "a disgrace to male and female nature." He sees these "delincuentes honrados" as typical Valencians. Though nowadays this sort of finely written abuse is more comical than threatening, Ford and other polemicists have molded many people's views.

Ford alleges: "The narrow streets of Valencia seem contrived for murder and intrigue, which once they were." For this reason, he says, a night-watch company, the "serenos," was introduced in 1777, "the first in Spain." In truth, the streets of Valencia's old quarter were and are no narrower than in any other Spanish city. In fact, the night-watch was first introduced in Madrid a decade earlier, when the enlightened despot Carlos III was trying to make the streets safer. Until the 1970s, all over Spain, these *serenos* with their huge jangling bunches of keys to all the houses in the street let people into their locked houses after 10 PM and called out *sereno*, "all well," on the hour all night. Under Franco, and probably in other times, most were police spies.

Casanova and Ford's views are unbalanced and unreliable, yet they to some degree underlie the extreme of how many non-Valencians see Valencia even today. Clearly, there are many other views and anyone at all will be more nuanced than these two.

One last, but not least, point on abuse. The hymn of the Valencian Community is little known. It was declared official in 1984. Its opening lines, oozing grandiloquent subservience, place the "region" clearly in the Spanish nationalist camp: "To bestow new glories on Spain, our Region knew how to fight." Valencian nationalists, *blavers*, put other words to this first line of the hymn: "All under the folds of our Royal Flag..."

---

71   Ford, p.648.

More scurrilous and sung by those with no regard at all for flags, kings, or patriotism are the words of the working class and peasants, reflecting not so much longing or ideology, but experience at the bottom of the heap: *Menja merda*…"Eat shit with patience, with spoon and fork…"

Criticism of Valencia comes not just from outsiders and cantankerous visitors: Valencians have a self-mocking, anti-authoritarian strain. To counter the negative views, here is Spain's most famous scientist, 1906 Nobel Prize winner Santiago Ramón y Cajal, who went from Aragon to work in Valencia:

> I found myself in a land that was new to me. With the mildest of temperatures, in whose fields aloe vera and orange trees flowered and whose souls harbored courtesy, culture and fine minds. It is not for nothing that Valencia is called the Spanish Athens.[72]

Surely this cannot be the same place as Casanova and Ford's city. They were looking, though, for different things.

ENTER BY TRAIN

How should we enter this city of some 750,000 inhabitants, with about a million more in its immediate hinterland? By boat is one possibility: on a ferry from nearby Eivissa (Ibiza) or on one of the cruise liners towering above quays that increasingly clog the harbor. Yet the boat will deposit you, though close to the new City of Arts and Sciences on the River Túria's dried river-bed, a good three kilometers from the old city center, built inland.

---

72   *Guía azul*, Gaesa, Madrid 2000, p.47.

By rail? To this day, I find it easy to disorient myself in this flat city: unlike Barcelona or Madrid, there are no visible hills or clear slope in the street to assist orientation. My confusion stems from my very first arrival by train from Barcelona. Though Barcelona lies to the north of Valencia, the railway circles the city through a tunnel and enters the station on the south side of the old walled city. For yet further confusion, this railway station on the south side is called the Estació del Nord, the North Station.

The North Station, like many stations, is a monument in itself, built in 1917 in the grand style. Miles Roddis wrote: "The exterior seems a cross between a mock castle and a rich, creamy wedding cake."[73] The ticket-hall is adorned by plants painted on the ceiling and *trencadís* mosaic. *Trencadís* is the style of breaking up pottery and sticking the broken pieces into cement. While, with its *art nouveau trencadís*, the station was competing with Gaudí's mosaic designs in Barcelona, in a side hall there is a plethora of exuberant, happy Valencian scenes. Colorful tiles show an idealized *horta*: oranges, a *barraca*, palms, bunches of grapes, cacti, roses, and dahlias; a canoe and a single-sail dhow-like boat from the Albufera lagoon; and cornucopias of fruit. In the middle section, a plump Valencian woman sells flowers, with the Micalet tower behind. These are the finest, brightest tiles I have seen in this city of colorful tiles. In such artistic outpouring, you can see the view the Valencian elite had of itself 100 years ago. The images are clichéd and prettified, but not untrue. The train leaves you at this station, designed to impress visitors newly arriving, right in the middle of the city: rail is by far the best entry.

---

73   Roddis, p.22.

North Station and bull-ring

Or by road? Easy. The AP7 runs along the Mediterranean coast of Spain, from France to Murcia. And the A3 from Madrid, entering the Valencian Community at Utiel and Requena, drops down into the city. Valencia has always been the closest sea to Madrid, Spain's capital city built near the geographical heart of the state on a moor bleaker than Emily Brontë's. Even before the railway, Valencia was the easiest entry and exit for travelers to the capital. It was through Valencia that the Bourbon Fernando VII disembarked in 1823, to repress a brief flowering of liberalism and restore the absolutist monarchy. And it was from Valencia that his widow, Queen Regent María Cristina, sailed to exile in 1840.

The A3—the Madrid highway—is the fastest, but least impressive entrance, with around ten kilometers of ribbon development on the city's outskirts. On each side of the road is a mix of small villas that have somehow survived, warehouses and factories from the 1960s boom, and roll-up buildings of the modern consumer world: supermarkets, sex shops, logistics centers, and the slick, shiny windowless hangars that house Coca-Cola, Heineken, or Estrella Damm beer's warehouses.

At Manises, famous since Arab times for its ceramics and surprisingly close to the city center, Valencia has an airport, too. Twenty years ago, Valencia was not on the tourist trail of great European cities. Now it is, though still lagging: you cannot yet buy a Valencia guidebook in Gatwick airport's bookshop.

Rail, road, air, or sea. No problems reaching the city. Once there, for the monumental old quarter, caressed by the green, waterless river, you have to walk. If you come by train, the south side of the old walled city starts across the road from the station. Here are most of Valencia's administrative and commercial buildings, the wealth in stone and adornment of any great city. Nearby are the fashionable shops of Carrer Colom.

My preferred entry is the Gothic bridge over the former channel of the River Túria on the opposite side of the old town from the North Station. The bridge is pedestrianized. As everywhere, this means no (or few) cars, but pedestrians plus wild cyclists, dogs, and Segways that pedestrians are obliged to dodge. Crossing this bridge gives you the imposing first view that people walking into the city centuries ago had: the Torres de Serranos, Torres dels Serrans, one of the medieval gates, built as gate, but also as awe-inspiring fortress, with battlements on its two towers underlining that the gate was to keep people out as well as let them in.

Such a huge gate, built with limestone ashlars, was constructed by city rulers who were confident in their present and future. It dates from 1392–98, at the dawn of the city's Golden Century. When the wall was knocked down in 1865, allowing the city's bourgeoisie to leave the pestilent, overpopulated city and extend their properties over the plain, only two of the twelve original gates remained, the Serrans and the Torres del Quart.

The Torres dels Serrans takes its name from its being the entrance for the Royal Road to Saragossa, leading up into the mountains. *Serrans* are people from the *serra*, people from the hills. The Royal Road will have seen kings and nobles in their carriages or on caparisoned horses, but also the poor from the infertile, cold villages of the Valencian and Aragonese mountains walking into the city to look for work.

The joined towers have had several uses. For 300 years from the 1580s the building was a prison, which is why it survived the demolition of the walls. It was a prison for nobles and gentlemen. Even the imprisoned have more or fewer rights according to their class—still true today. When General Milans del Bosch was sentenced to thirty years for bringing out the tanks onto the streets of Valencia in Spain's 1981 attempted coup, he then lived in comfort in a military prison. The numerous corrupt politicians and bankers now beginning to fill Spain's jails live separately from the common criminals, the plebs. The Torres de Quart, the other surviving tower, was also a prison: for women.

In the Spanish Civil War of 1936–39, the basement of the Torres dels Serrans was reinforced to house many of Spain's unrivalled collection of paintings, evacuated from Madrid's Prado Museum. On top of the basement rice husks were piled a meter high (rice, only in Valencia) under a further meter of earth, to protect against a direct hit. To the joy of art-lovers and the glory of Madrid's tourist industry, the canvases of Greco, Goya, Zurbarán, Velázquez, *et al.* survived the war.

Torres de Quart

Once through the Torres dels Serrans, a turn right takes you into the Carme quarter, the most romantic part of Valencia's old town. Blue domes of churches are glimpsed down narrow streets; you stumble on crumbling stones of the Moorish city wall (there is a stretch integrated into the bottom of a building beside a bakery on the Carrer Palomino, not 100 meters from the Towers); walls are often ochre; brown wooden doors into apartment blocks are wide, with inset lattice doors to step into courtyards; red geraniums hang from balconies. As you amble through the narrow, winding streets, you lose your bearings. A compass may be as useful as a map.

SILK

The Carme is for losing yourself and wandering on first visits. Little squares are frequent, the open space usually small and rarely square. Every commentator on Valencia talks of the calm and peace of these streets, a "friendly and light labyrinth, not too mysterious, dark, or damp," in the words of Valencian Joan Mira. Or Jason Webster: "There the streets were narrower, windier, and dirtier, giving a sense of the labyrinthine atmosphere of the medieval city, and a feeling of intimacy."[74]

The administrative center of the city is a bustling, busy place, but just a few blocks away, in corners of the Carme's little non-square squares, usually with a church on one side, you can sit on a bench to rest and watch the passersby and the city's white pigeons, much prettier than London's gray (pigeon-colored) pigeons.

Unlike similar old quarters in Barcelona or Madrid, the Carme is not overrun (yet) with hotels. Valencia's later-starting development as a tourist destination contributes to

---

74   Webster, *Or the Bull Kills You*, Chapter 2.

these quiet corners. The Carme has this century become a fashionable area of bars and restaurants, but this is night-life, the *lluna* or "moon" of Valencia. The night-life is called the *lluna* supposedly because those who arrived too late at the Torres dels Serrans to enter the city had to sleep out on the banks of the Túria under the *lluna*.

The Carme also meant abandonment. Only thirty years ago little had changed since the walls were destroyed. It was poor, dusty, and densely populated. After 1865, the nobles and bourgeois constructed spacious houses on agricultural land *extramurs*, outside the walls, so escaping cholera epidemics and surrounding poverty. Till the reform at the end of the twentieth century, the Carme, abandoned by the rich, slowly crumbled. Half-fallen houses, plots overgrown with weeds and broken bottles, and cracked and pitted walls proliferated among the rotting palaces converted to tenements. Some of this you can still see.

The Carme also had its factories. In Vicente Blasco Ibáñez's novel *La barraca* (*The Cabin*), girls and unmarried women rose before dawn to hurry along the paths through the *huerta* and over the Serrans bridge to the silk factories. Where now orange trees flourish on these paths alongside the irrigation ditches, mulberry trees to feed silkworms grew. Most factories were concentrated in the Velluters (velvet- or silk-workers) area, on the western side of the old town.

Silk was the major industry of Valencia from the thirteenth century until its collapse toward the end of the nineteenth century due to cheaper imports from Asia. So major was it that La Llotja dels mercaders, the Merchants' Exchange, Valencia's great Gothic commercial exchange on the Plaça del Mercat, became known in the eighteenth century as the Llotja de la Seda, the Silk Exchange.

There is some poetic symmetry in the silk industry being destroyed by Asian goods, for silkworms had originally been smuggled from Asia into Constantinople in the sixth century. Revealing the secrets of silk manufacture to foreigners was punishable by death in China. It is said that two monks brought the eggs of the silkworm (*Bombyx mori*) to Europe hidden in their walking-sticks. In turn, Constantinople guarded closely the secret of silk production until one Yahya al-Ghazal stole worms in 840 CE (this time hidden in a hollowed-out book, like pistols in gangster films), returning with them to Córdoba and breaking Constantinople's European monopoly. Valencia became for several centuries Europe's greatest producer of silk. Silk was not just fine stockings, dresses or foulards, but all kinds of clothing, including heavy priestly vestments and velvet. Silk is intimately associated with the rise of the fashion industry, for in the seventeenth and eighteenth centuries the rich who wanted to show off their wealth changed their clothes often. Color and originality of design replaced durability as the most desirable qualities in clothing.

Some 25,000 people were employed on over 3,000 looms in the city's silk industry at its peak in the late eighteenth century, just before industrialization. Fifty-six master-weavers, including twelve from Genoa and several Jews, had organized a guild in 1477 to control quality. They were men, while the laborers were young women. The guild of master-weavers received a Royal Charter in 1479. In the seventeenth century they successfully petitioned the king to have their skill defined as an "art." Thus, their Gothic headquarters at Carrer de l'Hospital 7, now a fine museum, is called the Higher College of the Art of Silk. Like many buildings in Valencia, this essentially Gothic building is overlaid with later Baroque additions.

The Silk Guild was so powerful that it had inspectors controlling not just the factories that were their members' property, but the streets of the Velluters district. It imposed straighter streets in the quarter, which now differs in its layout from the winding labyrinth of the Moorish city.

Fascism

The old quarter is packed with churches. What old Christian-dominated city isn't? Spain's rulers have been especially zealous in building churches and convents, for the country was the leader of the Counter-Reformation and forged its parlous national identity on the basis of the expulsion of Jews and Moors. Exclusion, not inclusion.

The weight of centuries of religious dominance expresses itself in these buildings. Often, when one perceives widespread use of contraception, the scarcity of nuns and priests, the legalization of homosexual marriage; when one sees topless bathing, nudist beaches, the huge gay rights and gay identity demos every year on the anniversary of Stonewall; or when one smells the heavy, herbal fragrance of marijuana drifting over the summer late-night/early-morning terraces of the Carme, it is easy to deceive oneself that Spain is a post-Catholic country. It would be a mistake: the country is divided right down the middle on these social issues. Centuries of ideology, expressed in the many beautiful churches, weigh heavily on the living. The Church adapts: for instance, many young people who live together for years end up getting married in church, with the bride in white. Spanish firms are world leaders in traditional wedding dresses.

Among the twenty-plus churches in Valencia's Carme district, there are two I will mention. First, the church on the Plaça del Carme, recently restored and open only a couple of evenings a week, has, on the left of the altar, a fresco painted in 1942. That man kneeling, but with an arrogant mien, looks familiar. Yes, it's Francisco Franco, the dictator. You can take it as a comic curiosity, but the picture underlines how the Church validated and applauded the cruelty and murders of the dictatorship. At the time this was being painted, there were still regular executions of Republicans in the woods of Paterna (see Chapter 14).

In 2017, forty years after the end of the dictatorship, the new City Council, run by the Compromís coalition, València en Comú and the Socialist Party together, changed the Francoist names of fifty-one streets in the city. These, in turn, had been renamed after the 1939 defeat of the Republic, which in turn, on the outbreak of Civil War, had renamed streets after revolutionary heroes. It's an easy gesture to change street names, but that doesn't mean that names are not important.

For example, a main street (and a hospital) is named after Dr. Peset, who managed Valencia's hospitals during the Civil War and was executed in 1941 by the Franco regime. Nearby was a street named after another doctor, Marco Merenciano, precisely the person who denounced Dr. Peset. Valencia's mayor Joan Ribó said, "It's hard to believe we are still honoring people linked to Franco's repression, which clearly isn't something occurring in relation to Nazism in Germany or Fascism in Italy."[75] Carrer Merenciano was one of the fifty-one streets renamed.

In a city with a higher proportion of fascist grouplets than elsewhere in Spain, the 2017 change was long overdue. The most high-profile stand against fascism till then had occurred in 1992, when the Dutch football coach Guus Hiddink refused to let a Valencia FC match proceed

75   Raphael Minder, *New York Times*, November 19, 2015.

until a Nazi banner was removed from the stadium. Hiddink won the skirmish but not the battle, for when he moved on to coach elsewhere, the fascists returned to the terraces. At Mestalla, Valencia FC's ground, to this day, Nazi chants are normal. Hatred for Catalonia is alive and well: *Puta Barça, puta Catalunya* ("Fuck Barça, Fuck Catalonia") is the normal chant when FC Barcelona visit. If you like soccer, go to Llevant/Levante, Valencia's other main socceer team and the more progressive club in its ideology and style. It wears the same blue and scarlet strip as Barcelona, thus in sporting terms defining itself against the centralist-unionist clubs like Real Madrid or Valencia.

There are more fascists in Valencia than elsewhere in Spain. Why is this? The extreme right defended the continuity of the dictatorship in the 1970s transition. In the early 1980s, fascists disappeared from sight in much of Spain, but in Valencia they did the state's dirty work, intimidating those on the left who, in the debate around the 1982 Autonomy Statute, recognized the *país valencià* as part of the *països catalans*. Intimidation is too mild a word: the pan-Catalanist Joan Fuster's house in Sueca was bombed twice, in 1978 and 1981. Homes of three other activists, bookshops (especially Tres i Quatre) and the university were also bombed. In gratitude for this "unofficial" support in what became known as the Battle of Valencia, the state has never investigated these numerous incidents with appropriate zeal. Extraordinary tolerance was shown to fascist groups. The most notorious incident was the murder of the young anti-fascist Guillem Agulló on April 22, 1993. Only Pedro Cuevas, one of the gang that knifed Guillem in Montanejos, was jailed for the murder. Sentenced to fourteen years, Cuevas was out in four. Today, fascists have again crept out from their lairs, confidence boosted by the rise in Spanish nationalism as an orchestrated response to the movement for Catalan independence.

SISTINE CHAPEL

To return to churches, the second not to be missed is Sant Nicolau de Bari, its entrance down an alley off Carrer Cavallers. It was reopened in 2016 after restoration financed by the Hortensia Herrero Foundation, set up by the art-lover and co-founder with her husband, Juan Roig, of Valencia's most successful supermarket chain, Mercadona. Hortensia and Roig are Spain's second-richest family, after Amancio Ortega and his daughter, the owners of the clothing multinational Inditex (Zara, Bershka, etc.). The Herrero Foundation also underwrote the restoration of the Silk Museum, mentioned previously (more on Mercadona in Chapter 17).

Sant Nicolau is known by propagandists as the Sistine Chapel of Valencia. The neo-Gothic exterior, seen on the Plaça de Sant Nicolau, around the corner from the entrance, contrasts with a Baroque interior, whose glory is the painted ceiling, bright with color and light after the restoration. Though I know people who deplore the vulgar, fat little naked angels, the sheets and robes waving in the clouds and the excess of religious mysticism, I agree with the propagandists. Comparison with the Sistine Chapel is not just boasting to foster local pride and to foment the tourist trade. It has its source in the comment of Gianluigi Colalucci, principal restorer of the Vatican's Sistine Chapel ceiling, that Sant Nicolau was the "Valencian Sistine Chapel." Gianluigi should know.

The painter(s) of the 2,000 square meters of ceiling skillfully disguised the Gothic ribs and vaults, using them to gain perspective and depth. The twelve "lunettes," ceiling paintings lit by windows, portray incidents from the lives of St Nicholas and St Peter Martyr, both icons of the Dominicans who owned the church. St Nicholas is also Santa Claus and there is an illuminating picture in a side-chapel of the saint silently pushing a bag of money through a hole in a house wall for the young woman inside to buy her freedom from a father trying to force her into marriage. The story's moral is that true saintly behaviour is to do good by bearing gifts anonymously. This is the basis for the legend of Santa Claus.

SILK EXCHANGE

A few blocks south of Sant Nicolau, twisting through tiny streets, with luck you emerge on the edge of the Carme district, behind Valencia's finest medieval building, dating from the late fifteenth century, La Llotja de la Seda (Silk Exchange) mentioned above. Théophile Gautier caught its quality in his 1840s travel book:

> ...the Great Hall, the vaulting of which springs from rows of columns of the utmost lightness, with spiral ribbings, has an elegance and gaiety of appearance rare in Gothic architecture, which is in general more suited to expressing melancholy than happiness.[76]

The *llotja* was a meeting-place for traders to buy and sell. The glory of this temple to commerce is the Transactions Hall, with eight "soaring, slim, twisted pillars, curling high like sticks of barley sugar" (Roddis). Or like ropes. These

---

76   Gautier, p.309.

thin columns rise fifteen meters to the ceiling where they open like palm fronds, "an ideal of perfection converted into tangible stone." There is a beautiful freestanding corkscrew staircase. The *llotja* has a tranquil garden of orange trees, too. A relief after so many churches. Neither Valencia's *llotja* nor cathedral was built in the heavy, dark, high Gothic of Castile's cathedrals such as Burgos or Toledo.

Tourists today enter the *llotja* through the back door, from the jumbled Plaça Doctor Collado, home to the city's best hardware store. The *llotja* contains a chapel, to pray that your ship comes in, and a prison for those whose ship sank and could not pay their debts. Upstairs housed the offices of the Consolat de Mar, which set and enforced the rules for foreign (i.e. maritime) trade. The inscription high in the noble, vaulted Transactions Hall is a paean in Latin to early capitalism:

> I am a famous house that was built in fifteen years. See how fine trade is when its words are not deceitful, when it keeps its promises and does not practice usury. The merchant who lives like this will have overwhelming wealth and also enjoy eternal life.

The front of the building gives onto the Market Square, site of executions and tournaments for hundreds of years. While the Plaça de la Mare de Déu concentrates religious and political power, this Plaça del Mercat, where the *llotja* faces the Central Market (described in Chapter 17), is commercial in theme. The streets around it are still full of small shops.

The view of the *llotja* from the center of the square where the Inquisition's bonfires were stoked shows the tracery and filigree of the stonework. Although the side to the left of the central tower (the debtors' prison), as you look from the Market Square, is higher than the right, the whole front is harmonious: its walls are smooth, the stone pale, the windows delicate and the ogives slender. The *llotja* is the only building in the city to be listed as a World Heritage Site (in 1996). In the words of the UNESCO Committee, it "dramatically illustrates the power and wealth of one of the great Mediterranean mercantile cities."

Its most spectacular features are the twenty-eight gargoyles that stretch out horizontally from all around the roof. Gargoyles' practical function is to protect walls by pouring rainwater out of their mouths onto passers-by in the street or square. Their religious purpose is to scare the populace by their monstrous appearance into remaining within the embrace of the Church. As they are high, take binoculars to appreciate the detail and beauty of the sculpting. You will then be surprised to see that the *llotja*'s gargoyles depict not only monsters but various sexual and scatological scenes, among them monks defecating and the violation of an animal. To the left of the roof (looking still from the Market Square), a bare-breasted nun is stroking her sex. To the right, a man with angel's wings is masturbating into a pot.

The carvings that ascend in two lines on each side of the main door are similar to the gargoyles, though not so sexually explicit. The official interpretation is that the images, both gargoyles and carvings, list sins that must not be committed by anyone entering the building. A snail (poor snail!) represents laziness; a lion, pride; a pig, gluttony; a greedy-looking merchant, avarice. As the fifteenth century was a time of mass illiteracy, images were used to educate and propagandize (not unlike TV adverts today). These conventional representations around the door are intermingled with all sorts of naked and sexually explicit figures. Sex for pleasure was the most sinful sin.

It is foolhardy to interpret a society 500 years ago through a contemporary prism. Yet it is very strange to warn against certain activities precisely by recreating them in such graphic detail. Can one not speculate that, while the *llotja*'s architect, Pere Compte, is in the history books, the anonymous stonemasons and sculptors also wanted to leave their marks? Could the man who for five centuries has been showing his naked buttocks and genitals as he fornicates with the wall, instead of warning against sin, be cracking a subversive joke against the powerful and wealthy? Perhaps these gargoyles and carvings represent a centuries-long streak of Valencian anti-authoritarianism, forerunners to the satirical *ninots* in the *Falles*. Whatever the interpretation, these "sins" are the greatest works of art in Valencia.

8: Valencia 2: Three Statues

To explore the Plaça del Carme, Sant Nicolau, the *llotja,* and the Velluters area of silk factories, as the last chapter did, you turn right after entering the Torres dels Serrans gate.

If instead you turn left, you leave the Carme neighborhood and find the Casa dels Caramels, the House of Sweets. Though it closed in 2016, this huge shop on the Carrer Mur de Santa Ana, with walls, pillars, and ceilings carved in multicolored sweets, is a fine example of the Baroque exuberance for which Valencia is famed. Falsely famed, complains the Valencian writer Joan Mira. Apart from the week of the *Falles*, Mira argues, "almost nothing fits [Valencians'] reputation for uncontrolled extroversion, for floral and decorative excesses."[77]

Mira is reacting to the facile cliché of Valencians' idle exuberance. He is right that this relatively prosperous region was built on the basis of hard agricultural labor and numerous small industrial workshops. Yet this does not contradict its people's love of noise, adornment, and color. The ceiling of Sant Nicolau, the tiles of the North Station and the House of Sweets are just some of a multitude of examples of "decorative excesses."

A block away from the sweet-shop (and not at all Baroque) stands the Palau de Benicarló, the seat of the Valencian Parliament (the Corts) since the post-dictatorship Statute of Autonomy in 1982. The Statute

---

77   Mira, p.11.

was the first time since Felipe V's abolition of the *furs* in 1707 that Valencia had a degree of self-government. The Palace has history: built for the Borja Dukes of Gandia, later a silk factory and then seat of the Spanish parliament when Valencia was the Republic's capital in 1936 and 1937. From the front, its Gothic austerity (a flat wall with few windows) recalls the palace of the Borja family in Gandia. Dating from 1485, its construction reflected and projected the family's pre-eminence among the Valencian nobility. Lucrècia's bare breast reflects still her evil reputation.

FALLES

And then, just two blocks away, we enter the heart of the city, if cities have body parts, the Plaza de la Virgen, the Virgin's Square, or the Plaça de la Mare de Déu, in Valencian still more explicit, Mother of God Square. This was both the Roman Forum and the Moors' city center, heart of the city for over 2,000 years in a way that the Plaça de l'Ajuntament, the Town Hall Square, grandiose though it is, is not. Pedestrianized again, now with marble slabs, after decades of traffic, the Plaça de la Mare de Déu encourages citizens to sit and stroll or meet at a café terrace. It is often said that this freedom is illusory, for on one side of the square stands the Palau de la Generalitat and on the other the cathedral and basilica. Temporal facing spiritual power. Yet here the Church wins hands down, for the Gothic Palau de la Generalitat stands sideways on to the square, sloping off down the mansion-lined Carrer de Cavallers (Street of Gentlemen). What dominates the square are the two religious buildings.

Cathedral from the Plaça de la Mare de Déu

On March 19, at the climax of the *Falles* week, some 20,000 *falleres* in their special silk dresses and *falleros* in colored waistcoats and pirate-length trousers pour through the square, piling flowers high as offerings to the Virgin. On the second Sunday in May, when the Virgin of the Dispossessed is taken out of the basilica and borne a few dozen yards to the cathedral, another huge crowd presses forward to touch the revered Virgin's vestments, even richer than the *falleres*'.

The *Falles* is Valencia's best-known festival, a spring celebration of fire and noise. On St. Joseph's Day, March 19, the enormous papier-mâché, plaster, and wooden structures, *ninots*, erected on most street corners are burned. The city's Falles Museum, near the City of Arts and Sciences, conserves the "best" *ninot* saved from the fire each year, but the exhibits are disappointing. They do not catch the anti-authoritarian satire of many *ninots* and reflect the tamer official promotion of the *Falles*. The *Falles'* roots lie in the Roman Saturnalia, when everyone stops working, starts drinking, and is licensed to mock everyone and everything and be mocked. One imagines that politicians like ex-Mayor Rita Barberá did not appreciate having her fatness and arrogance portrayed, yet there is pride, too: if a *ninot* is made of you, you've made it, you're an integral part of the city, instantly recognizable.

All year, the various *Falles* clubs prepare dresses (women) and *ninots* (men). There is a rich artistic tradition in the luxurious silk dresses of recent decades (under Franco poverty, they were simpler and uglier) and the elaborate, often surreal *ninots*, in Jason Webster's words, "caricature statues over five meters high made of wood or plaster then painted in bright colors."[78] It is an impermanent art form, like dance: months of labor disappear in a few hours of flame. All the senses are engaged in the festival: a riot of color in the dresses and *ninots*, the smell of sweat and gunpowder, the heat of the flames, and the noise of the firecrackers hurled—such a good joke—under people's feet and the official *mascletà*, fireworks on a string that rattle off in a crescendo of deafening noise. Gunpowder and noise accompany all lively parties in Valencia. It would be a good place to send soldiers for combat training. Jason Webster's first Max Cámara crime novel, *Or the Bull Kills You*, gives a fine vision of the modern *Falles*:

---

78   Webster, *Or the Bull Kills You*, p.80.

It was the penultimate night of Fallas—the *Nit de Foc*, the Night of Fire, when one of the world's largest firework displays was set off over the city sky. By now the night air seemed to be filled with one continuous explosion as the streets were crammed with people walking in groups, shouting and singing, some carrying plastic cups filled with whisky and cola, others clutching paper bags of freshly fried *buñuelos*. The *fallera* queens had lost their freshly painted look, the golden combs in the backs of their heads coming loose where they'd been jostled in the crowd…Costumes that had cost thousands to make and several months in the sewing were now close to getting trashed in the carnival atmosphere. The smell of gunpowder was omnipresent as child after child threw his *petardos* to the ground with a wild look in his eye, their crashing only drowned out as spontaneous *mascletàs* hammered out from somewhere nearby, shaking the cobblestones beneath their feet…Was this what hell was like, Cámara wondered? To live an eternal, never-ending *Fallas* fiesta, forced never to sleep and have your eardrums rocked again and again by an entire city of heaving, hysterical drunken partygoers?[79]

Webster's detective, Max Cámara, is from Albacete, which allows Webster to describe details of Valencian life through an outsider's eyes. This he achieves with relish and precision, making his books not just fine crime novels but sharp introductions to the city. Unlike many guidebooks, Webster's fiction has the great virtue of being critical: the only intelligent approach to a city one loves.

---

79   *Ibid*, p.342.

Just as there are people who live the *Falles* all year long, there are others who flee the city for the week of fire, smoke, and riot. Despite its satirical edge, it is now a somewhat conservative festival, with its sponsored clubs and official support. Just as the Saturnalia was tamed by the Church, so anti-authoritarianism is assimilated by the authorities. The *Falles* is undoubtedly deeply Valencian, but is also now a tourist festival.

The *Falles* is pagan, both in its origins and in its modern drunken rowdiness. Yet it is sanctified by religion, too. In Valencia, religion is a live political presence. Cardinal Cañizares, Archbishop of Valencia, who presides over these festivals, is an outspoken opponent of gay rights. According to him, the "Gay Empire" attacks the family. He has urged disobedience with laws on sexual equality. He has spoken out against the "invasion of immigrants". He considers abortion murder, and a more serious crime than sexual abuse of children. One concludes that he is on the far right of the Catholic Church. One should nuance, though, that not all his followers will share his views. The religious culture of Valencia is ferocious and distressing. Ultra-Catholicism is a powerful influence. Yet the basilica and all the other churches do not fill with the faithful on a normal Sunday. Most of the crowds who overflow the square at the *Falles* are there for tradition, a party, dressing-up, and a society's identity, without necessarily agreeing with either Cañizares or the Church. Thank God.

CATHEDRAL

If you sit on one of the many and expensive café terraces on the slightly raised section of the Plaça de la Mare de Déu, you see before you the Basilica of the Virgin of the Dispossessed and the cathedral. The basilica, to the left, is round, reddish, and symmetrical, whereas the cathedral on the right is low, jumbled and deformed, with its left side a circular three stories looking like part of Rome's Colosseum. On top is a platform for priests to watch events in the square and an enclosed bridge through which they can move between cathedral and basilica. If you finish your coffee and walk down the alley between the two churches, you can look on the left through a barred window and see at the far end of the basilica the Virgin of the Dispossessed in glory on her silver and gold throne. Rose Macaulay says that "the sumptuously jewelled image … [was] … carved for a lunatic asylum in 1410, by order of anti-Pope Luna."[80] Opposite, on the right of the same passage, there is a chapel set into the cathedral wall, dedicated to St. Vicent Ferrer who stands finger raised, hectoring (as usual) the crowds.

Valencia's cathedral has three great doors, one opening onto the Plaça de la Mare de Déu and two behind. The door on the Plaça de la Mare de Déu is Gothic; the one on the Plaça de la Reina, sober Romanesque, with a huge high door-knocker for someone on a horse and the carved heads of seven men and seven women reputedly representing colonists from Lleida who arrived with Jaume I; and the main door, also on the Plaça de la Reina, is exotic Baroque. The doors reflect the normal lapse of time to build the cathedral, but its basic construction, seen inside in all its unified simplicity, is Gothic. Here there is no jumble or deformity. Light through alabaster windows floods the long, symmetrical nave, as if it were an artist's studio. Unlike the dark, austere Castilian Gothic cathedrals that

---

80   Macaulay, p.94. Part of this asylum still stands in the Velluters district, once the Hospital dels Pobres Innocents, the mental hospital founded in 1409, one of the first in the world.

soar arrogantly toward God, this cathedral is longer and lower, a more homely form.

Many Catholic cathedrals possess limbs, nails, hair, or clothing of the saints. In Valencia cathedral, there is one such item: the brown, mummified forearm of St. Vincent the Deacon (not to be confused with St. Vicent Ferrer). Cathedrals vied to attract pilgrims, the tourists of ages past. Valencia goes one better: its great relic is the Holy Grail itself, the chalice that Jesus drank from at the Last Supper. In 1940 Heinrich Himmler visited the Montserrat monastery in Catalonia hunting for the Holy Grail, but no one told him to head for Valencia. Nor did Indiana Jones, foiling the Nazis' hunt for the cup, pass through the city.

The eggplant-colored stone cup was acquired in medieval times by Valencia from Huesca, in northern Spain, as collateral for a loan never repaid. In the Civil War a young couple risked their lives to hide it in their house in Carlet, to the south of Valencia city. In 2016 it was taken from the cathedral on a pilgrimage of thanks to that village. How the Church loves these stories of the humble defending its treasures!

Curiously, for so holy a Christian relic, on the chalice's base, which is another cup upside down, is an Arabic inscription from when it was mounted in the fifteenth century. The cup actually is Jewish, dated by experts to the first century of the Common Era. Who knows? There are other contenders: Glastonbury has one. There is no proof that Valencia's was the actual chalice Jesus drank from, but there is no evidence that it wasn't.

More interesting and absolutely genuine and very approachable, just along from the Holy Grail chapel, is a chapel dedicated to St. Francesc de Borja, which contains two paintings from 1788 by Spain's revolutionary painter Goya. Really, Saints Vicent Ferrer and Francesc de Borja are ubiquitous in Valencia. The paintings' strong lines, colors and faces make them immediately recognizable as Goya's work. On the left is a dark painting, showing an impenitent on his death bed. On one side, grotesque slavering devils drool at his imminent death, while St. Francis Borja fights, Holy Book held high, to save his soul. The picture is a close relation to Goya's dark cartoons of conflict and suffering.

The other painting, on the right, shows the saintly Borja leaving his weeping family to dedicate his life to God. It makes you think of the cruelty of suddenly in mid-life crisis upping and walking out on your family, even if it is for pious reasons. Perhaps, after all, Sant Francesc the Jesuit was the bad Borja, not Lucrècia or Pope Alexander VI.

Outside the cathedral, to the left of the Baroque door, you have to pay again to go up Valencia's cathedral tower, the Miguelete or Micalet. The Church, despite extensive state subsidies through tax relief and financial support for its schools and buildings, puts a charge on its monuments. Unlike Benidorm or Madrid, Valencia is blessed by having no skyscrapers. At fifty meters the Micalet, Little Michael, is not little at all, but the city's tallest building. There is no elevator, but 207 steps of a spiral staircase with hardly a passing point. If you're fit enough, the giddy ascent is obligatory. The platform at the top allows a 360° view of the city, from sea to hills and what remains of the *horta* among the suburbs and towns of the plain. You can see, as if it were on a model, the curving line of trees that marks where the river used to run and the new suburbs inland and seawards, blurring into mist or the haze of pollution. Yet Valencia is not a city of grand views from on high. Really it is a low city, full of corners and alleys, a blue dome glimpsed down a cobbled street, a gentle café on a deserted square, a detail painted on a balcony tile.

The platform on top of the tower is dominated by a great bell, which rang out for centuries to announce the opening and closing of the city gates. The Micalet has another tradition. At its foot, the poor from the hills, who had walked down along the Royal Road through the Serrans gate, might leave an unwanted child in past centuries. Not unloved, perhaps, but a mouth they could not feed. *Look up at the great bell*, they might say to the child, and slip away into the crowd. Here local traders could pick up child slave labor: errand-boys, cleaners, or victims of the sexual abuse we know more of today because before it was not discussed.

The old center of Valencia is large, cupped like a baby in the elbow of the Túria. The Carme and the area around the Plaça de la Mare de Déu are only a small part of this area. Though in other chapters there are descriptions and comments on parts of the old town, such as the city hall or the Central Market, numerous palaces, churches, bustling shopping streets, and sullen alleys are not mentioned in this book or touched on only in passing.

One mansion, not far from the cathedral, is highlighted by every visitor and guidebook to the city: the extraordinarily extravagant, Churrigueresque Palau del Marqués de Dos Aguas. This eighteenth-century style (named after the Catalan decorator Churriguera or Xoriguera) was extremely ornate Baroque. The mansion, started in 1740 and added to over the next century, is famous for its door, surrounded by sculptures in pitted, off-white alabaster. Snakes and alligators, flowing water, and twisted animals are carved in stone. On either side of the door two strong-bodied men are bent over: two Atlases holding up the world. Above the door a niche with the Virgin offsets any objections that the carvings might be too pagan. My first impression was that these extravagant sculptures had just been stuck onto an ordinary square

Atlas holding up the world: Marqués de Dos Aguas mansion

building, a cream cake thrown onto a white plate. On looking further (the building has two sides giving onto wide streets), it becomes clear that ornate decoration covers the entire palace. Ripples run through the stone. Bare-breasted women jut out above the windows (art justifies objectification of women). It is a one-off fantasy building.

Fantasy inspires strong reactions. Richard Ford (of course) disdained it as "a grotesque portal, a fricassee of palm trees, Indians, serpents and absurd forms."[81] The much more amiable Rose Macaulay adored it. Here are some excerpts from her lyrical description:

> ...one of the loveliest things in Valencia...exquisite and softly graded colours of this alabaster portal, changing in different lights from tawny to silver, lilac to maroon, green to pale russet...The sculptured luxuriance of the twined and wreathed fruit, foliage and serpents, the crouching Atlantean figures supporting the lintel, the beneficent females offering fruit and fish to the mother and child enshrined in a richly decorated recess above, is very exquisite and agreeable...richly curved windows, stone-balconied and elaborately shuttered.[82]

Now property of the state, the mansion houses the city's Ceramics Museum. This is disappointing if you hoped to see the gaudy, brightly colored tiles that adorn the North Station, but fascinating if you want to study the history of pottery in the area. The nearby towns of Mislata, Paterna, and Manises are the main sources of clay. Mass-production plates and pots of all kinds were exported

---

81 Ford, p.661.
82 Macaulay, pp.91-2.

from their potteries in medieval times throughout Spain and the Mediterranean. The museum explains, too, the manufacturing processes of "lustreware," fifteenth-century ceramics with a metallic sheen for Europe's royal and noble families. The building is the greater attraction than the museum. Macaulay concluded: "The whole effect is so beautiful that one is tempted to sit ... and gaze at it for hours."[83]

Strangling Thought

On the eastern side of the old town, in the Mar (Sea) quarter, three statues illuminate Valencia's development and conflicts. The sea is not close, but the name of the quarter comes from the Porta de la Mar, the Gate to the Sea, now in the middle of a roundabout, where the walled old town gave onto the river at the closest point to the sea.

The three statues are of a monarch, a philosopher, and a saint. Valencia's and Spain's tragedy is that the king and saint, temporal and religious power, together strangled the intellectual's voice.

The first statue, dating from 1890, is of the conqueror Jaume I, in the Plaça Alfons el Magnànim, known by everyone as the Parterre (flower bed in English), an attractive square with palms, giant rubber plants, heavy-smelling magnolias, and unusual "bottle" trees with deep green leaves. In spring this tree turns whitish with small bell-like flowers mottled yellow, pink, and red. It is odd that the square dominated by Jaume I's statue is not named after him. Several other squares in the city are similar: names of squares and statues do not coincide. It is like the North Station being on the south side.

---

83   *Ibid.*

Jaume I the Conqueror

King Jaume I rides his horse, looking to the left while he points to the right. Is this to imply that, like God, he could see in all directions? The inscription thunders in stone:

He entered Valencia as conqueror
Freeing it from the Muslim yoke
On Saint Dionysius' day
October 9, 1238

Words that underline that the Count of Barcelona did not *found* Valencia. He conquered it, which meant throwing out or enslaving the previous inhabitants. It emphasizes, too, the religious justification for this crusade, in case anyone might quaver at the crudeness of military conquest. He was a true Christian, for he freed the city from "the Muslim yoke." The Muslim yoke is a necessary falsehood, for Christians and Jews at that time could live in greater freedom under the Muslims than, later, Muslims and Jews under the Christians.

The second statue, just along the Carrer de la Nau, is in the center of the porticoed patio of the University of Valencia. This nineteenth-century building imitating a sixteenth-century one is the old university. The new one has been relocated to the more open spaces along the Avinguda de Blasco Ibáñez, near the Mestalla football stadium and toward the Malva-rosa beach. Until recently, humanities lectures were still given here, but now it is just the Rectorate's offices, library, and auditorium.

The bronze statue portrays Joan Lluís Vives, a scholar, on foot not horse, in a gown not armor, holding a book not a sword. The inscription is from 1880, much the same time as Jaume I's, but in Latin not Spanish:

To the most excellent scholar
And pre-eminent philosopher
Ionni Ludovico Vives

Joan Lluís Vives, thinker

Vives (1493–1540), born in that fateful time of the "discovery" of America and unification of Spain, was a humanist, educationalist, and philosopher. He came from a prosperous Jewish family in Valencia, which was forced to convert to Christianity, but still practiced Judaism in their private synagogue. His father feared the Inquisition (with good reason), and Vives, who was studying at the university where his statue presides today, was sent at the age of eighteen to complete his education at the Sorbonne. He never returned. His aunt and uncle were executed by the Inquisition and in 1526 his father was burned, too. His mother had died in 1508, before Vives left Valencia, but such was the zeal of the family's persecutors that they exhumed and burned her remains.

Suffering, unsurprisingly, from depression, Vives is often seen as a precursor of modern psychology, as his 1538 *De anima y vita* (all he published was in Latin) analyzed emotions and behavior from observation, for example itemizing the reasons why we might laugh or cry. In his day he was best known as a pedagogue, writing texts on the education of women and on how to teach Latin. He became a bestselling author throughout Europe, his *Linguae latinae* going through forty-nine editions within 100 years and *Instruction of a Christian Woman*, thirty-two.

Known as Ludovicus, Vives was befriended by Thomas More and appointed tutor to Mary Tudor, Henry VIII's daughter. When he took the side of Catherine of Aragon (Mary's mother) in her dispute with the king, he had to leave London and Oxford for Bruges, where he taught, wrote, and became a close friend of Erasmus.

Marrying Margarida Valldaura, also of *convers* (converted Jew) origin, and peaceful in Bruges, he came to perceive his longed-for Valencia not as home, but as the place of exile. It is a stimulating inversion of the normal definition of exile. In Bruges he lived, developed his mind, and won fame: Valencia was an impossible, fantasized alternative life. His *Collected Works* were not published in Spain until 1782–90, when a Valencian scholar Mayans i Ciscar edited them in Latin.

In Bruges he wrote *De Subventione Pauperum* (Subsidizing the Poor), an action plan against poverty, calling on society to provide support for the poor rather than their depending on alms. He can be claimed as a precursor of modern welfare states. He also made a distinction between the "lazy" and the "real poor." A real distinction it may be, but in this he anticipated the tiresome modern debates about the workshy and the deserving poor.

Ludovicus is hardly known today, but was as famous as Erasmus in his time. His life seems painfully contradictory. Jewish, he expressed his ideas in Christian terms. He served and defended Catherine of Aragon, a strong believer in her mother Isabel's expulsion and forced conversion of Jews and burning of secret Jews. An exile who never saw his family after the age of eighteen, he is a prime example of Spain's exclusion over the centuries of many of its best minds (see Chapter 15 on Max Aub). Henry Kamen, in *The Disinherited*, a study of Spain's exiled intellectuals, quotes Vives: "[In Spain] everything is darkness and night, no less in what is happening than in what I feel."[84]

Unity of the nation by military force and militant Catholicism, with exclusion of Jews and Moors, leaves no space for the independent research or free thought of someone like Ludovicus. Valencia University has honored the city's greatest thinker with the statue, but it cannot compensate for the pain of his life.

---

84   Kamen, p.22.

Right opposite the university is the Patriarca, a still-functioning Catholic seminary and a museum with, unexpectedly, three El Greco and two Caravaggio paintings. Its chapel is decorated with more magnificent tile-work, including a wicked, open-mouthed whale on the ceiling. You can hear Gregorian chant here at the 9:30 mass. Above the altar hangs a painting of the Last Supper by Ribalta, but at the climax of Friday morning mass, to impress the faithful, Ribalta's Supper is lowered on a pulley to reveal a painting of the crucifixion.

Like the university, the Patriarca has a two-story cloister. In the middle of its white marble columns the third statue presides: the seminary's founder Juan de Ribera, fanatical Archbishop of Valencia from 1568 to 1611. Like Jaume I he is seated, but on a throne not a horse. In the entrance hall, to the left of the main door, hangs a crocodile. This live gift to Ribera in 1600 from the Viceroy of Peru was stuffed on its death in 1606. It represents the silence fitting for a church or

The Patriarch of Antioch, scourge of Muslims

seminary, for crocodiles have no tongue. Thus, they neither talk nor laugh, but only cry—and this without sobbing out loud. Parents would warn their children with the saying: *Si parleu, a la pancha vindreu* ("If you talk, it'll gobble you up"). Maybe crocodiles could be put in public libraries—those that are left—today. Another curiosity is that in the Patriarca library, though how it got there no one seems to know, is the very last manuscript of Vives' friend Thomas More, written in his cell while awaiting execution.

The name of the seminary comes from Ribera's prominence as an anti-Muslim preacher, which earned him the exotic title of Patriarch of Antioch. His religious job did not prevent him becoming Viceroy of Valencia and head of its army in 1602, thus conjoining religious, political, and military power. Against the Kingdom of Valencia's economic interests, the all-powerful Juan de Ribera pressured the king and in 1609 achieved his lifelong aim of the Moors' expulsion. Thus, the third statue completed the work of the first statue, the city's conqueror Jaume I.

As an afterthought to the three tall statues, in the Plaça del Patriarca in the wall of the university is a fountain with the statues of Ferdinand and Isabella, the monarchs who united Spain and expelled the Jews in 1492. One might think there is nothing especially controversial about a city commemorating with statues a well-known, long-dead king and queen. The particular position and history of Valencia can be glimpsed in the sensitivity of those who advocate the unity of the *països catalans*, outraged that the statues of these two centralizers of the Spanish state, who set off the long process toward destroying the rights of Catalonia and the *país valencià*, are commemorated in the heart of Valencia city. "Gratuitous obsequiousness before Castilian-centrism ... wretchedness of spirit ... intellectual indecency," thunders the usually calm Joan Mira.

Russafa

These three statues are near the eastern edge of the old town. Continuing south-east is the Eixample, the Expansion, where the bourgeoisie and a new middle class, escaping overcrowding and cholera, started to build their houses 150 years ago. Its streets are laid out in straight lines, in sharp contrast with the twisting streets of the old town. This was the period of *art nouveau* and the Eixample contains many examples of fine apartment blocks with touches of that style. This building fashion, most closely associated with Barcelona and Gaudí, needed a wealthy bourgeoisie wanting to show off their wealth in the *coup de fouet* (the geometric forms suggesting the curves and twists of nature), the richness of decoration, and the frequent use of motifs with fruit and vegetables that characterize *art nouveau*. Its materials typically combined brick with marble, wood, and ceramics.

The *art nouveau* jewel of the Eixample is the Colom Market, formerly a normal neighborhood food market, now converted to cafés (including an *orxateria*) and restaurants for those with jobs, leisure, and money. Its cast-iron structure makes it a light, airy building, like an open cathedral. It has *trencadís* mosaic and Valencia's normal colorful ceramics on its pillars. The market vies with the North Station discussed above as the finest *art nouveau* building in the city.

Just on from the Eixample is the old village of Russafa. The Moorish kings built a legendary palace and garden here, though no trace but the name remains. Russafa was the first village of the *horta* to be absorbed by the city. Although no greenery is left, the village structure is still evident in its narrow streets radiating out from its market and church. This is a market of gray cement, ugly as the Colom and Central Markets are beautiful, but it has no pretensions except for the freshness of its food. It is a fine example of a local market.

Russafa is Valencia's bohemian quarter, the kind of area that most big cities have: a mix of old working class, immigrants, and students. The novelist Jason Webster lived there for several years:

> Lying just to the south of the old centre it [Ruzafa] was no longer the refuge of drug dealers it had once been, but Moroccan grocery shops sat next to Chinese wholesalers of cheaply made clothes and antique dealers selling Art Deco furniture. Cámara liked it for its friendly, village-like atmosphere.
>
> Architecturally, like much of Valencia, it was a mixture of elegant, brightly painted eclectic apartment blocks—five or six storeys high, with tall narrow French windows and ornate iron railings—standing next to younger, more awkward siblings: ugly, brown-brick structures from the 1950s and 1960s, with bright orange awnings and aluminium doors.[85]

The last time I was there, in 2017, sheets unfurled from windows urged people to keep quiet at night and respect residents' rest—an unequivocal sign of its growing popularity as a night-time destination for the young. And a poetic anarchist slogan adorned many a wall: *Antes nos mataban y ahora no nos dejan vivir* ("Before they killed us and now they don't let us live"). This, an equally unequivocal sign of the neighborhood's continuing tradition of dissidence.

---

85   Webster, *Or the Bull Kills You*, p.35.

9: Valencia 3: Along the Dry River

A return to the Torres dels Serrans, starting point for the two preceding chapters, places us on the sixteenth-century stone bridge of the same name. It is now one of twenty-three bridges over the waterless river, the curving line of green through the gray housing seen from the top of the Micalet. Down on the ground, the hint of country in the city becomes glorious reality. The drying and landscaping of the river is Valencia's most successful change to the cityscape of recent decades. Cities are always obliterating fields and forests, but no other city I know of has removed its river.

The flood of October 14–15, 1957 killed eighty-one people. The only area not affected was the former Roman Forum, now the Plaça de la Mare de Déu. The city (named Valentia = Courage) had been founded in 138 BCE a few miles south of Saguntum, then in its pomp, by 2,000 discharged Roman soldiers. They had the wisdom to build on the slight hill on the wide plain.

Over the centuries, floods periodically destroyed bridges and inundated Valencia. This was and is also a problem for other places on the coast, subject to torrential autumn rains in the nearby mountains. Both Alcira, on two rivers, and Alacant suffer recurrent floods. That of 1957 was the worst of all. After the disaster, a new river was cut to the south of Valencia. At first, a multi-lane highway was planned for the dried-up riverbed, but surprisingly the space was eventually used for a six-kilometer park meandering through the city center.

Visitors often imagine that the river would have flowed strongly before its diversion, like any normal river. In fact, it was often waterless. In *La barraca*, set in the 1890s, Blasco Ibáñez has his main character, Batiste, attend a horse fair:

> As always, the Turia river was almost dry. Some seams of water, escaping from the water wheels and dams that refresh the plain, formed snaking curves and islands in the burning, dusty soil that looked more like a desert in Africa than a river bed.[86]

To the Catalan painter Santiago Rusiñol is attributed the phrase when being shown Valencia's river 100 years ago: "It's a good location for one."

The Túria, like the several other rivers on the Mediterranean coast, has reservoirs upstream for drinking water and then feeds the intricate system of ditches and channels that irrigate the *horta*. This means that when these rivers draw close to the sea they carry very little water. In heavy storms the water roars spectacularly over hard, dry ground, sometimes flooding, as the Túria did in 1957.

The Serrans bridge is roughly halfway along the six kilometers of the new urban park. You can walk, run, or bike up or down this dry river. Children fill the playgrounds. Dogs do what dogs do on the grass: gambol, sniff, and shit. In the sunken park, the noise of traffic is muffled. People sit, stroll, play sports, and practice Tai Chi. This chapter follows the river, commenting on some of the buildings on its banks. Heading inland from the Serrans bridge, on the left as you go, slipping into the Carme quarter again, the first stop is the museum to Josep Benlliure (1855–1937).

---

86   *La barraca*, p.199.

Benlliure's name is not one that resonates around the art world, though he is one of Valencia's best-known painters. The painter's house-museum is more interesting than the painting, for it explains and shows the life of a bourgeois painter, who was very good but not original. Benlliure followed fashion rather than creating it, as his contemporaries like van Gogh or Gauguin did. His brother Marià was the extremely productive sculptor of statues all over Spain (including Juan de Ribera sitting in the Patriarca seminary's cloister). Valencia is home to fine painters, such as Ribalta, Sorolla, and Benlliure, but to no world-famous names, except Josep Ribera (no relation to the patriarch). It has produced no Velázquez, Goya, or Picasso. Pictorial genius in Valencia is most and best seen in its ceramics, and its sculptural talent in the temporary creations of the *Falles*. This could say something about a commitment to living in the present and going out in a burst of flame, but maybe this is too fanciful.

The three-story Casa Museu Benlliure is the home, built in 1883, where the painter, his wife Maria and four children lived. It is strange to wander through the homes of dead people, especially one whose office, dining room, bedroom, and studio have been conserved much as they were. You can sense, with the pleasant shiver on feeling how the decades rush by but we are still here, how the well-off lived a hundred years ago.

The house contains not just Benlliure's work, but the furniture and decoration of the time, sculptures by his brother and canvases of his contemporaries, including Sorolla. Behind the house is a delicious, romantic garden, a rare privilege in the over-populated old town, with Benlliure's studio at the back. The walled garden is narrow and long. Palms, a lemon tree, and mandarins are wrapped around by thick creepers that form a vegetation awning against summer heat.

The studio at the bottom of the garden is not what I had anticipated: a simple summer-house, bare but for stacked canvases, the easel, paint splashes, stained cloths, and light. No, this studio is a chapel dedicated to the painter himself. Benlliure was a collector or, one might say, desecrator of ancient sites. Romanesque windows and door, brought back from Italy, front the solid two-story studio, which is cluttered with antiques, tapestries, costumes, musical instruments, and pictures covering the walls. The studio was not just a private space, but a stage set to impress clients, who would be ushered through the lush garden and into the artist's impressive lair before deciding to have their portrait painted for a fat fee.

In 1879 Josep Benlliure settled in Rome, where he stayed for thirty years. Here he encountered the work of Marià Fortuny, Rome-based painter from Reus in southern Catalonia, and adopted his style. Though Fortuny had died in 1874, his high-earning work still dominated contemporary taste. It was defined by Oriental fancy, color, and precision of line. In the 1880s, Benlliure became known throughout Europe, painting in the style and fashion of Fortuny. These genre paintings of daily life, detailed portraits of gardens, and taverns, with touches of fantasy and the exotic, caught the public mood.

In the 1890s, though, the style began to slide out of fashion. Benlliure sought to adapt, incorporating features derived from Sorolla. His color and line recorded scenes of the Valencian *horta* in a more Impressionist style. He continued to paint, but was no longer a big seller. From 1904 to 1912 he accepted a salaried job as head of the Spanish Fine Arts Academy in Rome. Later, in 1922, he became director of Valencia's Fine Arts Museum. The fascination of the Benlliure House-Museum is twofold. It lets us peer inside a wealthy household of the time. It gives, too, a rare insight into the difficulties and career of someone who was obviously a very good painter, but not a great original. Throughout his long life he continued to paint but never repeated the success of the 1880s.

Josep Benlliure's younger brother, Marià (or Mariano in Spanish) (1862–1947), was and is more famous. Also a master of nineteenth-century realism, Marià sculpted some 100 large, public statues all over Spain of the great and good, both religious and political figures, most of them still in place. Like Josep, he lived in Rome, in his case for two decades from 1881. When he returned to Spain, it was to Madrid, where reputation and contracts were to be found, though he was buried in Valencia's Cabanyal Cemetery alongside his parents. Most of Marià Benlliure's work stands in the streets of Spain, but some can be seen in his brother's house and in the Sala Benlliure of Valencia's Fine Arts Museum, result of the sculptor's donation in 1940. In the latter are some brilliant terracotta heads of famous figures of his time, moulded by the sculptor's strong fingers, not by chisel and hammer.

There is another great sculptor present in Valencia. This is at the IVAM (Institut Valencià d'Art Modern), just by the Torres de Quart, a little further upriver from the Benlliure House-Museum. The IVAM is a striking modern glass-and-concrete building, with a length of city wall tucked away as heritage in the basement. It devotes a special space to Julio González (1876–1942), with some 400 sculptures, including his famous *Woman in Front of a Mirror*. While Marià Benlliure's imposing bronzes were rooted in the pompous realism of nineteenth-century military and political fame, González was trying to fly, to free sculpture from its mass and weight.

González never lived in Valencia. Born in Barcelona, he spent most of his life in France, very much part of the great art revolution of the first decades of the twentieth century.

The Valencia connection is due to the 1985 donation to the IVAM by his granddaughters of this valuable collection of one of the century's most famous sculptors.

It was collaboration with Picasso in the late 1920s that set González on the production of abstract work in cast iron. Though abstract, his sculptures are recognizably based on the human figure. Catalonia has a long tradition of artisan ironwork; González introduced its techniques to fine art, "drawing in space." Despite the crude strength of iron, González welded in his best work delicate, light pieces that seemed to float—just as, in another medium, the architect Santiago Calatrava (see page 192) conjured the effect of weightlessness from enormous steel sheets and cables.

Moving on, upstream, still on the left of the river and just outside the old town, is the Jardí Botànic (Botanical Garden). This dates from 1802, though many trees, plants, and bushes were brought from previous sites. The outstanding Spanish botanist of the Age of Enlightenment, Antonio Cavanilles, author of *Observations on the Natural History of the Kingdom of Valencia* (1786), was responsible for developing the garden's stock. He had bad luck as Marshal Suchet's invading troops tramped through it in 1812. In the twentieth century the garden fell into disuse, an abandonment that was the fate of most botanical gardens in Spain. Cavanilles' garden in Madrid, beside the Prado Museum, was similarly left to grow wild until as recently as the 1980s. The age of classification of plants was the eighteenth-century Enlightenment, but the early twentieth century showed little interest in conservation of nature or education about the natural world. Now, awareness of the loss of diversity and of the importance of the environment means that botanical gardens are flourishing again. Valencia's is a small bulwark of protest against the destruction of the natural world along the Mediterranean coast.

The Botanical Garden was restored in the 1990s. It claims 4,500 species, covering aquatic and tropical plants as well as Valencian ones. The garden has that cool beauty created by high brick walls distancing the city traffic. In the long summer, it is a refuge where water flows by benches under the shade of 200-year-old trees.

The Botanical Garden's research building was host to the signing of the agreement between the Socialist Party and Compromís that led to the coalition that took control of the Community of Valencia's government in June 2015, removing the PP from twenty years of power. Headlines in newspapers about the "Botànic government" or "Conflict in the Botànic" can be confusing. The plants are not in dispute, just the coalition partners.

The dry river then curls away from the old town, through sports pitches and playgrounds, with bicycles and joggers in their shiny, tight-fitting colors passing constantly. The walk upstream ends at the Parc de la Capçalera, the Head-of-the-River Park, where the ex-river opens out into a wet lake where you can pedal a boat shaped like a swan, beside an artificial, wooded hill and benches where the homeless sleep among the reeds and bushes. On the left are the railings of the Bioparc, where animals run relatively free, not confined in cages. It is designed so that visitors cannot easily see the ditches and fences, which gives the feel of being out in open country with the animals.

Just before reaching the Parc de la Capçalera, you can turn off to the left into Mislata, one of the city's outer neighborhoods, an old village of the *horta* incorporated into the city. Here the City History Museum is located, one of the few museums outside the center. And here too is a remarkable site, Valencia's old Model prison built to Jeremy Bentham's design, with a central panopticon and its several wings, now completely restored in scrubbed red brick to house various departments of the Valencian Autonomous Community's government. Many people want to see politicians in prison. Here, though, in these palaces of recycled cells, it is civil servants who are confined.

SEAWARDS

Going the other way from the Serrans bridge, toward the sea, is a more varied and stimulating walk. The second bridge from the Serrans is the Trinitat, which leads to the Trinitarian Convent of Poor Clares where the writer Sor Isabel de Villena (see Chapter 3) was abbess. Just beside the convent is the Fine Arts Museum. It looks like a castle, but was a convent, then a military hospital before transformation into the museum in 1946. Its collection, like many in Spain, is based on the religious art confiscated from churches on the 1838 Disestablishment.

The museum's most popular section is the first floor devoted to Spanish art, with the great names we are predisposed to revere: El Greco, Murillo, Goya, and a self-portrait of Velázquez. Perhaps more interesting, because not to be found elsewhere, are the very extensive rooms of Valencian painting, featuring work by the Baroque artists Juan de Juanes (1523–79), Francisco Ribalta (1565–1628), and Josep de Ribera *Il Spagnoletto* (1591–1652).

Ribera is the most famous of these painters. Born Josep in Xàtiva, then probably studying with Ribalta in Valencia, he left in 1610 for Italy, where he received his nickname: he was short of stature as well as Spanish. In 1616 he reached Naples, where he married a Neapolitan and stayed the rest of his life, working mainly for the Spanish viceroys. He is attributed with the bitter phrase that his homeland was "a loving mother to foreigners and a cruel stepmother to her own sons." Famous throughout Europe in his day, Ribera was the heir to Caravaggio's "tenebrous" (dark) and very detailed realist style. Ribera used light and dark to create a dramatic, sinister atmosphere. He revealed the coarse texture of ordinary objects in thick layers of paint. His reveling in the gruesome details of the martyrdom of the saints earned him Richard Ford's comments:

> He became the leader of a gloomy though naturalist school, and was a painter-monk, formed by taste and country to portray the church-militant knights of Santiago, the blood-boltered martyrdoms, attenuate ascetics, and ecstatic Faquirs of the province of San Vicente Ferrer, the forerunner of the Inquisition.[87]

Yet *Il Spagnoletto* was not only a religious obsessive. There are many non-religious paintings and he developed from the Caravaggio style into more colorful Baroque art, becoming a decisive influence on his near-contemporaries Velázquez, Murillo, and Rembrandt. Of all the Valencian painters he is by common assent the greatest, Valencia's "Old Master." His best-known painting today is the portrait of the fifty-three-year-old Magdalena Ventura, *The Bearded Woman* (1631) (now in Toledo), notable for his treatment of his unusual subject not as a freak, but with empathy. A hundred years ago, Havelock Ellis was less prejudiced than Ford and fought to express in words how Ribera moved him: "The robust vigor of Ribera's art is compensated and completed by his essential tenderness…somber and deep tones of emotional color…the most superb and original colorist of Spain."[88]

---

87   Ford, p.640.
88   Havelock Ellis, pp.120-4.

The Fine Arts Museum also has space devoted to Valencia's more recent painters, the "Impressionists" Sorolla and Pinazo. Sorolla is discussed in Chapter 13. The work of the less-known Ignacio Pinazo (1849–1916) throws up several questions. In 2016–17, he was treated to a year-long centenary exhibition in the IVAM, with huge posters and publicity. Commentators wrote of how this painter, unjustly neglected for decades, was now receiving deserved recognition. Pinazo's 100 paintings and 600 drawings held in the IVAM's cellars were put on display for the first time in decades.

The questions are: in an area with no indisputably great painter (except *Il Spagnoletto*), is Pinazo being promoted for the tourist trade and Valencian pride, i.e., after a century of being undervalued, is he now being overvalued? Or was he really the equal of any other Spanish painter of his time, but was undervalued because he did not go to Madrid or Paris and lived his life quietly in a village in the *horta*? And do Valencians only value those who triumph elsewhere: Ribera in Naples, Sorolla in Madrid and New York, Blasco Ibáñez in Hollywood, or Calatrava all over the western world? In the country of loud explosions, does anyone look at a quiet man's paintings?

Ignacio Pinazo, unlike the Benlliure brothers, was born into a poor family. His mother died when he was seven and his father and stepmother when he was sixteen, all of cholera. Brought up by his grandparents, he earned his living in practical artistic trades: baking, painting tiles, decorating fans, and making hats while studying at free evening classes to be a fine-arts painter. Success came in the 1870s and he too could visit Rome. Fleeing another cholera epidemic, in 1885 he settled in Godella, in the *horta* north of Valencia city.

Pinazo is the most purely Impressionist of the Valencian painters. His early work features traditional historical scenes (some of these large, long canvases can be seen in the Ceramics Museum in the Marqués de Dos Aguas Mansion), but his stay in Rome on a scholarship from 1874 made him a more intimate painter. Though often seen as a nineteenth-century artist like Benlliure, a traditional painter of nature and country life, his techniques are modern, characterized by rapid, often broad brush-strokes, quite likely due to his training in various kinds of commercial art.

He has never been highly valued in the art market and the pre-exhibition storage of his work in the IVAM cellars is no different from the treatment of his forty paintings held but not shown by Madrid's Prado. His reclusion in Godella and his independence led to undervaluation. Pinazo was not one to follow fashion or court fame. Yet several critics rate him highly: quite the equal of Sorolla or the Catalan Impressionists, Ramon Casas, and Rusiñol. I do not know if Pinazo was before undervalued and is now overvalued, but it is worth spending a little time looking at his work and thinking about the answer.

Right beside the Fine Arts Museum, the large Royal Park, the Jardins de Vivers, is ideal for a stroll after a session staring at paintings. The Moorish rulers built a palace and gardens here with water flowing and falling intricately among exotic trees and animals. The palace was wantonly destroyed at the start of the nineteenth century, supposedly to prevent Suchet using it as a base in the same 1812 invasion that trampled the Botanical Garden and left cannon-shot holes in the Torres de Quart. The destruction of the palace was to no avail, as the city was taken anyway. Nor is the reason given for its destruction clear, as numerous other buildings outside the old walls were left standing, such as the Fine Arts Museum itself or the Trinitarian Convent, right beside the park.

Following on down the riverbed and bearing right at its elbow onto the forearm, walkers reach the imposing

Palau de la Música. It is the first of the major new buildings of the bottom part of the river-park. Unlike the museums and gardens mentioned above, this is actually in the old riverbed, not alongside it. Opened in 1987, the Palau de la Música was part of a state-wide plan to open a concert hall in all of Spain's provincial capitals, particularly suitable for musical Valencia, where every town has its band.

The Palace of Music is a fine auditorium, but not as striking as the giant Gulliver nearby, roped to the riverbed, sprawling on his back and looking like a *ninot*, a papier-mâché figure from the *Falles* festival. This magnificent playground has the children as the Lilliputians, investigating the giant fallen to the riverbed from another world. Gulliver has numerous twisting, hidden slides and secret staircases in the folds of his clothes. Strong thread binds him. Even strands of his hair can be used as slides.

And then, a few hundred meters from Gulliver, hero of Dean Swift's satire on human futility, we come to the City of Arts and Science, which is both a glory of modern Valencia and evidence of continuing human folly. The city's rulers wanted to provide their city with a second Golden Century. They got glitter, but little gold.

Our Guggenheim

Fifteen years ago, on a first visit to the newly opened Príncipe Felipe Science Museum, I overheard a middle-aged woman proudly tell her friend: "Now we've got *our* Guggenheim." The new Guggenheim Museum in Bilbao was in the news in the 1990s for the flair and originality of its building (designed by Frank Gehry) rather than its contents. In the global tourism market, cities now compete for customers. The magnificent buildings designed by "trophy" architects, centers of culture that *must* be visited, put a city on the map. The woman felt that now Valencia could compete with Bilbao. She was showing pride in her city. She was also reflecting the arguments of the ruling PP: that these buildings were necessary in order to attract tourism and so make the city prosperous.

Tourism is a double-edged sword. One can argue the line of the PP and it is generally right: prestige buildings do attract visitors. Visitors are needed, for traditional industries have declined. We have to compete with Bilbao, with Barcelona, with Madrid…But then what do these visitors/tourists do? Who do they benefit? They sleep in hotels and eat in restaurants, bringing profit to hoteliers and restaurateurs. They buy postcards and souvenirs and sometimes expensive goods too, bringing profit to shopkeepers. Tourism provides numerous jobs, but not good or stable ones: most jobs in the tourism industry (waiters, cleaners, *kellys*, shop assistants…) are precarious and low-paid, with exploitative conditions.

Tourism also alters the shape and rhythm of a city. It can change a city definitively, making its residents feel alien. Not yet and not so much in Valencia, for it lags behind Barcelona or Madrid as a tourist attraction. Whole neighborhoods have not yet been given over to hotels and Airbnb tourism apartments, with local residents and small shops priced out. This is a process far advanced in Europe's great tourism cities and in Valencia the process is under way. Tourists already dominate the streets between the Plaça de l'Ajuntament and the cathedral. These are lined with ice-cream parlors, pizzerias, restaurants with plastic menus outside with sickly photos of sausage, chips, sangria, and fried eggs, and—my particular objection—cafés with red plastic chairs.

"Over-tourism" is exacerbated by the recent phenomenon of huge cruise ships putting in to Valencia: so high they tower above the dock wall and port installations. The tourist industry complains that visitors sleep and eat on board these floating leisure palaces and so spend little money in the city, while residents bemoan the cruise passengers clogging the pavements.

Tourists are drawn, too, to the six new futuristic steel and glass buildings that make up the City of Arts and Sciences, Valencia's Guggenheim, at the uncompleted bottom of the river-park: uncompleted for lack of money. The riverbed ends beyond the new buildings in rubbish-filled lots and a wall separating it from the docks.

These six buildings are the Palau de les Arts Reina Sofía (opera house), the Hemisfèric (3-D cinema), which leads into the Príncipe Felipe Science Museum with the 300 meter-long Umbracle beside it. Further down are the Àgora and the Oceanogràfic (Aquarium).

Flown in from outer space? Calatrava's City of Arts and Sciences

Between the Science Museum and the Àgora an elegant bridge with a 125-meter slender needle with taut filaments like a harp's crosses the dry river. The needle is the highest tower in the city. In fact, "highest" is the main objective of the City of Arts and Sciences. It is not primarily designed to show great art or teach good science, but to be the highest, the biggest, and the best. Its purpose, however pretty one may or may not find the buildings, makes it vulgar.

Here is a brief summary of the buildings. Google and the tourist guides will expand on any and all of them. The Opera House, 230 meters long and seventy meters high, is second only to Sydney's opera in its style and capacity. The building is covered by two laminated steel shells weighing over 3,000 tons, 163 meters wide, and 163 meters long. The architect Santiago Calatrava's achievement is to give this building of great weight and size an eerie effect of airy lightness. It does actually look something like the Bilbao Guggenheim, with its overhanging metallic roof.

The Hemisfèric "broods like a huge, heavy-lidded eye over the shallow lake that laps around it" (Miles Roddis). Lying squat on the water, its aluminium shutters open like eyelids to reveal the eye of knowledge. Its oval exterior, 100 meters long, houses a cinema and planetarium. Visitors are drawn into the virtual reality of IMAX films by angled seats and a vast, concave screen. Dating from 1998, it was the first of the river-city's buildings to open.

The Príncipe (Prince) Felipe (he's now king) Science Museum was opened in 2000; it is 220-meters long, looking like the skeleton of a whale or a futurist cathedral. The building is the thing: the exhibits are standard. The arches, the buttresses, and the lake in front of it create the effect of a building in tension, a live building held down like Gulliver by its steel wires.

L'Umbracle beside it was designed as the entrance to the river-city. It has an underground car park, on top of which the long greenhouse mixes plant species indigenous to Valencia and sculptures. The plants were chosen to change color with the seasons. The still unfinished Àgora is a covered plaza, an adaptable space.

Lastly, the Oceanogràfic (by Félix Candela, the only building in the City of Arts and Sciences not designed by Calatrava) is an aquarium, with different water environments—the Arctic, tropics, or Red Sea—and some 500 species of fish. It is said (by the City Council) to be Europe's biggest (certainly bigger than the key competitor, Barcelona's!). Here you can walk along underwater tubes and eye the unblinking fish that saunter idly around you.

You can approach these new buildings, the centerpiece of the new Valencia, in wonder or with skepticism. Both the emotion and the thought are needed: to marvel at the daring and beauty of them and to look critically at what they are.

CALATRAVA: FLOWN IN FROM OUTER SPACE

The architect of the City of Arts and Sciences is Santiago Calatrava, born in 1951 in Benimàmet, a former village now on the northern edge of Valencia city. This Valencian is now one of the half-dozen most renowned architects in the world.

Rowan Moore wrote in *The Guardian* of the "flamboyant Spanish architect":

> Calatrava is a maker of trophies, popular with cities keen to raise their profile with structures like bridges and railway stations whose functional purposes become the occasion for the display of curving, flying, hanging, waving shapes that he

likes to compare to skeletons, or birds, or trees, or other things of nature. Sometimes his buildings have moving parts, roofs that open or sunshades that unfurl.[89]

In this modern world of cities competing with each other for tourism and business, famous architects are those who provide spectacle. When you get a Calatrava, you get a bridge or building that looks like a Calatrava, just as an El Greco or Lucian Freud painting looks like a Greco or a Freud. Architecture, though, is not painting. A painting exists on its own terms, but a building should fit in with its surrounds, not be imposed on them.

It is easy to be rude about Calatrava, and below I will be. The negative side of his work can be summarized in three brief points: i) he is notorious for bringing in projects way over cost, ii) he is unluckily affected by numerous problems in his buildings, often involving lawsuits, and iii) he is renowned for his overweening ego.

First, his skills and quality should be celebrated. Calatrava studied civil engineering after architecture. He is a sculptor and painter, too. His creations are big: he is the architect of bridges, opera houses, museums, and now the world's highest tower. His work is often brilliant, technically very complex. What first brought him a reputation was the 1987 Bac de Roda bridge in Barcelona. It joins two working-class neighborhoods divided by railway lines. Calatrava is a romantic architect. This bridge soars across the tracks, all aglow and white. This is public, functional art bringing glamour and beauty to people's lives. All his bridges soar: powerful steel cables look like delicate threads. Steel sheets weighing thousands of tons seem to float in the air.

---

89   *The Guardian*, February 5, 2017.

The Turning Torso in Malmö, a tower that twists around itself like an embarrassed teenager, is one of many spectacular buildings. Calatrava is fond of comparing his buildings to nature, such as the whale or elephant skeleton of Valencia's Science Museum; or the oculus of glass and steel, the Transportation Hub at Ground Zero of the World Trade Center in New York, which looks like, in his own words, "a bird freed by the hands of a child." The Tenerife opera roof is an Atlantic wave breaking. His latest project, to be the tallest tower in the world (830 meters), in Dubai, "is inspired by the delicate veins of lily leaves."

To return to Valencia, Calatrava's opera house is the centerpiece of the City of Arts and Sciences. Calatrava spent fourteen years on the project and construction. This man who works in solid sheets of steel and glass is characteristically poetic about his work:

> Because of the time spent, its size, and because it involves music, this project is the most intense and the one I've devoted most time on, so far. It represents a correlation between spectator, musician, and artist.[90]

It sounds good, though the artist-architect's meaning is not easily grasped. Descriptions of the opera house are many and inventive: an egg yolk flowing from a cracked shell, a trilobite, a warrior's helmet, a ship's prow, or: "An arresting, glimmering white building that looks as if it could have just flown in from outer space, surrounded by pools of cool, blue water."[91] This is a beautiful building. Why need it fit

---

90   (Consulted December 17, 2017) https://www.designbuild-network.com/projects/valencia-opera/
91   Nick Meo, *Telegraph*, July 28, 2012.

in with its surroundings? A great building can dominate its surroundings, which just have to sit unnoticed while everyone stares at the building. Yet it has not been exempt from problems. The most glaring example of design failure was the seating. Seats behind pillars had no view of the stage. Even more striking than this error was Calatrava's truculent and now famous reply, as characteristic of him as his budget over-runs: "There are seats without a view in Milan's La Scala and this doesn't matter because people go to listen and learn rather than see."[92]

Two hundred seats had to be removed, reducing the number to 1,500, making it no longer bigger, but smaller than other opera houses in Spain. Further problems have assailed the building. A heavy storm in October 2007 flooded it, causing sixteen million euros of damage. This was not the fault of Calatrava alone. In fact, Calatrava's firm had warned of this danger, as the opera is at the lowest point of the dry river. Though now the water no longer pours off the mountains as it did in 1957, it can still race five kilometers along the riverbed. The firm had warned of it, but no measures had been taken by the City Council or Calatrava himself. After the flood, seven million had to be spent on a protective wall.

And the opera's ceramic cladding, the *trencadís* inspired by *art nouveau*, began to bulge and then drop off in late 2013. "As an architect, you do not have control of who will build the building," Calatrava lamented stoically: "…Even if you do not deserve any blame, you have to stand there, like the captain of a ship." He is to some degree right, yet of course the architect has overall responsibility. The builder's name is forgotten: it is a Calatrava building. And surely someone of Calatrava's stature makes sure he gets the builders he wants.

---

92   Castillo Prats, p.296.

These mishaps combined to make people start to question Valencia's own architectural genius. Was it really worth spending so much to have "our Guggenheim"? In the years of boom till 2008 money seemed to grow like oranges, on trees. Now, the new Botànic government is having to pay for the upkeep of these white elephants and probably wishes that the opera house could be flown back to outer space.

So how much was spent?

Building	Budget (million euros)	Final Cost (million euros)
Opera House	109	378
Science Museum	62	168
Àgora	41	102
Hemisfèric	18	32
Umbracle	14	36
Assut de l'or bridge	23	60
Oceanogràfic	39	200
Others (landscaping, fees, repairs etc.)		c.120
City of Arts and Sciences: TOTAL	308	c.1,100

The Oceanogràfic, the Aquarium, is the only part of the complex that breaks even. Accordingly, it has been privatized! The Generalitat wants to sell off the rest, as it is faced not only by debt interest but by maintenance bills. Calatrava is not an ecological architect. He makes no effort to adapt his buildings to local conditions and his huge, high, hollow spaces cost enormous sums to heat. Not so important in sunny Valencia, but these same glass and steel structures also cost large sums for air-conditioning.

Calatrava's fees ran at 100 million euros, forty-two million more than originally budgeted. They were paid to Calatrava's accounts in Switzerland where his firm is based and are thus exempt from Spanish VAT. In addition, cost over-runs benefited Calatrava, as he was paid 12.5 percent of the extra expense. It was the PP that came to power in 1995 that favored him by introducing this clause. Under the original agreement with the Socialists, Calatrava would receive 11 percent of the agreed budget, not of the final cost. Thus, for every euro he ran over budget, he received an extra twelve and a half cents. The more he spent, the more he earned.

Calatrava is a man of great charm and dynamism. It is said that when he is summoned to be reproached for soaring costs, he walks out of the meeting with yet another project under his arm. Valencia's own, he became very much the PP's architect, the man who could make real its wildest dreams. He and President Francisco Camps added the Àgora to the river-city in 2004, though its purpose was never clearly defined. It was opened officially in 2009 with the men's professional tennis tournament, part of the ATP World Tour 500 series. For years it was unfinished, as well as extremely underused. Some 1,300 tons of material for the roof, wings that were to become a mobile butterfly, loiter on a nearby site, rusting. Much, it is said, has been stolen. The material had been bought but could not be installed because there was no money left. In addition, the Botànic government was doubtful about the butterfly wings' safety. In Oviedo Calatrava had to pay three and a half million euros in compensation because one of the wings of his Conventions Palace fell off. In 2018, however, scaffolding was up on the Àgora. The la Caixa Foundation had come to the rescue, investing eighteen million to open a CaixaForum, a free-access exhibition and museum space. Part of one of Spain's biggest banks, CaixaBank, the Foundation has opened to acclaim CaixaForum buildings in several other cities of Spain.

Calatrava made a lot of money from the City of Arts and Sciences. His practice has been sharp, but it leads onto a deeper question about the political strategy of the PP in Valencia and the party's corruption, subjects of the next chapter. The wonderful six-kilometer river-park through the center of the city ends at Calatrava's City of Arts and Sciences. His extravagance, ambition, and arrogance symbolize this period of wasteful splendor. Santiago Calatrava is an apt representative of the modern Valencia. Not Pinazo.

10: The Party's Never Over

"Estoy en política para forrarme"
(I'm in politics to line my pockets)

Vicente Sanz.[93]

The City of Light[94] film studios and school was the third major project of Eduardo Zaplana's presidency (1995–2002), alongside the City of Arts and Sciences (Chapter 9) and Terra Mítica (Chapter 6). As usual, the PP announced the studios with unreal fanfares and over-the-top rhetoric. These would be the most advanced studios in Europe, with 11,000 square meters of studio space and the latest technology to compete with London's Pinewood Studios. Located just south of Alacant, near the airport, its budget was 240 million euros and, in positive comparison with the City of Arts and Sciences, it "only" overran by thirty-four million. The cost of maintenance, however, was a ruinous million a month. And it was chronically underused. Thirty-seven films were shot between its opening in 2005 and 2012. By 2010 it had lost eighty-four million euros.

The studios fell foul of the European Union, which ruled after a complaint from Pinewood that the use of

---

93   Formerly president of the PP in the province of Valencia, Sanz was secretary of RTVV, Valencia's public radio and TV company, from 1995 to 2010. He was later found guilty of sexual abuse of several journalists.
94   A name normally associated with the city of Paris, but linked here to Alacant's Roman name *Lucentum*.

public money represented unfair competition with other film studios. "A private lender would not have granted credit for the project, because cash-flow was insufficient to cover the investment." The EU sentence in 2012, ratified in 2014, forbade use of the studios for fifteen years, later reduced to five. The Generalitat tried to sell the buildings. Despite praise from Ridley Scott and Francis Ford Coppola, neither Coppola himself nor anyone else wanted to buy them. Since 2014 the studios are closed, the installations are deteriorating, and Alacant's Hollywood dream is a nightmare of legal conflicts. The Botànic government is trying to sell it off in lots and is planning to use one area for the reopened Valencian TV channel.

ANTI-CATALANISM

The PP governed Valencia for twenty years, in which time it is calculated that it spent at least five thousand million euros on projects like the three launched under Zaplana above and on the major events associated with the period of Francisco Camps as president of the Generalitat (2003–11).[95]

Camps (born 1962) brings to mind Tony and Cherie Blair, who supposedly sat down in a London restaurant in the late 1970s and worked out how their lives would go. Cherie would earn big money as a lawyer and Tony would seek political power. In the early 1980s Camps used to meet with student friends in a bar called the Agujero (Hole) near the Mestalla stadium and the University Law Faculty. These law students plotted out their political careers; they became known as the *clan del Agujero*. Two of the friends became *consellers* with Camps twenty years later. Camps has never

---

95   Figure of the Valencia Institute for Ecomonic Research (IVIE), cited in Castillo Prats, pp.507-8.

worked at anything other than politics: creating a career in the City Council, in the Generalitat, and as a member of the Spanish Parliament. Tall, elegantly dressed, slim, he is known, among ruder names, as the *curita*, the little priest, due to his religious faith, ready smile, and Messianic belief in his own virtues.

After the rough and tough Zaplana, Camps at first seemed a breath of fresh air. He was well-mannered, suave, and, unlike Zaplana (who is from Cartagena, in Murcia), was able to speak Valencian and often did. Camps distanced himself in style from Zaplana, but the political content turned out to be much the same. He continued with the vote-winning theme of anti-Catalanism: the Catalans, along with the Socialists, slowed down the highway connection to Madrid; the Catalans denied Valencians drinking water by refusing the canal to transfer water from the Ebro; they were linguistic and cultural imperialists. Whereas Zaplana created big buildings, Camps oversaw big events: the pope's visit, the America's Cup yacht race (though this involved very big buildings, too), and Formula One motor racing on a street circuit.

Camps, once the shining white knight of Spain's PP, backer of Prime Minister Mariano Rajoy and tipped to succeed him, is now repudiated by his own party. An illuminating incident occurred when he appeared before the Spanish parliamentary commission investigating the illegal financing of the PP on March 5, 2018, seven years after his forced resignation. Camps answered a question from a member of parliament for Esquerra República de Catalunya, Ester Capella, as follows: "The *país valenciano* does not exist. I cannot accept this insult." He who was president of the Comunitat Valenciana for eight years says it does not exist! It is even more surreal when the words *país valencià* (or *país valenciano*) appear in the 1982 Statute of Autonomy, ratified in 2006 when Camps was president. Camps, of course, was not denying that Valencia existed, but was rejecting the left's terminology.

Camps' response to Ester Capella underlines how Zaplana, Barberá, and he built the PP's success on a story of standing up for Valencia against Catalan imperialism. This was their political project, nurtured from Camps' student days in the Agujero, at the time of what is known as the Battle of Valencia. It is worth looking at this conflict to understand Camps' ideological roots.

In the 1936–39 Civil War and the 1970s transition, Valencia was a leftist stronghold, an important anti-Franco area. By the early 1980s, however, reaction in this "highly susceptible, insecure and fragmented society"[96] was striking back in a fierce debate over Valencian identity. For the new post-Franco Statute of Autonomy (1982), the left wanted the name *país valencià* and the right, *Reino de Valencia*, the Kingdom of Valencia. "Valencian Community" was a compromise.

The Battle of Valencia was waged not only with words and mass demonstrations, but with physical intimidation. The house in Sueca of Joan Fuster, whose *Nosaltres, els Valencians* (We, the Valencians, 1962) is the Bible of the large minority who argue for the cultural and political unity of the *països catalans*, the Catalan-speaking lands, was bombed in 1978 and 1981. The Tres i Quatre bookshop, a center of anti-Franco meetings and identified with the unity of the *països catalans*, was attacked eight times by fascist groups asserting the Spanishness of Valencia. (Tres i Quatre means "three and four" and refers to the three main areas where Catalan is spoken, i.e., the Balearic Islands, Valencia, and Catalonia, and the four red stripes on the flag.)

---

96   Enric Juliana, quoted in the Introduction (Maceda, p.11).

The Valencian nationalists of today are known as *blaveros* or *blavers*. Descended from regionalist parties, the *blavers* were encouraged by Spain's right-wing parties during the 1970s transition from dictatorship to democracy in order to divide the Catalan-speaking lands. The *blavers'* name comes from *blau* (blue) and refers to their insistence on a blue fringe to the Valencian flag to distinguish it from the four bars with no blue of the Catalan flag. Their argument goes right back to the foundation of the Kingdom of Valencia in 1238. It runs as follows: the Moors were tolerant of other religions, so did not interfere with Christian and Jewish cults as long as these did not attack Islam. Thus, since the many Christians in the area before 1238 did not use Arabic, they must have used a Romance language that, like Catalan and Spanish, developed from the break-up of the unity of Latin on the fall of the Roman Empire. Thus, the roots of Valencian are different from Catalan. Valencian, the *blavers* say, is descended from Occitan, especially through the Templars who were given refuge in the region; whereas Catalan was a branch of Provençal.

Both radical *blavers* and believers in a Greater Catalonia, the *països catalans*, are in general agreement that Spanish (*castellano*) is not the language of Valencia. Where they differ is that the *blavers* argue that the main danger to Valencian identity is Catalan imperialism. Thus, they are ferociously anti-Catalan. Throughout the 1980s and 1990s María Consuelo Reyna, in her daily columns in the paper *Las Provincias*, inveighed against Joan Fuster and his co-thinkers.[97] As, in the Battle of Valencia, the *blavers* had argued for the term "Kingdom of Valencia," I asked a radical *blaver*, who preferred to remain anonymous: "But who is your king?"

97　"The Catalans want to steal our paella!" was her most famous phrase.

"We reject the Bourbons who abolished our *furs*. We return to before 1707. We are a kingdom without a king."

The Valencian PP is happy to accept the Bourbons and does not call for a kingdom without a king, but the party's ideology is a milder form of *blaverisme*. The anti-Catalan crusade has resulted in the Community's flag with blue fringe, insistence that Valencian is a language separate from Catalan, and *comunidad* instead of *país* (land) in the area's name. This demagogic assertion of Valencian identity against Catalonia conceals the subservience of the Valencian right to Madrid, to Spanish nationalism.

THE POPE, RACING CARS, AND YACHTS

Pope Benedict XVI (did the visit remind Ratzinger of his namesake Benedict XIII, Papa Luna?) attended the fifth World Meeting of Families in Valencia on July 8–9, 2006. Both City Council and Generalitat spared no expense. The Meeting, with a million people anticipated to acclaim the pope, was planned like a sporting event. Yet not everything can be planned: the pope's visit was overshadowed by Valencia's worst metro accident. On July 3 at the Jesús station, forty-three people died. Official reaction was to blame the dead driver and downplay the incident. Nothing was to interfere with the positive publicity of Valencia as a great city and Camps kissing Benedict's ring, with the king and queen present at the huge outdoor mass in the Túria riverbed.

The accident, though, would return to haunt the PP. The victims' families refused to keep quiet. They demonstrated for years on the third of every month, despite attempts to buy their silence. The PP's leaders showed their caliber by rejecting a formal investigation and refusing to meet the families. Finally, Jordi Évole's 2013 television program on the accident stimulated widespread disgust at the PP's callousness and was a principal factor leading to its fall in 2015.

There is a motor-racing circuit at Xest (Cheste) a few kilometers inland from the city, but Bernie Ecclestone, the Formula One boss, and Camps wanted an urban circuit, like Monte Carlo. The elderly Ecclestone played hard and dirty. He announced two weeks before the 2007 regional election that he would bring Formula One to Valencia only if Camps won the election. Camps promised voters that the circuit would cost the Generalitat "not one euro" and would be better than Catalonia's Formula One circuit at Montmeló. He duly won the election. A company, Valmor Sports, was set up to administer the race. The first Grand Prix took place in 2008 and Valmor found that the business was not so profitable. Around 115,000 attended the first race, but only 51,000 in 2012.

The Generalitat spent eighty-nine million euros on conditioning the circuit. It then had to take over the payment to Ecclestone's Formula One Administration of twenty million a year—the fee for the rights to host the race. Finally, bankrupt, in 2012 Valmor was bought by the Generalitat for one euro, which meant that the latter had to assume the former's thirty-four million euros of debt. Víctor Maceda, journalist with the weekly *El Temps* and author of the informative and reliable *El despertar valencià* (Valencian Awakening), reckons that "the presumed zero cost of Formula One ended up at 286 million euros."[98]

Only five Grand Prix took place. After Camps fell, his successor Albert Fabra canceled the contract with Ecclestone. Imagine how many potential schools and health centers were consumed in the burnt rubber and exhaust fumes of five car races. The Valmor case has ended up in the courts.

---

98   Maceda, pp.110-1.

Veles e vents, David Chipperfield's sandwich building,
in Valencia's new America's Cup harbor

Camps' third great event was the America's Cup, a
prestigious race for millionaire yacht owners that attracts
the jet (or yacht) set to watch it every three or four years.
In 2003, a Swiss yacht club became the first European team
to win the cup in the 152 years since it started off the Isle
of Wight in 1851. As there was no sea in Switzerland (the
Société Nautique de Genève practiced on Lake Geneva),
the SNG chose Valencia to defend the cup in 2007. Eleven
yachts competed to be the challenger to the holder and then
the SNG successfully defended the cup. The contests lasted
from April 16 to July 3, 2007. In the February 2010 defense
of its title, the SNG lost the knock-out races—litigation
had reduced the field—against the Californian Golden
Gate Yacht Club.

The Valencian interest in the America's Cup had ended, as the winning team flew back to San Francisco with the cup. Though the hope of Camps and Rita Barberá that Valencia's new yacht marina and village would be a permanent headquarters for the America's Cup was dashed, the marina has greatly increased Valencia's capacity for hosting the yachts of the super-rich. The main building was the spectacular *Veles e vents*[99] for VIPs, an illuminated giant white sandwich, designed by David Chipperfield. It languished half-used and half-empty (like the Àgora) until in 2016 Heineken took the building for seven years to develop into a gastronomic center.

The consortium set up to finance the harbor building in 2003 borrowed 313 million euros from the government. In 2016 the loan was written off as irrecoverable.

WE ARE THE BEST

One of the most surprising features of these twenty years of PP domination is what is called in Spanish *autobombo*, self-praise or blowing one's own trumpet. "The Community has reached unprecedented international standing." "We are leaders, we are the best." "If someone comes to our country and wants to know what Spain wants to be in the future, come to the Valencian Community." "The Valencian Community is envied by everyone." All these are quotes by Camps. On October 9, 2005, Camps proclaimed "Valencia's new Golden Century."[100]

---

99 *Veles e vents, Sails and Winds*, title of the famous Ausiàs March poem.
100 Castillo Prats, pp.257-8. I have stolen all these quotes directly from this book on how the PP "sacked" Valencia as surely as Hannibal sacked Arse.

He protests too much. It makes one wonder who it was who lacked a positive self-image. Maybe it wasn't the Valencian people at all, but Valencia's conservative politicians, who have a compulsive need to sing their own praises. They took out full pages in the press:

> The Formula One race is the latest in a series of great sporting events that have awoken the city's tourism potential and has knocked on into strengthening tourism in the Valencian Community. A territory that has in the past concentrated its visitors at its beach and sun resorts and that has now, with this new event, positioned itself in the *pole position* of world tourism.[101]

One of Camps' saddest statements was his justification for the politics of big building projects and events: "Big events are like magnets for new foreign investment."[102] However, there is no evidence for this oft-repeated mantra. The Castelló airport, Terra Mítica, the Formula One circuit, the new harbor for the America's Cup, the City of Light, all lost money and failed to attract investors. Most telling are the figures from Spain's National Institute of Statistics. Here is Castillo Prats with a compelling argument:

> If Spain's GDP was 100, the Valencian Community was at 96.5 points in 2000, it dropped to 92.3 in 2005 and to 88.6 in 2009 ... Growth in GDP placed the Valencian Community below the state average during Camps' rule.[103]

---

101   *El país*, June 19, 2010.
102   Maceda, p.257.
103   Castillo Prats, p.258.

Maybe the average Valencian felt better, but they certainly became poorer as all the great buildings were rising and the major events were taking place.

It is true that tourism has grown. Valencia city has become an attractive destination and the beach resorts continue to flourish. Some of this can indeed be attributed to the big events that put Valencia in the news.

The economic crisis of 2008, from which the Spanish people have not recovered, hit Valencia particularly hard. In 2012 the Valencian Community needed a two-billion-euro bailout from the central government. The collapse of the construction bubble threw hundreds of thousands out of work and left unfinished buildings, ghostly reminders of a false dawn, all along the coast. Hospital wards closed, local taxes rose, and nearly 50 percent of Valencia's young people

The cost of prestige events: primary care center in pre-fab (Oriola)

are un- or under-employed. Many have emigrated. While hundreds of thousands of elderly northern Europeans migrate to the Valencian sun, tens of thousands of the *país valencià*'s youth migrate to work in northern Europe. Particularly damaging is that, during the construction boom, many left school as soon as they could to earn good money. Now these people, little more than a decade later, are on the scrapheap with few educational qualifications.

Education, health, and social services are starved for cash. This unattributed phrase became a popular refrain: "We are becoming beggars in a city of expensive wonders." The Botànic government entered in 2015 to find the coffers not just empty, but full of bills. The PP in twenty years had presided over a drop in the living standards of Valencians and bankrupted the government. This was the economic model of Zaplana, Barberá, and Camps.

I have talked of Zaplana and Camps. The other figure of the Valencia PP's triangle of power was Rita Barberá (1948–2016), mayor of the city from 1991 to 2015. On November 23, 2016, Rita Barberá died of a heart attack in a room of the Hotel Villa Real in Madrid. She was in Madrid to appear at the Supreme Court, voluntarily but as someone under investigation for corruption.

Barberá was the principal political architect of the great leap forward of Valencia as a tourist city, transformed during the two and a half decades of her mayoralty. And she was a symbol of a certain corrupt way of doing things that had ended with her now less popular Partido Popular losing power in both the city and Valencian Community in 2015. Backhanders, filtering public money to the party, money laundering, "gifts" received, commissions for building contracts, suitcases (and pianos) full of cash, all this was the grisly story of the Valencian PP coming apart at the seams during the last few years of Barberá's life.

Barberá was an expansive extrovert who dominated the Valencian political scene with the force of her personality. She won six successive elections. During her rule, the city changed, in many ways for the better. The old quarter underwent a facelift. The port expanded. The suburban train, tram, and underground network, Metrovalencia, was extended. The City of Arts and Sciences was built. The long Túria garden was improved. Emilia, the mayor in Jason Webster's *Blood Med*, is based closely on Barberá:

> She was a maverick and knew that many Valencians supported her because she championed the city, wearing her identity as a Valenciana like a badge of honour. No scheme was too grand, no project too costly for Emilia and her home town, not even now, when the coffers were bare and the debts threatening to drown the place for generations to come. For all her faults—her tackiness and authoritarian instincts—the city had become almost her personal fiefdom: her position was never seriously threatened... *Valencia, soy yo* went the joke. In the style of Louis XIV, Emilia believed that she was Valencia.[104]

CORRUPTION

It was not just that the PP had bankrupted the Valencian Community with vainglorious projects and buildings. The party had also stolen. The PP in Valencia has been involved in so many cases of corruption that Compromís leader Mónica Oltra defined Valencian democracy as

---

104   Webster, *Blood Med*, p.177.

"kleptocracy" and Ximo Puig said there are so many court cases that they should just be called "the PP case." They are interested parties, of course. Oltra built her career as the courageous leader of opposition to the PP in the Corts and became vice-president of the Valencian government after the Botànic Agreement of 2015.[105] The Socialist Party leader Puig became the president. Interested parties, but not wrong.

The Socialist member of the Corts Eva Martínez said in 2011: "I'm convinced that this money has been siphoned off, because it's absolutely impossible that a project budgeted for three or four hundred million euros spends one thousand three hundred million, however many additional features and improvements there are."[106] She was referring to the City of Arts and Sciences. This is just one scandal of many. It is not the new Golden Century, but corruption for which the Zaplana, Camps, and Barberá regimes will be remembered. There is barely a senior person in the Valencia PP who has not been charged with corrupt practice. Judge de la Mata called what was then Spain's governing party a "criminal organization." He is not the only judge to have done so.

There is one case, Imelsa, that has produced a truly weird character. Imelsa was a public company, Impuls Econòmic Local (Local Economic Stimulus), depending on the Diputació (Provincial Council) of Valencia. As its name implies, Imelsa was set up to develop the economy. Its director Marcos Benavent misunderstood his brief and stimulated his personal economy. He was accused in 2015 of

---

105   A fine speaker, Oltra became popular for stunts such as wearing a t-shirt with a photo of Camps and the legend in English "Wanted. Only Alive" in the Corts in May 2009. She was trying to oblige Camps to attend the Corts for questioning.
106   Castillo Prats, p.293.

having diverted through false invoices at least 561,000 euros to a company specially set up for this purpose. I say a "weird character" because Benavent repented of his crimes and confessed all. He admitted to having been a "money junkie." This besuited, dynamic middle-aged conservative was suddenly transformed into a long- and white-haired hippy with earrings and beads, calmly talking in the interviews he gave about how meditation and ecology were now his thing and he was much happier for it. In all, 115 people imputed in the Imelsa swindles are awaiting trial.

Benavent was the right-hand man of Alfonso Rus, Mayor of Xàtiva for twenty years. The Valencian-speaking Rus liked to boast he had no academic qualifications, but this did not stop him from being as corrupt as the university-educated parliamentarians. There is a disgusting tape of him joyfully counting dirty money. Rus was an enthusiastic reactionary: he stopped Raimon (see Chapter 2) singing in Xàtiva, while spending large sums of public money on refurbishing the bull-ring and hiring Elton John and Julio Iglesias, among others. Rus also refused to withdraw the title of honorary mayor of the city from the dictator Franco.

Here are two examples of the practice of buying votes through favors: three days before the 2015 elections, Rus provided contracts of 400 euros a month to sixty-two unemployed people in Xàtiva. In the previous election, he trebled the annual subsidy to the Association of Bulgarians in the city: 300 duly registered to vote. The self-made Rus was unmade by Benavent's confessions.[107]

Marcos Benavent is not the only "penitent." Ricardo Costa, member of the Corts from 1995, when he was only twenty-four years old, and the former general secretary of

---

107   Maceda, pp.164-5.

the PP in Valencia, admitted in 2018 in the trial of the Valencian part of the "Gürtel" corruption case (see below) that the PP was financed illegally, most often through donations from businesspeople in exchange for contracts. Known as "Ric," Costa set the cat among the pigeons by requesting that Spain's prime minister, Mariano Rajoy, be called to give evidence and claiming that Camps knew all about the dirty money. When Esteban González Pons, one of Camps' lawyer cronies from the Agujero bar and PP leader in the European Parliament, advised Ric in 2009 to be discreet, Costa replied: "In the PP, the party's never over."

It is tempting to provide dozens of anecdotes of PP corruption in Valencia. They have their comic sides, but it is a tragi-comedy, for this was public money being stolen and the results are schools in prefabs, hospital wards closed, expensive buildings that cannot be maintained, and massive debt interest payments. The victims of the theft of public money are the great mass of Valencian voters, many of whom unfortunately voted for the very people who robbed them.

I will confine myself to the main cases:

1. **Gürtel.** This is the most famous corruption case in all of Spain. The strange name is because Gürtel means Belt in German, which is Correa in Spanish: the leader of the corrupt gang is Francisco Correa. Basically, through fourteen companies in Valencia, such as Orange Market, the Madrid-based Gürtel clique received 4,894 million euros in public contracts from the Generalitat, in exchange for bribes in cash or in kind. They were responsible for organizing numerous events, such as the pope's visit. They received inflated payments due to the ascendancy that their Valencian

leader Álvaro Pérez, *el Bigotes* (Moustachio), acquired over senior figures, especially Camps, who called Pérez his "intimate friend."

2. **Brugal.** Bribery, extortion, and illegal use of influence. Ángel Fenoll started in the 1980s collecting rubbish with his father on a mule and cart in Oriola. Friend of successive Mayors of Alacant and Oriola, he held the rubbish contracts for these cities. The Oriola tip straddles the border of the provinces of Murcia and Alacant provinces. For years, Fenoll played off inspectors by telling them the tip was registered in the other province. This huge tip operated for sixteen years without a license. At its peak in 2007, Fenoll's company Colsur had 700 employees. Fenoll bribed elected officials systematically and recorded all his conversations. When he thought someone else might be recording him, he arranged meetings in a sauna. Naked, it was hard to conceal a wire. For the investigating journalist Víctor Maceda, the rubbish case of Oriola is the purest example of corruption in Valencia. Political, business, and financial power were divinely interlinked. The Brugal case has caused dozens of PP officials and politicians to fall, including the Mayors of Alacant and Oriola and the president of the Diputació d'Alacant, José Joaquín Ripoll.[108]

3. **Enrique Ortiz** owns 70 percent of buildable land in Alacant. Insatiable purchaser, builder,

---

108   Maceda, *El Temps*, January 29, 2013. Author's interview with Maceda, January 24, 2018.

contractor, Ortiz had outstanding relationships with PP politicians. He would give expensive presents, including apartments and vacations or find jobs in his companies for politicians' relatives. He is facing various prosecutions.

4. **EMARSA**, the public company running the Pinedo sewage treatment plant for Valencia city and surrounding towns, was robbed of at least twenty-five million euros. Esteban Cuesta, a nurse with no experience of management, was appointed manager. He employed Romanian women "as translators." No contracts. No translations produced. It transpired that eight "translators" were put up in five-star hotels. Twenty-five people were indicted in 2015 for fraud.

5. **Piano case.** The friend of Zaplana, Luis Fernando Cartagena, Mayor of Oriola from 1987 to 1997, received a donation from the Carmelite nuns for social purposes. He placed the bag containing 49,000 euros in the piano of his office and used it for personal expenses. Sentenced to four years in jail.[109]

6. **Solidarity case.** Stealing from nuns and the poor may seem rather degenerate, but it gets worse. Rafael Blasco, *conseller* in all the Valencian governments of Zaplana and Camps, became head of the Conselleria for Solidarity in 2008. For three years his department budgeted money for third-world projects. Most of it never arrived: 833,000 euros for a water project in Nicaragua was used to buy

---

109 Maceda, p.150.

property in Valencia; 297,000 euros against sexual violence and child labor in Malabo, too. A hospital in Haiti after the earthquake was never built (four million euros). The cynicism of these thieves is seen in the words of Blasco's confidant, the businessman Augusto Tauroni through whose companies much of the "aid" was channeled. Tauroni was recorded telling Blasco: "We have to prioritize our own stuff before anything for the blackies."[110] Blasco was sentenced to six and a half years.

7. **Nóos.** This "non-profitmaking" institute run by the king's brother-in-law, Iñaki Urdangarín, received swollen contracts from the Generalitat. Urdangarín was sentenced to six years in prison.

8. **Taula.** Fifty people from the PP in Valencia City Council, including employees and seventeen councillors, were indicted in 2016 for money laundering to provide illegal financing for the party. Illegal financing is, of course, a way of buying elections, just as effective though not as direct as giving funds to the Bulgarian Association of Xàtiva.

9. **RTVV.** Known for its adulation of PP leaders and denial of space for opposition voices, Radiotelevisió Valenciana abused all rules on public-service broadcasting. By the time of its closure in November 2013 it had a debt of 1.3 thousand million euros. Its directors and executives were cronies of the PP presidents

---

110   *Ibid*, p.170. In Spanish: "Hay que priorizar lo nuestro antes que lo de los negratas."

and are involved in various corruption cases.

How did the politicians of the PP think they could get away with it? The corruption in the Valencian PP affected "every level in the party, every leader and every administration," in Mónica Oltra's words.[111] Their control was near-total. They won elections at all levels of the administration: towns, cities, regional government, and the Generalitat. They controlled the television and press. They thought they controlled the judiciary. They felt immune. History was on their side, too: their predecessors under the Franco dictatorship had done the same.

Four points to end this chapter. First, there has been a general attitude in Spain that Valencia is particularly corrupt. Rafael Chirbes, scourge in his novels of corruption, reminds us that corruption is not specific to Valencia: "The myth of the Valencian Community's corruption has grown because they hadn't the same power as other communities to stop information, but the Gürtel comes from Madrid."[112] The Madrid PP has had an enormous number of high officials involved in several corruption cases. In Catalonia, Jordi Pujol, who was president from 1980 to 2003, admitted tax evasion and his seven children are all accused of various crimes, including receipt of commissions for awarding public contracts, tax evasion, and money laundering. Barcelona's Palace of Music was used to divert money to Pujol's ruling party, Convergència, and to enrich individuals. In separate cases, Catalan Socialists and other members of Convergència have been found guilty of corruption. The Socialist Party in Andalusia operated (operates) an extensive web of clientelism. In short, the

---

111   Castillo Prats, p.439.
112   *El confidencial*, August 17, 2015.

Valencian PP has been exceptionally corrupt, but it is not alone.

Second, most cases of corruption, such as in Madrid, Catalonia, Andalusia, and Valencia, occur when the same party is in power for a long time. In addition, both the building boom up to 2008 and wasteful big-spending projects favored corruption. Money sloshed about with lack of control.

Third, why should we be surprised at government corruption? We live in a system that prizes and admires the person who lusts after and accumulates money over and above collective health and welfare. With such ideas dominant, it would be unusual if there was no corruption.

Fourth, it is often said that people get the governments they deserve. If they vote time and time again for the PP, even when corruption cases had emerged, it means they think, *if I was in power, I'd do the same.* This is to misunderstand the nature of control and manipulation by a ruthless ruling party. The Valencian PP controlled the media. It gave its people spectacle and development at a time when the opposition was woefully weak. The period from 1995 to 2008 was one of unprecedented boom and growth in the economy, which the PP was happy to attribute to its own good management.

The Valencian people were slow to break with the PP, but they did. Camps had a big majority in 2011, just two months before he was forced to resign, but in 2015 the PP lost hundreds of thousands of votes. It was the government that was corrupt, not the whole of society; though, we should be warned, corruption as a government habit creates an atmosphere at all levels of society.

Today's Valencian Community

11: Alacant: Luminous and the Place of the Tragedy

"The palms! They were gilded by a morning sun"

Jean Genet, *The Thief's Journal*

I was fortunate to have a host in Alicante/Alacant, with 300,000 inhabitants the *país valencià*'s second city. Mariano Sánchez Soler has written several well-researched and incisive books explaining how many of those who dominate Spain's economy today made their fortunes under the Franco dictatorship. As did the Franco family itself. Despite the change of political regime in 1977, economic power remained intact. Journalist and poet, Mariano is also a writer of hard-boiled crime fiction.

We meet in a café behind Alacant's main food market, on the raised, pedestrian-only Plaça 25 de Maig. The square's name commemorates the 300 killed and near-thousand injured in the fascist bombing of the city by planes based in Mallorca on May 25, 1938. More died that day than in the destruction of Guernica a year earlier. Mariano is white-bearded and short-sighted and holds forth with enviable energy and enthusiasm. He worked for many years in Madrid as a journalist, but has always been drawn back to Alacant, his home town. His passion for the city makes him fiercely critical of the destruction of its past by speculation and angry at the neglect of the present. His book *Alacant a sarpades* (Rough Sketches of Alacant) is one of the city's essential texts.

221

Mariano's book opens with a reflection on the city with two names: Alicante/Alacant read the road signs as you approach. Al-Lacant is the Arab name and leads naturally to Alacant. The change of an "a" to an "i" and the addition of an "e" is part of the steady, centuries-long castilianization of the city. Now you barely hear Valencian in the street. "In Valencia city it's sixty-forty Castilian to Catalan speakers," Mariano tells me. "In Alacant, it's seventy-five against twenty-five." He may be optimistic.

Mariano was brought up in a Castilian-speaking family. When he reached university in Madrid, he found to his shock that Catalans and Valencians were ridiculed alike for their accents and origins. They were *polacos*, Poles, the common insult for Catalan/Valencian speakers. "I had thought I lived in the south-east, in a Spanish city. In Madrid they set me right. Suddenly I was a foreigner."[113]

Mariano's reaction was to subscribe to *Avui*, launched in 1976 as the first legal paper in Catalan since before the Civil War, and to take a correspondence course in Valencian. A stubborn response. Only by learning the language, he felt, could he properly become the *alacantí* he already was. It was not a nationalist gesture, but rather a rejection of Spanish nationalism.

For the first-time visitor, Alacant is a city as attractive as its resonant names. Rose Macaulay, mobbed in 1949 by people unaccustomed to seeing a woman driving a car, loved it:

> Curved whitely round its great ship-crowded harbor and beach, with the luxuriant fringe of palms along its waterfront, and its tiers of white, flat-roofed eastern houses climbing behind, Alicante is a handsome, luminous, oriental city and port.[114]

---

113   Cadenes, p.72.
114   Macaulay, pp.108-9.

Luminous, white, African, palms. There is a darker, less light-filled part, too, and Macaulay, noting the number of streets named after Franco's generals, does not forget that José Antonio, the founder of the Falange, lived, was arrested and, on November 20, 1936, shot in Alicante. Like all the *país valencià*, Alacant was a Republican city till the end of the war. In *Campo de almendros* (Camp of Almond Trees), Max Aub recorded a chilling date: "This is the place of the tragedy: by the sea, under the sky, on land. This is the port of Alicante, March 30, 1939. Tragedies always happen in a particular place, on a precise date and at an hour that permits no delays." In stark prose, Aub recalls the end of the Civil War, when thousands of fleeing Republicans, the rank-and-file who were not flown out by Soviet planes, massed on the Alacant waterfront. General Gambara's Italian troops were entering the city. The remains of the Republican army had only one destination left: concentration camps. Only the very old are left to remember now and the tourists who mass around the castle and Postiguet beach and fill the pretty bar and restaurant terraces that spill over the narrow streets of the old quarter are unaware of this history.

Alacant is not a place of monuments: no Sagrada Família, no Prado Museum, no City of Arts and Sciences. The old quarter crouches beneath the Santa Bàrbara Castle on the huge yellowish Benacantil crag that looms over the city. The crag, just one more of the many mountains that reach the coast all along the Valencian coastline, and its castle, "crowned with a sentry-box hanging boldly over the abyss,"[115] assisted the establishment of the city on the shore: it could be defended in the sixteenth century against pirates. Traders settled there; the city grew.

---

115   Gautier, p.306.

The ruined castle on top has everything you could wish for in a castle: turrets, dungeons, cafés, a museum, and views overlooking the town. Ruined, because it was blown up in the War of the Spanish Succession. In 1964 the abandoned ruins were partially restored. A tunnel was drilled into the hill from the side nearest the beach and a lift installed. Foreign tourism was starting.

Inland, behind a brief plain, gray mountains sprawl. You can appreciate how Alacant is built at the end of a long ravine. Though the bare-looking mountains suggest aridity, in September or October torrential rains flood the city, even today lifting the sewerage covers off their holes. In 1985 five people were killed. All along the Mediterranean coast, dry river-beds can be converted in a few minutes to roaring torrents that carry cars and people into the sea. *Alacantins* stay indoors when the autumn storms fall.

The Postiguet beach and the port are closely attached to the city. You step off the Explanada, esplanade, with its 400 palm trees and you are on the city's intimate, daily beach. Alacant does not turn its back on the sea. The eighteenth-century city hall is in a noble square only two blocks from the beach, whereas Valencia's municipal buildings are two kilometers from the sea. Walk down the Rambla past its elegant soft buildings with curved edges and white balconies, giving the street an air of the French Riviera, and you reach the beach or the port, where you can catch a ferry to the island of Tabarca or to Oran, just over the water in Algeria.

Foreigners and natives alike emphasize Alacant's intimacy with the sea. Alacant's best-known novelist Gabriel Miró (1879–1930), an elegant prose stylist, wrote:

My city is shot through with the Mediterranean. The smell of sea anoints its stones, shutters, books, hands, hair. And the sky of sea and the sun of sea glorify the roof-tops and towers, its walls and trees. Where you can't see the sea, its presence is divined in the victory of light and the air that creaks...How I love you and how filled I am by this so sweet blue flame of Alicante![116]

The esplanade was built on land reclaimed from the sea by the destruction of the city walls. In 1848, the 400 palms were planted: palms are not native to Spain, but they flourish there and give to Alacant its air of the South, their fronds curling down into the light. Jean Genet, romantic vagabond in the 1930s, wrote:

> The palms! They were gilded by a morning sun. The light quivered, not the palms...on the shores of a quiet sea and plunging into it; white mountains, a few palms, a few houses, the port and, in the sunrise, a cool and luminous air.[117]

Now that the Rambla is not a proper *rambla*, where pedestrians stroll (or ramble), but is a normal road of car noise and fumes, the esplanade, with its enormous *ficus*, rubber plants (or trees), their hanging tendrils searching for soil, street market (post-hippy trinkets and beach-wear/wares), café terraces, and casino, serves as the Rambla. Its line of houses, varied in height, color, and style (some *art nouveau* ones), fits together, an elegant and rich ensemble. Its pavement, inaugurated in 1958, swirls along in imitation of the front along Rio's Copacabana beach. Dull, subdued Francoist Alicante was making a statement of intentions: it wanted tourists.

---

116   This quote from Miró's *El mar, el barco* (1921) is taken from an Alacant tourist leaflet.
117   Genet, pp.63-4.

The biggest *ficus* in Alacant grows in the romantic nineteenth-century square just behind the esplanade, the Plaça Gabriel Miró, recently restored after decades of neglect. The square's junkies and prostitutes have been squeezed out, to haunt some other less visible street. The large post office, an *art nouveau* building overlooking the square, has also been rehabilitated. Gabriel Miró is well served by his square's handsome flat-fronted apartment blocks with tall windows and narrow iron balconies, thick foliage and a famed central fountain with a statue of a woman with a long-necked jar sprinkling water over a faun.

The oldest quarter, by both castle and beach, maintains its narrow, hillside streets. Museums, offices of the City Council, and rehabilitated buildings stand alongside tumbledown blocks and rubbish-filled lots: it is in a process of stuttering gentrification. The two main churches are worth a visit. The St. Nicholas cathedral, started in the seventeenth century, has a cloister with a garden of fine columns and ironwork. The Church of Santa Maria is earlier than St. Nicholas. It was built on two levels on the site of the mosque, as usual. Its Baroque door of winding pillars contrasts sharply with the most sober Gothic exterior. Rose Macaulay wrote: "Santa Maria...standing in a white plaza near the sea, with a most beautiful Churrigueresque portal, very richly carved, with twisted columns...a charming balustrade and a deep blue dome."[118]

Good word, Churrigueresque, the longest in this book. It means exaggerated Baroque, a building hung heavily with curling, twisting adornments, like the Marqués de Dos Aguas mansion's doors in Valencia (see Chapter 8). You get a great view of this fourteenth-century church from the roof-garden of La Milagrosa Bed & Breakfast, on the

---

118   Macaulay, p.109.

opposite side of the square. La Milagrosa (The Miraculous) welcomes non-residents up to this comfortable roof-terrace with long-leaved plants, sofas, and bar.

MISSION IMPOSSIBLE

An attractive city? For most visitors, the intimate seaside centere of Alacant is. For others, such as Núria Cadenes in her book *Vine al Sud! Guia lúdica del país valencià* (Come South! Leisure Guide to the *País Valencià*), the city is depressing:

> Coming in by railway into Alacant it's hard to find any joy. There's a rubbish-tip beside the rails. And barren land further on…A skeletal tree. Building sites with plastic and glass. And blocks of apart-ments, in the hard, hard, hard development style.[119]

By "development style" she means the thousands of high-rise flats built in the 1950s and 1960s to accommodate immigrant workers from Spain's interior. All cities are like this, yet her words are a salutary corrective. Tourists too easily head for the old center and main streets, where money is spent on upkeep, and forget where most people live: neighborhoods without fine houses or restaurants that you may observe from the railway or glimpse from the air-conditioned coach speeding from airport to hotel.

Even in Alacant's smallish central area, it is clear that speculation, cheap building, and bad taste have spoiled the city of Mariano's childhood. Most spectacularly, the thirty-story Tryp Gran Sol hotel, on the Rambla and a block back from the esplanade, dominates downtown Alacant. Tryp

---

119   Cadenes, p.70.

used to be a firm of people who sold hotel rooms on the internet, but now they run many of these hotels too. The Gran Sol (Great Sun) was originally a 1960s Meliá hotel. José Meliá (known as "Don Pepe") started off as a Barcelona travel agent and made a fortune with a chain of hotels taking advantage of the 1960s tourist boom and relaxed planning laws for friends of the dictatorship.

Another hotel right on the dock is still a Meliá and boasts four stars. This gives great views of both the Postiguet beach and the harbor, but blocks the connection between the two for *alacantins*. From inside the hotels, looking out, the views are beautiful; from the outside, concrete brutalism. The saga of this apartment-hotel dates back to 1964. Don Pepe was an intimate of Franco and it was not hard for him to start negotiating for building on public land owned by the port authorities. Mariano wrote in an article: "The building of the Meliá is a complete lesson in how a city's

Hotel Tryp spoiling the esplanade at Alacant

most emblematic seafront can be privatized, by changing laws, twisting wishes, and deliberately taking decisions whilst knowing they were illegal."[120] Finally, in the 1970s, the Meliá was built, dwarfing the port buildings. In 2001, this *fait accompli* was at last fully legalized as an enormous block of luxury hotel-rooms, apartments, a shopping mall, and 259 parking spaces. The harbor, too, has changed: no longer small boats, but luxury yachts. Unlike the Cabanyal in Valencia, the fishermen's quarter of low-rise houses under the castle, giving onto the beach, was replaced by a road and a line of six-story apartment buildings.

Change is inevitable under a system that chews up neighborhoods and flings up new ones for profit. We all want time to stop and long for the lost city of our childhood. That's nostalgia. The real fight is, accepted that the city is in constant change, to control what kind of development. Are those pretty new houses where once there were slums, are they for the new rich or for the previous inhabitants? Or, do we allow unplanned tourism, restaurant tables blocking streets, and hotel rooms where once there were peaceful apartments? Do we dare to seek to control tourism?

Tourism brings money into the city, money that goes into the pockets of the owners of Tryp and Meliá and provides precarious jobs and low wages for thousands of room cleaners and waiters. Don't believe that tourism benefits its workers. Since 2014 there have been new associations of room cleaners, or *kellys*, as they call themselves from the Spanish (*las*) *que limpian*, women who clean. As tourism grows, there are more *kellys*: today some 250,000 in the Spanish state. *Kellys'* associations have made these precarious, ill-paid workers more visible. They have begun to fight for their rights all around tourist Spain: it makes

120   *Cuarteto de Alicante*, p.479.

a big difference whether you have to clean three rooms per hour or four. With the new labor law brought in by the PP government in 2012, conditions have deteriorated. Instead of having a yearly calendar so that they can organize their lives, *kellys* (like waiters, like nearly all sectors of hotel work) are often on call, or on one-week contracts. They earn on average two and a half euros per room.

In August 2018, they won in the courts the right for certain illnesses, such as Carpal Tunnel syndrome (caused by repetitive movements such as cleaning mirrors above your head), to be recognised as job-related. *Kellys* are calling for a quality standard, whereby a hotel is publicly recognized if it follows good practice in its labor relations. Yolanda García is a spokesperson for the *kellys* in Benidorm. "If there are illnesses, it's because of the frenetic pace of work…People come back to their rooms drunk, break things, move furniture, and you've got ten minutes to clean when you need half an hour." Though she is critical of the British ("It seems they come with the attitude that anything goes"), the responsibility, she is clear, lies with hoteliers and government. "You have to do twenty-five or thirty rooms in five hours. If you don't finish, you have to carry on unpaid in your own time. It's Mission Impossible."[121]

COMMERCIAL CITY

Alacant has never been a manufacturing city. It has a tobacco factory and is known for its *salazones*, salted fish: tuna, sardine, herring, cod. Try in a bar the *budellet*, salted tuna intestine, or the *huevas*, the roe. Thus, its rather weak business class is known as the *burgesia bacallà*, the cod

---

121   Quotes by Yolanda García taken from the newspaper *ABC*, April 9, 2018.

bourgeoisie. It is a city of services. There are other towns in Alacant's hinterland that manufacture things: toys in Ibi and Castalla, shoes from Elda, *turró* from Xixona, grapes (and wine) from Novelda, shoes from Villena—Christmas industries.

If not a manufacturing city, Alacant has aways been a commercial one. Tobacco was imported from 1765 on, when the prohibition by the Spanish Crown on Catalans (including the Valencians) trading with America was finally lifted, privilege reserved till then for Spain's Atlantic ports. Despite this prohibition, Alacant grew into a big port. On the southern edge of the Catalan lands, Alacant became the main import-export route for Madrid's burghers and Spain's rulers, who preferred not to have their commerce dependent on Catalonia. From the sixteenth century, luxury goods from Milan, Florence, or Venice flowed through Alacant: sheets, cloth, embroidery, mirrors, glass, gloves, ottomans. And wines and wool from Castile went out. As the port of Madrid, its links, both physical and emotional, were more with the capital than with Valencia city, an attitude and relationship reinforced in the nineteenth century by the railway. Madrid's first rail connection with the sea was to Alacant. And the train was not just for trade: the Alacant coast became known, and still is, as the *playa de Madrid*, Madrid's beach.

As explained in Chapters 6 and 12, the coast north of Alacant, the Marina, and to the south became not just Madrid's beach, but one long international resort. Vacationers from all over northern Europe found a tourist industry quite happy to enrich itself and ruin its own back garden in order to accommodate them. Among the tourists came long-term residents, usually retirees lusting for the sun and living on pensions which went further (in the 1970s and 1980s) in poorer Spain.

Criminals came too. There was no extradition treaty with Britain before Spain joined the Common Market in 1991 and it was easy for retired villains to mingle in with other elderly foreign residents in their villas and pubs where they could watch all the English soaps. Among these residents was a most distinguished writer: Chester B. Himes (1909-84), author of the eight violent and humorous Harlem crime novels. His detectives are Coffin Ed Johnson and Gravedigger Jones. The funeral director is called Exodus Clay; it is sardonic (black) humor.

Author of the great anti-capitalist novel *If He Hollers Let Him Go*, Himes had to be humorous, I suppose, to get through the violence of white supremacy that drove him out of the United States. "Being born in America doesn't make you an American," he said laconically. After six months in Alacant, he and his English wife Lesley settled at the Pla de Mar residential complex in Moraira, a quiet beach town just up the coast, where he wrote his two volumes of memoirs and could contemplate the Penyal d'Ifach. There is a monument to him on the front at Moraira. It is said that in his last years, ill with Parkinson's, he sat in front of his chalet with a shotgun on his lap staring down all passersby, but that is probably crime novel readers' projection. He was buried in nearby Benissa.

Retirees, criminals from the North, and Chester Himes are not the only foreigners to seek refuge in Alacant and its coastal towns. *Pieds noirs*, white Algerians fleeing independence, flowed off the ferry from Oran in 1961 and 1962. Some 25,000 of them were of Spanish origin, children of émigrés in previous generations. Recognizing right-wing co-thinkers, the Franco dictatorship gave them Spanish passports and residence with no impediment. The legend goes that the governor greeted them off the boat with two baskets, one for them to dump their weapons, the other to pick up residence papers. For decades, Jean-Marie Le Pen, former colonial soldier in Algeria and leader of France's National Front, held election rallies in Alacant.

ANARCHIST ALCOI

> And I repeat once more: I'm from Alcoi
> My flag contains no blue
> I say loud and clear that I speak Catalan
> And I do so in the style of Valencia.
>   Ovidi Montllor, "Ballad of the Tired Man"

When you drive inland from Alacant, the road rises rapidly. On the other side of those bleached bare hills behind the coast, the landscape changes. Dusty soil and stone facing the sea turn to green on the inland side, where thick pine forests cover countless steep valleys with villages huddled by the stream at the bottom. Some are now towns, like industrial Ibi, the Spanish state's main toy-manufacturing center, or Xixona, the world center for *turró*, the Christmas sweet made from almonds (see Chapter 17). The streets of Xixona (pronounced "Shishona") are broad and the houses of the *turró* manufacturers wide too and elegant with fine ironwork on the balconies. Richard Ford praised the "almond-cakes," but advised that: "The Spanish women, as those in the East, are great consumers of dulces or sweetmeats, to the detriment of their teeth, stomachs, and complexions."[122] From here, *turró* is dispatched all over the world in winter in little balsa-wood cases closed by tacks. In summer, the town's inhabitants spread out over Spain, selling its other industry: ice cream. Xixona hides a treasure,

---

122   Ford, p.635.

a fifteenth-century bread oven, still in use, five meters deep and high enough for a person to stand. Ask to look at it (on the Carrer Raval). The proprietors go out of their way to assist.

From Xixona, take the mountain road to Alcoi. This fearsome route winding above a precipice is called the Carrasqueta. We drove up it warily through the terraced almond groves, for rain was spotting the windscreen and cloud obscured the peaks. Bikers roared past, feeling virile and immortal as they leaned around the wet curves. Stop at one of the look-out points and view the long coast north of Alacant. The jumbled farmhouses immediately below are tiny: it is like looking down on a Christmas crib. On top, just fifteen kilometers from the coast but at 1,100 meters, the mountain flattens out to a plain covered by a holm-oak forest, *carrasca* in Spanish, giving its name to the road and mountain pass. The trees are twisted and ghostly, trunks gray with moss and lichen. Their branches, bare of leaf in winter, reach out to startle the passerby.

To the right of the road, in the forest, lies an exclusive restaurant-hotel, Pous de la Neu. Its library boasts 2,000 volumes on food; it has a small botanical garden. The name refers to the several snow-pits around the restaurant, constructed some 400 years ago. In those times before electric fridges, snow packed in winter in the pit provided ice for the city below, right to the end of summer.

On the other side of the Carresqueta pass lies Alcoi, one of Spain's earliest industrial towns despite its isolation in the mountains and lack of raw materials, except water. It is a very particular place, renowned for bitter class struggle in the nineteenth century. Paper, engineering, and textiles were Alcoi's main industries. Paper and textiles developed because of the abundant water cascading down three rivers to drive mills and factories. Just one waterfall, the Molinar, roaring down a ravine, moved in 1795 twelve paper mills, seven flour mills, and thirteen fulling mills (for cloth).[123]

A century later, as engineering developed, coal was needed: the railway built from Gandia brought coal to Alcoi and Alcoi's goods to the sea. Nineteenth-century factory conditions were as appalling as in Britain. Figures from 1873 record that 42 percent of children died before the age of five. Twelve-hour working days were normal.

In 1821, the textile workers of Alcoi had the honor of leading the first great working-class strike in Spain. When the introduction of improved machinery in the textile and paper factories led to dismissals, some 1,200 armed men overwhelmed the city's police and burned most of the factories and their machinery. Though it was a mass struggle doomed to failure in its aims, as the use of more profitable machinery cannot be halted, the tradition of collective struggle was successfully introduced. Alcoi's great worker-poet, Ovidi Montllor, called his city *poble tossut i obert* ("a stubborn and open town"). Its tradition is to fight hard (stubborn), but this enclosed, mountain-ringed town has been open, host to international ideas and visitors, anarchists in particular.

These were the working-class visitors. The other side of the coin of the major manufacturing town was its rulers' wealth, reflected in the sumptuous town hall on the Plaça d'Espanya. Yet the main staircase exhibits two strange exhibits that you cannot miss as you climb to the offices and the council chamber: enormous paintings of the

---

123   (Consulted February 20, 2018.) https://rutasyvericuetos. blogspot.com.es/2011/07/el-camino-del-agua-el-molinar-de-alcoy.html

murder of the mayor, Agustí Albors, by enraged workers on July 10, 1873. During a general strike to raise wages by 20 percent and reduce the working day to eight hours, the Republican Albors ordered police, to open fire to disperse a demonstration in front of the town hall. One worker was killed and several injured. Demonstrators attacked the building. Mayor Albors, police and his supporters barricaded themselves inside. After twenty hours they were forced out by fire and smoke. The mayor was dragged down the street and thrown off the bridge into the ravine.

It is, to say the least, unusual to portray the killing of the mayor in the entrance to the town hall. The powerful main picture, dating from 1995, is by the local painter Ramón Castañer. It shows the workers, faces distorted by fury, and only the white leg of the mayor being dragged along the street. Keeping the victim off-picture makes the image all the more powerful. Why would modern politicians commission a picture like Castañer's? Are they so sure that anarchist revolution is just history? Or perhaps it is a modern reminder to politicians to tread carefully: the white leg in the black sock could belong to any of them.

The revolt became known as the *Revolució del Petroli*, as petroleum torches were used to set fire to the town hall and nearby houses of the mill-owners. The smell hung for days over the city. This was the time of the First Republic, from 1873 to 1874, and Alcoi was the headquarters in Spain of the anarchist International Workers Association (AIT), with 2,591 affiliates in the city alone. After the death of the mayor, Alcoi declared its independence from Spain and was governed by a committee of public safety, in effect a workers' government, for three days until the entry of federal troops and the subsequent repression. Executions and jail followed. But the revolt was not unsuccessful for the mass of workers, as the local manufacturers, shaken to their boots by events, heaped all the blame on the conveniently dead mayor and raised salaries and reduced the working day. Much of the story is told in the 1983 novel of the Alcoi writer Isabel-Clara Simó, *Júlia*.

A tangent reflecting Alcoi's anarchist tradition concerns Robert Capa's photo *Falling Soldier* of a militiaman shot while charging forward on the Córdoba front on September 5, 1936. It became the most famous photo of the Civil War, representing both courage and defeat. The soldier was identified many decades later as twenty-four-year-old Frederic Borrell, a volunteer with the anarchist militia from Alcoi. Borrell wore the particular uniform sewn by the collectivized textile factories of the city. Some say that Capa's photo was posed, but this unresolved controversy does not alter the presence of anarchists from Alcoi fighting for their freedom far from home.

The model collectivization of Alcoi's industry at the start of the Civil War is discussed in Chapter 14. In the 1970s transition, Alcoi's militant tradition revived. A number of economic-political strikes sought both to improve wages and conditions and to bring an end to the dictatorship. The paper industry remains and one of its prime products is paper for rolling cigarettes. In the streets of London or New York, joints are rolled in paper from Alcoi, from packets often adorned with hip mottos in English.

Alcoi is ringed by hills, whichever way you look. It is known sometimes as the city of bridges, because of the number of them spanning the great central ravine, a cleft in the rock, "open like a horse-shoe with its toes in the air—gray and ochre and a stony presence that dominates everything," in the words of Núria Cadenes. It is a tough town and no town for old men and women. The best secret of this industrial city is its wild beauty: the forested hills enclosing it or the porticoed square hidden behind the town tall, the Plaça de

Alcoi, ringed by hills

Dins (the Square Within), secret because access is on foot down alleys, through narrow stone arches. It is not an obvious, open, traffic-filled square, like the Plaça d'Espanya in front of the town hall. The Plaça de Dins was the old cloister of the monastery, which was converted into the town hall when Church properties were disestablished in 1838.

Today, when anarchist revolution is a memory so confined to history it can be portrayed on the town hall's main staircase, Alcoi is best known for its "Moors and Christians" festival. These commemorations, involving thousands of elaborately costumed warriors in long-rehearsed maneuvers, are held all over Alacant province: at La Vila Joiosa, for instance, the Moors arrive by sea and are repulsed on the beach. Rose Macaulay was there seventy years ago:

> Painted scaffolding, with tiers of seats, adorned
> both sides of the main street, and Moors
> and Christians, turbaned or armoured, rode
> caparisoned horses or donkeys...Both sects were
> very gay; it was interesting to see the handsome
> brown Moors of Villajoyosa making so merry
> over the defeat of their relations so long ago.[124]

The Alcoi festival, stretching over three days, commemorates
the 1276 defeat of al-Azraq (the Blue-Eyed One), the final
defeat of the Moors in the area. Tradition has it that St. George
himself appeared to help the Christians and so the spectacular
festival takes place around St. George's Day, April 23.

As is the case with the *Falles*, all year people (women)
sew costumes for the Moors and Christians. People
(men) compete to enter one of the societies that take
part in the processions and massive battles. You might
think that Christians beating the hell out of Moors every
year has something of racism in it—and you would be
right. The participants and local governments justify the
commemoration as tradition and explain that acting as a
"Moor" is just as popular as being a "Christian." For those
involved in the festival all their lives, the racist subtext may
be hard to grasp. The spokesperson of the Spanish Islamic
Federation was clear: "In a democratic Spain, where all
religious confessions are represented, these celebrations of
conquest must disappear."[125]

The "handsome brown Moors" watched by Macaulay
at La Vila Joiosa were Valencians dressed as Moors. The
descendants of the real Moors are not so merry over their
defeat.

---

124   Macaulay, p.107.
125   *El mundo*, October 5, 2006.

What a Brutal Life!

Climbing the hill from Alcoi's Town Hall, there is a long wall with portraits and quotations from poets, among them the actor and singer-songwriter, Ovidi Montllor (1942–95). His verse on the wall is:

Poqueta cosa és
i moriran sense ella
L'hortet, el riberol
Quina vida més bèstia!

"It's not so much/yet they'll die without it,/the little garden, the river bank./What a brutal life!"

Ovidi's life, beliefs, and songs have made him a hero for the pan-Catalanist movement. From a working-class anarchist family, Ovidi is one of the few people known just by his first name. On the twentieth anniversary of his death from cancer, the radical part of Catalonia's independence movement celebrated Ovidi with exhibitions, talks, books, and his music. The verse on the Alcoi wall catches the melancholy (the poor without the most basic pleasures) and the combativity (the outburst of the last line) that make Ovidi so attractive. Influenced by Brassens and Leo Ferré, Ovidi's songs denounce injustice, but are lyrical. His voice is indignant, yet warm.

Ovidi is the most radical of the generation of singer-songwriters who sang in Catalan in the 1960s and 1970s, helping to create a huge social and cultural movement against the dictatorship. He moved to Barcelona in 1968, where his fellow-Valencian Raimon (see Chapter 2) helped him find gigs. In 1975, during Franco's last days, he and the Mallorcan Maria del Mar Bonet shared a famous concert of protest songs at the Paris Olympia, songs in

Catalan though both were from Catalan lands that were not Catalonia. Ovidi became an expert in Valencian poets and put many of their verses to music, something that Paco Ibáñez (a Basque brought up in Valencia) did with Miguel Hernández, among others, and Raimon, with Ausiàs March and Salvador Espriu. They were a cultured and politicized group of working-class singers.

In the 1980s Ovidi pursued a successful career as a film actor, in part because he could no longer make a living from singing. The mass movement of singer-songwriters from the 1960s and 1970s had subsided and Ovidi was sidelined and neglected in the mass media. His performances as a singer gained enormously from his ability as an actor. He could fuse song, movement, and poetry. Since the PP lost Alcoi town hall in 2011, Ovidi has had a plaque on his birthplace (Carrer Sant Joan de Ribera, 15) and a street, student hall of residence, and community center named after him. Radical poets are usually safe to package after death. In Ovidi's case, his uncompromising politics make him still, twenty years on, a loved and hated figure.

Just as he, Raimon and other Valencians expressed in song and poetry the struggle against Franco, so a younger generation of political singer-songwriters formed the cultural soundtrack to the movements that in 2015 expelled the PP from the Valencian government. Some 200 groups and individuals organized themselves in an assembly. They called it, of course, the Col·lectiu Ovidi Montllor.

In February 2015, Esquerra Unida (United Left) put forward a motion in the Valencian Corts that the government declare 2015 the year of Ovidi. The PP used its majority to reject the motion. Its representative Mayte Parra (one-time Mayoress of Ibi, near Alcoi) accused Ovidi of "humiliating the language of the Valencians" by having sung that his was "a flag with no blue in it" and that what he spoke was "Catalan in the style of Valencia." The indignant Parra insisted: "We say to him that our land is the Community, our language Valencian and our flag contains blue because we are Valencians, and not Catalans."[126]

Nothing clearer: Valencia is the modern Communitat valenciana, nothing to do with the *països catalans*, "Catalan lands," and our language is quite separate from Catalan. The PP continues to seek political benefit from its anti-Catalanism. Twenty years after Ovidi's death, Mayte Parra was still polemicizing with him, such is the power of his presence. One of Ovidi's most famous phrases ironized on the PP's political use of the language question:

> There are people who are ill-pleased that people speak, write, or think in Catalan. The same people who are ill-pleased that people speak, write, or think.

---

126   Maceda, p.229. Raquel Andrés, *La Vanguardia*, August 10, 2015.

12: Umbrellas of the Desert

I n his *Catalan Cuisine*, Colman Andrews wrote:

> The town of Elx (Elche in Castilian)…is famous
> for three things: an immense grove of date palms,
> 100,000 of them or more (the largest such grove
> in Europe by far), the stunningly beautiful *Dama
> de Elche*, a prehistoric polychrome bust of a
> woman—elegant, proud, elaborately accoutered,
> mysterious—discovered in the nearby ruins of La
> Alcudia in 1897…and *Arròs amb Crosta*.[127]

One can forgive Andrews, entranced by food, for raising
Crusty Rice to the level of the palm forest and Iberian
head. Instead, Elx's third feature of fame should surely be
its Mystery Play. This liturgical drama with music from the
thirteenth century is performed each year in two parts on
August 14 and 15 in the city's Santa Maria basilica. In 2001,
UNESCO declared the *Misteri* one of the Masterpieces of
the Oral and Intangible Heritage of Humanity.

Sacheverell Sitwell found it "a formalized religious
ceremony, as curious as any in Christian Europe…There are
picturesque processions through the town, and at the climax
Baroque cupids in the form of living children are lowered
from the ceiling. It is a rustic masque…"[128] This patronizing
comment fails to catch the passion and excitement of the

---

127   Colman Andrews, pp.64-5.
128   Sitwell, p.171.

Play, unchanged in centuries. Crowds push forward to see processions carrying the dead Virgin through the streets before the performances. It is rancid Catholic propaganda. The Jews are the criminals. No women perform: female parts are played by boys. It is propaganda and it is also engrossing theater and deep-felt popular tradition. The Elx Mystery Play dramatizes the Assumption of the Virgin Mary. The basilica has a dome especially adapted for the lowering of children and the rising of the Virgin into Heaven. Mariano Sánchez Soler is a fan:

> I tell you, and this is an atheist's view. The Mystery Play is remarkable, it has incredible plastic power. It's hot in August, the seats are hard and it lasts for over two hours, but it doesn't seem long. It's enthralling and it is the oldest performance in the Catalan language to still exist.

Such mystery plays were common in medieval Europe, but they were forbidden in churches in the seventeenth century. Elx's priests appealed to Pope Urban VIII, who not only granted them dispensation but ordered that their play be performed indefinitely.

DATES

For Ibi, Xixona, and Alcoi, you drive into the hills. If you leave Alacant in a different direction, toward the southwest, only twenty-five kilometers away lies the *país valencià*'s third city Elx, with a population of some 200,000. The city is partially embraced by an oasis of palm trees in the unfriendly, bare, dusty hills. Here starts the driest part of Spain, the provinces of Almería and Murcia, which reaches up to Elx. It is quite unlike the castle-topped mountains to the north or the fertile *horta* around Valencia city. Ted Walker felt: "Elche is an oddity. The old city of white, cubist houses grew up amidst the famous grove—or was it the other way around? ... a higgledy-piggledy effect of low, flat-roofed dwellings half-hidden among the trunks."[129]

The low flat-roofed dwellings are mainly in the Raval de Sant Joan, the old Moorish quarter. Otherwise, the buildings at Elx, both in the old town and spreading across the plain, are much as in any Spanish city. Jan Morris, in tired cliché, called it "half African in temper." Rose Macaulay also saw the "low, white, flat-roofed Arab houses" across the river and felt "the African air." Travelers responded genuinely to the changes in weather, housing, plants, light, and smells as they moved south, reaching Alacant and especially Elx, but they showed their longing for the exotic in expressing these changes as "African." The image of southern Spain has suffered from visitors' predisposition to find vivid difference, parallel to the "Orientalism" of writers on Asia and the Middle East.

What really makes Elx so strange is its great palm grove, irrigated from the River Vinalopó that passes through the city in an ugly concrete channel. It is said the Phoenicians planted the trees, to use the dates on their trading trips across the Mediterranean. For sure, the Arabs irrigated it. There are palms along the esplanade at Alacant and a *palmerar*, date-palm grove, imitating Elx's on the coast immediately south of Alacant. Oriola has its palm grove, too. There are palms on the beaches at Benidorm or La Vila Joiosa, indeed in most coastal towns, but these are for adornment and atmosphere. Nowhere in Europe is there a *palmerar* to equal the size of Elx's. You step out of a modern

---

129   Walker, p.190.

Spanish city and in minutes you are wandering through a forest. Slim, tall palm trees are handsome. And they have many uses: dates, palm oil, alcohol, brushes, hats, baskets, and the palm hearts used in salads.

Today, this Moorish forest's main use is a Christian one: the fronds that decorate balconies on Palm Sunday, the Sunday before Easter, are sold all over Spain from Elx. Palm Sunday commemorates the Gospel story of the strewing of palm fronds before Jesus's donkey when he rode into Jerusalem. It is widely believed, too, that they protect against lightning strikes. Female trees produce the fruit and male ones are used for fronds. The long fronds—they can measure five meters—are tied and kept out of the sun to turn them yellowy-white.

The palm forest at Elx

The *palmerar* is reckoned to have some 200,000 palms, though I have seen 300,000 and 100,000 cited. Around 1900 there were a million, but these have been whittled away by building. The palms are fiercely protected, but they touch the city center on Elx's western side and partially surround buildings and streets. Speculators are always trying to carve off an edge for a block of apartments.

There is a two-kilometer walk marked out through the palms, starting in the Hort del Cura, the Priest's Grove, or Garden, a botanical garden where you can buy sweet, cheap dates and baskets woven with strong, flexible palm fiber. Dates are picked from October to January, which is why they have become linked to Christmas in Britain. Richard Ford described them: "When ripe they [the dates] hang in yellow clusters underneath the fan-like leaves, which rise, the umbrella of the desert, like an ostrich plume from a golden circlet."[130] The pre-World War One traveler, Edith Browne, shared Ford's enthusiasm:

> The trees present a magnificent spectacle with their deep golden clusters of fruit on tawny stems hanging around the summit of the trunks, beneath the shadow of sun-flecked green plumes…Now watch the pickers…He winds his legs round a tree, knots his bare feet, takes a grip with his hands and clambers up the 60-foot branchless trunk as dexterously as a monkey.[131]

In the Hort del Cura the prime exhibit is the Imperial Palm, a single trunk branching into seven shoots. Normally several palms grow from a single root system, but this specimen is

130   Ford, p.630.
131   Browne, p.88.

unique because the division into different trunks occurs two meters above ground. It was named after the Austro-Hungarian Empress Sissi who visited in 1894. There is a bust of Sissi, though the legendary imperial beauty cannot compete with the Lady of Elx, reproduced by the garden's pond.

The walk through the palm grove is flat, easy to do, and fascinating. From the Hort del Cura it is marked out by arrows on the ground and walls. There are palms of many different species, ages, and heights. They can live for up to 300 years. They are especially flexible, bending in the wind and sudden driven rain, then springing upright again. The walk leads along paths between low walls that enclose *horts* owned by different proprietors. If you are a touristy romantic, you can take a horse-drawn carriage. At several points, the blue dome of the basilica rises above the tree-tops.

THE IBERIAN LADY

The third great feature of the city is the Dama d'Elx, the head and shoulders of an Iberian woman, dating back to the fifth or fourth century BCE. Discovered in 1897 at L'Alcudia (now an archaeological park) on the south-east edge of Elx, the limestone sculpture is fifty-six centimeters high and weighs sixty-five kilograms. Jan Morris raved about her extraordinary beauty and made the rash claim that she is the authentic ancestor of Spanish culture:

> The Lady of Elche, who is plainly Iberian with strong Greek blood, is representational, to be sure—vividly, rather alarmingly so. But she is truth slightly heightened, clarity with a shot of mescalin: and much of the art that has succeeded

her down the centuries, like the society itself
that gave birth to it all, has this quality of being
lifelike, but more so—intenser, taller, more
vertical, perhaps more real than reality.[132]

The Lady's most distinctive feature is her "huge cartwheel
ear-rings"(the aesthete Sitwell) or "two ammonites connected
to a cone" (Ted Walker), giant circles that shield each side
of her face. They are in fact curled tresses. This hair style is
often compared to Princess Leia's in the original *Star Wars*
or the rolled-up Mallorcan doughnuts known as *ensaimades*.
By such jokes we seek to make the mystery of this statue,
as enigmatic as the Mona Lisa, familiar. The Dama d'Elx is
not the only Iberian bust of a woman to be found. In nearby
Guardamar, a fragmented bust was discovered in 1987 and
stuck together again. And there are half a dozen others from
south-east Iberia, all of them impressive and mysterious, but
none so well preserved as the Dama d'Elx.[133]

A fourteen-year-old boy, Antoni Macià, digging the hard
earth on August 4, 1897, struck stone with his mattock. He
and his companions were accustomed to finding Roman coins
or pottery, for they were working the land just outside today's
Elx, where the Roman colony of Ilici had flourished, but the
complete head and shoulders they uncovered was something
else. A French archaeologist, Pierre Paris, was in Elx to see the
Misteri. He bought the Dama cheaply and, a month later, it
was on exhibit in the Louvre. It stayed there until 1941 when
the Franco regime did a deal with the Nazis, exchanging it for
a painting by Greco, one by Velázquez, and a Goya tapestry.

---

132   Morris, p.46.
133   In 2007, the "Dama Ibèrica" was placed in the middle of
a roundabout near Valencia city's Beniferri metro station. An
eighteen-meter-high gaudy imitation of the Dama d'Elx, it is
made of 22,000 tiny bright-blue tiles, each a miniature lady.

It was exhibited in the Prado until 1971, when it reached its present destination in Madrid's National Museum of Archaeology. Return to Elx? Unlikely. Like Picasso's Guernica, which is yet to take up the position reserved for it by Frank Gehry on a Bilbao Guggenheim wall, the Lady of Elx is too valuable a tourist attraction for the capital to let it go. In art, too, Spain seeks to centralize. The deal made by Franco in 1941 suggests the importance to Spanish nationalists of this earliest Iberian artwork. Jan Morris' association, in the quote above, of the Lady with the Spanish character reflects the dictatorship's mystic, non-scientific view of a pure Iberian-Spanish character, incarnated in the Dama d'Elx.

You can see what Jan Morris means, but you probably need that shot of mescalin to really believe it.

DISHONEST BEACHES

Elx is not on the coast, but twelve kilometers of beaches south of Alacant belong to Elx City Council. This coast is quite unlike the resorts of the Marina to the north of Alacant, where the mountains tumble down to the shore and high-rise apartments and hotels are squeezed into the remaining space. The Elx, Santa Pola, and Guardamar coast are dominated by sand dunes. Access to the beaches is over long wooden ramps to protect the mobile dunes, where grass is sown to bind the sand-hills to the ground.

The tourist leaflets do not give an honest view of Elx's beaches. They show handsome wooden walkways over the dunes to the yellow beach and blue sea. This is true, but false. The pretty photo has a context, but this the glossy leaflets omit. If you actually stand on one of these beaches and look back, new high-rise vacation rentals dominate the hills. Elx's coast is a shock. It is totally built up, even more densely than around Calp or Benidorm, for here behind the beaches there are no mountains. Every bit of ground is covered. And if you then look out to sea from the beaches of Elx, there is no relief: you see the city of Alacant to the left and, on the other side of the bay, another promontory, Sant Joan, covered too in apartments.

South of Elx's beaches, just past Santa Pola, the road runs spectacularly across salt pans, wide shallow lakes beside bright-white pyramids of salt. Sea water is evaporated in a series of lakes until only salt is left and it can be swept up into the pyramids. The pans and the dunes between Santa Pola and Guardamar de Segura, the most southern Valencian-speaking town on the coast, are now protected as a nature park.

From Santa Pola you can travel the four kilometers to Tabarca, the only inhabited island of the several on the Valencian coast. This island, almost bare of vegetation, belongs administratively to Alacant. Once a pirate hideout, then in the eighteenth century settled by Genoese who had escaped slavery in Tunis, Tabarca entered a long decline until recently

Pyramid of salt, Santa Pola

revived for tourism drawn by its marine fauna and flora.

Guardamar has overcome two disasters to become the most interesting and relaxing town on the coast south of Alacant. It has conserved its small-town identity. Destroyed by an earthquake in 1829, the village was then rebuilt nearer the sea, but shifting dunes poured sand into the streets and houses and across cultivated fields. The engineer Francisco Mira was hired in 1896 to save the town and worked there for the next twenty-eight years. His ideas and the labor of the town's inhabitants erected barriers and planted trees, as many as 600,000 pines and also 40,000 palms and 5,000 eucalyptus, to hold the dunes in place. This *pinar*, the pine dunes, covers 800 hectares, a greater area than the town itself. The two-kilometer walk through the trees, giving shade on a hot day, to the great pier and lighthouse at the mouth of the River Segura is a tourist experience worth a dozen discotheques. Francisco Mira's feat is commemorated by colored tiles explaining his work on the wall of the avenue named after him that runs alongside the *pinar*. Generations of schoolchildren have been educated in the importance of the *pinar* by planting trees each year.

The *pinar* has enabled Guardamar to conserve semi-wild beaches and avoid high-rise construction along the front. It is a back-to-front town, as its tall apartment blocks rise inland from the *pinar*, on the River Segura, not on the shore. Between the *pinar* and the beach are a row of two-story houses, known as the Houses of Babylon. Another Guardamar disaster meant that Babylon had to be abandoned in February 2017: a storm swept away the beach and wrenched concrete from the houses. The residents blame the pier at the mouth of the Segura for the constant erosion of the beach, preceding and leading to this disaster. Ever-shifting dune and beach systems are particularly vulnerable to the changes in currents caused by breakwaters and piers.

VERY STRESSFUL

The next town, sixteen kilometers south, is Torrevieja/Torrevella, located between two big salt lagoons, the pink and the blue, and the sea. Between its residential estates and the main town itself Torrevieja now has some 90,000 inhabitants, making it the fifth largest city in the Valencian Community—and the fastest-growing one. It had a brutally simple growth formula. All land was reclassified for building except for the lagoons and the lagoons' environs, which were created a nature park. In 1990 Torrevieja had 23,000 inhabitants; in 2000, 50,000. Remarkably, over 50 percent of its inhabitants are foreign-born. The biggest group is British, with 13,000 registered voters, i.e., permanent residents. There are Russians, Swedes, Germans, and Dutch (retired and richer), and Africans and Latin Americans (workers and poorer). Since many with second homes do not register and some people leave without removing their names from the registry, figures are approximate.

In 2016, there were 296,000 registered British citizens who had lived for more than twelve months in the Spanish state. Of these 121,000 were over sixty-five (40 percent). A great many have retired to their dream of Mediterranean life in coastal towns such as Torrevieja/Torrevella, Xàbia (also with over 50 percent of its population foreign) and Oriola (with around 19,000 registered Britons on its coastal residential estates). In contrast, there were 116,000 Spaniards in the UK, though these are younger and usually do not own property. They come and go more easily and numbers are probably much higher than the figure quoted.[134]

Torrevieja is a prime example of the huge emigration of elderly north Europeans to the Mediterranean coast, facilitated by the right to health service facilities in Spain

---

134   Alan Travis, *Guardian*, June 29, 2017.

of EU citizens. The 2016 Brexit vote threw British residents into turmoil. They feared that if there were no reciprocal agreement, they would remain without access to free health care. To be elderly, without the desire or money to return to Britain and facing exclusion from health care, is a dire scenario. In addition, the immediate effect of the Brexit referendum (in which most of the British in Torrevieja had no vote) was to cause sterling to fall against the euro. As a result, the 108,433 Britons in Spain who received UK pensions in 2016 faced a cut of 10 to 15 percent in their real value.

Sid Williamson, former Labor Party representative in Torrevieja, told me in May 2018: "You ask for an opinion on Brexit and I can't give you one, because the government don't know what they're doing. It's absolute chaos. Different ministers express different ideas. The rational solution, of course, is a reciprocal agreement on healthcare."

The task of the British consul in Alacant, Sarah-Jane Morris, in numerous mass meetings of British residents along the coast, is to allay fears. She affirms that everyone registered and living legally in Spain at the time of Brexit will have their healthcare and annual pension increases guaranteed. She warns against scaremongering and advises people to only believe official channels.

"When there is no clear position from the British government, assurances that everything will be alright are worthless," responds Sid. "It's a very stressing time, very, very stressful. Everyone's upset. There's no voice for our point of view. Some people have sold up, but of course most can't, even if they want to, as the value of property has fallen in Spain and continues to rise in the UK."

However the Brexit negotiations are concluded, what is certain is that the British government's vacillations and contradictions have caused a great deal of stress among elderly British people in the Valencian Community.

PART THREE:
Twentieth-Century Blues

The *horta*: field of *xufes*, Alboraia

Blasco Ibáñez's mansion on the Malva-Rosa beach

13: The Spanish Zola and the Light-filled Barbarian

"Distant from the painting of intellectualized contents and messages, [Sorolla] never wavered in his search for the visible truth, the realism of the senses"

Begoña Torres

I am lucky enough to have found a 1919 edition of Vicente Blasco Ibáñez's 1898 novel *La barraca* (*The Cabin*). The author and publisher (the same person) writes the introduction. He explains that in 1895, after helping organize massive anti-monarchical demonstrations, he was on the run. He took refuge in the home of a sympathizer who ran a wine shop near the port. Kicking his heels in the upstairs room, its curtains drawn while police searched the streets, he decided to write a story. After several days, Blasco's supporters smuggled him out of the country dressed as a sailor. Returning later to Spain he was arrested and spent eleven months in jail before he was elected a Member of the Spanish Cortes and parliamentary privilege freed him.

A while later, Blasco, the Republican member of parliament, was haranguing a mass audience in the port. After the meeting a young man approached and handed him a manuscript. He recognized the wine shop owner and the manuscript was what he had written in the few, but long, days of his refuge in the upstairs room. *La barraca*, as it was, was published to little response: the novelist was at the start of his career in parliament and politics occupied him more than promotion of literature. Only some 500 copies were sold. Then a French translator stumbled on a copy in San Sebastián and wrote to him from Bordeaux, asking permission to translate it. Blasco was so busy that he did not reply to several letters, but finally scribbled four lines authorizing translation. A few months later he was amazed to read in the paper that *La barraca* was the season's sensation in Paris, which then led to belated success in Spain.

This introduction, this short account of himself, reveals much of who Vicente Blasco Ibáñez (1867–1928) was. First, he is a romancer. He loves embroidering stories about himself. He loves projecting himself as a man of action. Second, many of these stories are true: he really was on the run, in exile, in jail, and then in 1898 in parliament. Third, he did write fast, with the gift of concentration among the multiple attractions of his daily life. And fourth, he was a rabble-rouser, a charismatic orator. "He liked to stir up the masses, he felt good in the middle of crowds, he was sensual and passionate. Against Castilian hardness and sobriety he chose Mediterranean exuberance," wrote the Valencian novelist Manuel Vicent.[135]

Blasco Ibáñez was a famous and popular writer in his own day, both in Spain and internationally. Like many prolific authors who were popular, he is seen by the arbiters of literary taste today as second-rank: a writer of colorful adventures of the Valencian *huerta*, of little depth. Much of Blasco's enormous output, historical novels or his Madrid stories, justifies this view, but his best, the five Valencian novels, are fine portraits of his time. And more than just documentary sources for what Valencia was like 125 years ago, they are acute social and psychological stories about poverty and doom, close to the naturalism of Zola. In these

---

135   Manuel Vicent, introduction to *Entre naranjos.*

books, written in half a dozen years, he tackled the main themes of his city and land.

These are the five. *Arroz y tartana* (Rice and Carriage, 1894) studies the merchant class around Valencia city's central market. *Flor de mayo* (Blossom in May, 1895) tackles the fishermen of the city's Grau and Cabanyal quarters, with those sea storms and calms that Ausiàs March had portrayed as corresponding to the surges and falls of human feeling. *Entre naranjos* (1900) is set south of Valencia city in Alcira, among the orange groves of the Júcar (Xúquer) River, showing the clash and attraction between bohemian and bourgeois, between an opera singer and a rural political boss. *La barraca* (1898) dissects the violent passions of the *huerta*; and *Cañas y barro* (Reeds and Mud, 1902), the rough lives of rice farmers and fishermen on the Albufera lagoon (see Chapter 17).

The five Valencia novels are often dismissed as merely local color and depressing, schematic, fatalistic stories of primitive feelings, rather sub-Zola. The author himself came to look down on them and moved on to what he felt were novels with more universal themes, the best-known of which is *Los cuatro jinetes del apocalipsis* (The Four Horsemen of the Apocalypse, 1916).[136] The reverse is true. The books that are most local, most intensely rooted in the land he grew up in, are the most "universal" in their themes.

Blasco the writer has two great qualities: his action sequences and his descriptions of nature. These visual strengths contribute to why so many of his books were adapted to cinema: the orange groves, the city bustle, the *huerta* spring vividly from his books; and the set-piece action scenes are easily translated to cinematic language.

---

136   This novel about World War I sold massively in the United States and is often cited as contributing to that country's 1917 entry into the war.

He was a contemporary of Valle-Inclán, his fellow-Valencian José Martínez Ruiz "Azorín" (from Monóvar, near Alacant) and Unamuno, the "generation of 1898," meaning that these writers reached their artistic maturity in that year when Spain lost its colonies: the Philippines and wealthy Cuba. Unamuno called on the intellectuals and politicians of Spain to "regenerate" the poor and defeated country. These intellectuals believed in education as the key.

Blasco did not disagree with the need for education and regeneration, but he had little in common with his literary generation. No elitist, he was a different kind of writer. He was swept into parliament that year, 1898, on the crest of a Republican mass movement. He fought hard to rebuild Spain, not in the terms of his fellow intellectuals, but as a man of action, a political leader.

As well as a political figure, Blasco Ibáñez was an enormously successful writer, which fed the envy of his literary contemporaries, not "men of action" and mostly impoverished. Blasco knew how to market himself and his wares. His novels sold in tens of thousands and were translated into most European languages. He made and spent a lot of money, another reason why others, scraping by on newspaper articles, looked at him askance. If he is so popular, he cannot be any good. Manuel Vicent wrote:

> He had the supreme pleasure of making himself hated. Other writers argued with their cat over a sardine, while an unimaginably successful Blasco Ibáñez visited Madrid, with all his novels optioned by Hollywood...and without taking their pride into account insisted on inviting to lunch scribblers who he assumed were starving to death.[137]

---

137   *El País*, May 4, 2014.

The story goes that when news of his death on January 28, 1928 reached Madrid, the long-bearded, one-armed maestro Valle-Inclán responded in the café where he held court: "Blasco dead? No way. Just self-publicity."

The books became successful movies. Greta Garbo played the lead in *The Torrent* (1926), a silent adaptation of *Entre naranjos*. *Blood and Sand* (published in 1908) earned him big Hollywood money in 1922 with Rudolph Valentino as the bullfighter. A 1941 remake starred Tyrone Power and Rita Hayworth. The 1989 version with a sultry Sharon Stone still circulates on early-morning TV (the best is the music by Paco de Lucía). Yet *Blood and Sand* is much subtler than these clichéd films of fiery, beautiful women and a proud, doomed matador. The novel examines the effects of sudden wealth and fame on an uneducated young man brought up in poverty. It is a story applicable to any bullfighter, boxer, or footballer trying to cope with adoration and success.

Blasco was always in motion. He set up a newspaper *El Pueblo* in 1894, in which several of his Valencian novels were serialized, and founded a publishing house, Prometeo, in 1916 with his son-in-law Fernando Llorca. He was heavily involved in translating and publishing the classics. Here is the moving tribute of the Madrid working-class writer Arturo Barea in *The Forge*, his autobiographical novel of childhood in the first two decades of the twentieth century:

> The priests at my school said that he [Blasco Ibáñez] was one of the worst anarchists, but I did not believe it. Once he had said that nobody read books in Spain because the people had not enough money to buy them; and I thought he was right, because our school books were very expensive…He opened a bookshop in the Calle de Mesonero Romanos and started making books. Not his own books, since he

said that would not be fair, but the best books you could find in the world, and every copy was sold at thirty-five centimos. People bought them by the thousand and when they had read a book, they sold it to the second-hand bookstalls where the children and the poor bought them. That was how I had read Dickens, Tolstoi, Dostoevski, Dumas, Victor Hugo, and others.[138]

The great writer understood the hunger of the poor to read. He broke the control of the Church over what was available to read. He published the realist nineteenth-century novels that were not available in Spanish translation due to the Church's censorship.

He made fortunes from his writing and lost a fortune setting up utopian socialist settlements in Argentina. He named the new cities Cervantes and Nueva Valencia. When he reached Buenos Aires in 1909, 50,000 people greeted "the Spanish Zola" on the quay. He was a leader of fashion, too, popularizing two-tone shoes and the Blasco collar—an open-necked shirt not unlike those worn by Oscar Wilde.

THE CABIN

I return to the Valencian novels and, in particular, *La barraca*, the great novel of doomed nobility of the character that he wrote in the room over a bar while on the run. *La barraca* gives a view of the *huerta* near Valencia city in the last years of the nineteenth century. The peasants live in the typical huts of whitewashed adobe and thatched roofs, so steep that the eaves almost reach the ground. Two slits like the arrow-

---

138   Barea, p.85.

shooting holes in medieval castles run air through the loft where wheat or corn is stored. The men and their sons work the land around the *barraca* from morning to night. The women cook, wash, look after babies, and clean the house. Girls walk to work in the city's silk factories.

The land is not theirs, however, but belongs to a city landlord. The peasants are humble before their landlords and fierce with each other. Shotguns hang behind the door of each *barraca*. They have a keen solidarity with each other, but it is a twisted solidarity. The novel's simple, linear plot turns on how the people of the *huerta* scapegoat a vulnerable family rather than combat the landlords.

The opening chapter of *La barraca* contains much of the novel in embryo, a sign of careful composition that gives the lie to the author's account of rapid, frenetic writing. Maybe, though, he carried a story for a long time in his head until it was ripe, then set it down complete. The chapter carefully sets the scene. The dress, huts, and fields of the people of the *huerta* are explained. The fertility of the land contrasts with the ill health of the young Pepeta. The beauty of the land contrasts with the vengeful envy of its people. Pepeta gets

A *barraca*: Valencian small farmer's house

up at 3 AM and takes the vegetables to the city market. She comes back and returns to the city, this time with her cow. She tours the city, taking milk to her customers.

The miserly landlord is known as a *judío*, a Jew, used several times as an insult. Blasco probably shared this prejudice, as he referred to the miserly usurer Don Jaime in *Entre naranjos* as a Jew, though he is (officially) a Christian. Berber pirates are also present in the folk memory of the *huerta*. Its people's Christian upbringing includes memory of the supposed sins, warranting their murders, and expulsions, of Jews and Moors.

Rural tragedy unfolds, as the participants seem unable to do anything to avoid their miserable destinies. This is the "naturalism" associated with Zola. As Manuel Vicent puts it, "Blasco is still a nineteenth-century writer, while his fellow-writers had begun to glimpse the ruptures that were to define the new age."[139] (Not unlike the Benlliure brothers, one might argue). Despite the sharpness of his writing, this old-fashioned feel to his books can make for stodgy reading: he is too explicit, rather than suggestive. He is a novelist following a thesis.

La barraca is like a huge medieval fresco, in which the background characters are sketched in rapidly, caricatures of avarice (the landlords), vanity (the schoolmaster), or goodness (Pepeta or Teresa). Then, in the foreground are the mass of laborers, moved to violence and harassment by ignorance, spurred on by the clever, idle Pimentó, or in the next instant moved back to tears and kindness by the death of Teresa's youngest son.

In the center of the fresco stand Batiste, Teresa's husband, and Pimentó. Pimentó is boastful and malicious; the outsider Batiste is hard-working and noble, only wanting to provide for his family and get on with everyone.

---

139   Vicent, Introduction to *Entre naranjos*, p.10.

In these two figures Blasco goes beyond caricature. Batiste is weighed down by responsibility and at times enraged by injustice, but has a placid, balanced character, until the constant aggressions convert him into someone provocative and rash. Pimentó starts off as just a loudmouth, but as the novel develops he shows that he is not just a bragging coward. Again, self-righteous at first, Pimentó comes to doubt whether he is right, though the circumstances, the weight of generations of behavior pressing down, push him to further crime.

The reader knows that tragedy awaits Batiste and Teresa, yet the tension is maintained throughout. It is a book published right at the end of the nineteenth century and is an adventure story in the nineteenth-century tradition, with no touch of the modernism that Valle-Inclán was bringing to Spanish literature. This should not make us think it is simplistic. Description, action, and tension are key to making people read. The psychology is acute. And the subject matter lets us see, all too infrequent in literature, the lives of rural laborers.

THE FRIGHTFUL CHALET

Valencia has a legendary beach, the Malva-rosa to the north of the port. Behind it still stands, battered but undefeated, the Cabanyal quarter, the old fishing families' neighborhood, which has miraculously survived speculators' attempts to destroy it. The Cabanyal is a small district of two-story houses (some are just one-up, one-down) on a grid system. The fishing nets used to be laid out to dry and be repaired on the straight streets. Many of the houses are painted brightly or adorned by colorful tiles. Idiosyncratic details, balconies, ironwork, or gargoyles, make it a place to wander, like the Carme, though poverty, drugs, and lack of investment make it like the Carme thirty years ago. It still retains something of a village atmosphere: people will sit out in front of their houses on hot nights. Rita Barberá found it hopelessly old-fashioned and unprofitable. She wanted to knock down 1,600 houses and drive the Avinguda Blasco Ibáñez through it to the sea, but she was stopped by the 2008–11 Socialist government after a powerful local resistance campaign. As in the *palmerar* of Elx, though, builders keep chipping away at the edges.

Like the Cabanyal, the Malva-rosa has survived. It is an ancient beach from before mass tourism. These were beaches of rickety sand-strewn restaurants, bathing clubs, and villas with their gardens giving onto the sea. Times and usage have changed, but it is still a town beach, where the houses and streets run down naturally to the sand, with no huge tourist hotels.

It was also a beach with a fishing fleet, where the sailing boats were drawn up on the sand. On the Carrer dels Pescadors in the Cabanyal, there is still a Casa dels Bous (Oxen Stable) in front of the Llotja del Peix (Wet Fish Market). The oxen were used to haul the fishing boats in and out of the water. Both Oxen Stable and Fish Market are in a lamentable state of disrepair, apart from a restored blue-and-yellow sundial and the date 1895 on the former. You can see the boats, bathers, fisherwomen, and oxen in Sorolla's many paintings of the Malva-rosa. When he was working there, he kept his easel and brushes in the Casa dels Bous. The two buildings are not now actually by the beach, for the sea has withdrawn in the past 100 years.

On the Malva-rosa and the adjoining Las Arenas beaches, running three kilometers north from the harbor, fish and shellfish restaurants cater for the Sunday lunch crowds. Here several colorful houses of the bourgeoisie of 100 years ago still line the sand. Among them, toward the end of the Malva-rosa, stood Blasco Ibáñez's "chalet," a 450-square-meter three-story mansion in a mixture of styles. One could say, as vulgar, lively, and diverse as Blasco himself. Joan Mira expostulates: "He had a frightful chalet with caryatids built…and would wander along the beach without a tie, with a cigar in his fingers, allowing himself to be admired by bathers and fishermen."[140]

Commissioned in 1902, the noble house has a large garden behind and wide terrace on the middle floor, where the writer had his office, with a view toward the sea if he ever had time to glance up from his long desk of Carrara marble with lions for its four feet.

The house is not the original. In 1939 the victors of the war expropriated it as a leisure club for the Spanish Falange. In the 1980s the Socialist City Council decided to restore the house, but its condition was so ruinous that it was knocked down and rebuilt in the 1990s according to the original plans. The chalet is thus not the original but the exterior is a faithful reproduction of it. Inside, the layout is quite different, now a small museum dedicated to Blasco Ibáñez and a center for study of his work. The chalet is brash and the contents are slight, but it is well worth a visit. The photos of the writer and his family of three sons and wild-looking daughter with the great name Libertad Blasco-Ibáñez Blasco (1895–1988), the colorful covers of his books' first editions, the diary of his travels, his desk—all there for us to marvel at his energy and life. Nothing on his politics, but a house-museum is a place for homage, not for awkward, often divisive questions.

Blasco is still a live political firework. In rebuilding the chalet, in naming the main avenue to the beach after the writer, the post-dictatorship Socialists of the 1980s were making political points. Their federalism was similar to Blasco's, though they could not say so; there were radical noises, but no federalism at all and subservience to Madrid.

---

140   Joan Mira, p.153.

Blasco Ibáñez's politics were of a specific kind: anti-monarchical, calling for a democratic Republic; anti-clerical, for the separation of Church and state; at times revolutionary-sounding, with elements of socialism. Later, in Argentina, he attempted to found socialist communes. In *Entre naranjos* he criticizes in explicit leftist terms Rafael's grandfather, "who had amassed the family fortune through fifty years of slow exploitation of ignorance and wretchedness."[141]

To be against the monarchy in these years after its 1874 Restoration was revolutionary and dangerous. It meant opposing the whole system of political bosses who fixed elections and kept "order" on behalf of the upper class in every town and village. This system particularly exercised power through the Diputacions (Provincial Councils), which oversaw town budgets, appointed or dismissed officials, and gifted construction contracts. It is a system of clientelism which still, to some degree, exists today. It can be seen in the case of the Fabra family (Chapter 5), who ran the Diputació de Castelló for over a century.

Most importantly, with Blasco Ibáñez we can grasp something of the complex Valencian national question. Blasco was in favor of greater autonomy for Valencia, but fiercely against the teaching of the Valencian language. The pan-Catalanist Joan Fuster is hard on Blasco: "Blasco called himself a 'federalist,' but his federalism suffered from total disconnection from the region's concrete realities."[142]

Fuster argues that Blasco diverted the proletariat from radical Republicanism or anarchism to his own party, based on the urban middle class and artisans. In turn, Blasco's Republicans were subservient to Madrid parties. It was a

---

141   *Entre naranjos*, p.33.
142   Fuster, p.273.

particular form of Valencianism, identifying the Community with Spain, rather than asserting its independence as a nation (or region) or affirming its identity as part of a linguistic and cultural entity with Catalonia and the Balearic Islands, the *països catalans*.

One should add that, in the thirty years that "Blasquism" dominated Valencia city's municipal politics, it strengthened street-fighting thuggery as a back-up to political argument. Blasco's was an attempt at a reactionary solution to the "national question," similar to that of Alejandro Lerroux in Catalonia. Lerroux started out organizing masses in Barcelona's streets in the early twentieth century to fight for workers' rights, the Republic, and federalism and ended up as prime minister in 1933–35, leading a right-wing coalition government.

The PURA, Blasco Ibáñez's party, led by his son Sigfrid after his death, supported the Lerroux government, which collapsed in the mid-1930s through its political contradictions and the notorious Strauss and Perlowitz scandal.[143] These two foreign crooks bribed ministers to persuade the government to license a roulette wheel that could be manipulated by a button. The scandal, in reality much less serious than many scandals of the last few years, was nonetheless sufficient to bring down the Lerroux government and destroy its ally the PURA. From 104 members of parliament in the 1933 elections, Lerroux's Radical Party fell to five in February 1936.

The sorry end of Blasquism was that several of the PURA's leaders became high-ranking officials of the Franco regime after 1939. Blasco Ibáñez's was a classic populist movement, based on leftist rhetoric. In short, its main

---

143   Based on this pair of crooks' names, the word *estraperlo* entered the Spanish language, in particular to describe black market fraud in the 1940s years of hunger.

functions were to head the Valencian working class away from anarchism on the one hand and from national aspirations on the other. Revel in Blasco Ibáñez's best books, but beware of his politics, however radical and fiery he could sound.

Light

For the clearest view of Blasco's contemporary and friend, Joaquín Sorolla (1863–1923), Valencia's best-known twentieth-century painter, you have to go to Madrid. Just off the Castellana in a classy neighborhood, Sorolla's house and garden are big enough not to be dominated by the blocks of apartments that now loom on either side. The Sorolla family moved to this house built to his specifications (Paseo del General Martínez Campos, 37) in 1911. His parents had died of cholera when he was two. One can surmise that the house and its paintings, which overflow with contentment with his wife Clotilde, their two daughters, and a son, were the personal triumph of creating the home and family he had not had.

The luxurious house shows how much Sorolla earned. He painted the King of Spain; he painted President Taft of the United States; he painted numerous society women. He was commissioned by the Hispanic Society of America to do a series of huge paintings on the different regions of Spain for the sum of 150,000 dollars. This society, founded in 1904 on West 155 Street, Manhattan, by Archer Milton Huntington to promote Hispanic culture, is the greatest museum of Spanish art outside Spain. Huntington was the son of a shipyard and railroad millionaire and dedicated himself, as heirs of ruthless businessmen sometimes do, to culture, spending the family millions on his passions for Spanish art and rare books. He invited Sorolla to exhibit there in 1909 and, out of the 356 pictures shown, 195 were sold. The five-month show made Sorolla internationally famous and paid for his Madrid house. From 1911 to 1919 he painted fourteen murals of *The Provinces of Spain* for Huntington. Some say the effort led to the stroke in 1920 that ended his active life.

In New York he is one of the greats, hung alongside Velázquez and Goya. Nowadays, though, he is not quite so highly valued and in recent Sotheby's auctions of Spanish art (2006 and 2010) some of his work failed to reach the reserve price. Though he was more sophisticated, by general agreement more skilled, certainly more famous, than his contemporaries Josep Benlliure and Pinazo, he was not part of the great revolution in painting led by Picasso. Nevertheless, today he is Valencia's talismanic artist, with hotels, streets, and the city's new high-speed train station named after him.

Sorolla was a little younger than Pinazo and the Benlliure brothers. When he went abroad in the 1880s, it was not to Rome but to Paris, where the Impressionists influenced his style. As prodigal in painting as Blasco was in writing, he was the author of some 2,200 catalogued paintings. He kept some of the best for himself. They can be seen in the handsome Museo Sorolla, which is a fine mixture of Sorolla's work and a lived-in home.

When we visited, there were a dozen eight- or nine -year-olds being taken around by a museum monitor. She was brilliant. I learned more about painting by standing behind the children and pretending not to listen than by reading an art book. She sat them on the floor in front of a famous Sorolla of a naked boy leading a horse out of the sea onto the Malva-rosa beach and got them talking. What color's the horse? White, of course! But what other colors? The children (me too) began to look. Their hands shot up. Yellow—green—gray—black—purple. We were learning to observe, to see the nuances of color on the horse. Sorolla is drawing white on white paper, but it's not just white: for that you'd leave the paper blank.

"Now look at the beach, children. The sand is yellowy, a warm color, and the sea is blue, a cold color. What's that fleck of white on the boy's shoulder? It's the fierce sun glistening on his wet skin. And why is he as naked as the horse? He is poor, so he went into the sea without clothes." "He's wearing a hat," a girl says. "And the horse is wearing a bridle," a boy adds. "Yes," said the monitor, "neither of them is completely naked. They balance each other, as they are joined by the rope the boy holds to lead the horse. And what's there in the corner, in the background?" "Cows?" a bright girl wondered doubtfully. "That's right, cows. They're oxen, not cows for milk, but working cows, oxen that pull the fishing-boats up onto the sand or into the water."

The monitor made me look. Sorolla was painting the heat of the sun and the chill of the sea, the fierce light and shadows cast. To paint Mediterranean light, as Sorolla did, you show shade, always there as people in the bright sun create shadow. A hat or a rope casts shadow, too.

Children looking at *The Horse's Bath* in the Sorolla Museum

Or in the several paintings of bathing huts, the light draws stripes on the people inside as it enters through the horizontal slats in the wooden blinds. Why are the stripes in front when the slats are behind? Because there are more blinds we cannot see. And not just blinds: look, there's light flowing through the roof.

Room 2 in the Sorolla Museum is his studio. The biggest room, it reaches through the house's upper floor, so that light pours through windows under the roof as it does in Valencia's cathedral. Here he received his clients, so it is densely hung with his work. His paint brushes are still there. In the studio's star exhibit, *Boys on the Beach*, three naked boys lie in the water. It is a simple picture, quite naturalistic, but with touches of abstraction in the contrasting light and shadow and the swirls of water. Begoña Torres, author of the most recent Sorolla monograph, wrote of it: "The appearance of spontaneity and fluidity shows us his mastery of a really complex technique that is able to capture the magical effects of light on wet bodies."[144]

Two wealthy women in straw hats stroll by the sea, in long white dresses, one with a white parasol. In another canvas, three working fisherwomen stand, large, forceful, the breeze ruffling their white clothes and tipping the waves with white. As with the horse, the shades of white are everywhere. Sorolla is a painter in love with the outdoors: the colors of the Malva-rosa and of Xàbia where he sometimes vacationed: oxen, sailboats, children running, the boys naked, often in the sea with the water shimmering over them in the sunlight.

Velázquez became the great master for Spanish painters in Sorolla's time. Sorolla traveled to London in 1907 to copy the Rokeby Venus and came back to paint

---

144 Begoña Torres, p.173.

a similarly sensual painting from behind of his naked wife Clotilde. It seems startling in early-twentieth-century Spain that Sorolla should paint his wife (rather than a model) in the nude, but remember he had been to Paris, he knew the Impressionists, he had seen paintings such as Renoir's of his wife Aline in *The Large Bathers*. And though he lived in Madrid, he was a Valencian, freed by light and fire from dour priest-ridden Castile.

In later years he lived by painting the famous and wealthy. This was the time of a new industrial bourgeoisie rising and male industrialists would pay for prestige portraits of their wives. These are often in darker colors: he was not only a master of shades of whites and bright light. They are also, unlike most portraits commissioned by the rich, quite realistic. He eschewed flattery. The people wear their best clothes, but their looks are by no means enhanced. His painting of Blasco Ibáñez shows a fat man wearing black, looking more like a shabby priest than the politician and great writer. It is an affectionate portrait, though. Sorolla transmits warmth—and not just in the multiple portraits of his family.

In his earlier days he painted a number of realist pictures of mild social protest: of workers, peasants, the handicapped, and exhausted prostitutes being taken by a woman to their next brothel. Sorolla, though, was not a radical painter. He was a bourgeois painter: this is not meant as an insult, but refers to both his form and content. He is, though, an original. He painted what he saw (not adapting what he saw to what would sell, as Josep Benlliure sought to do) with a magnificent technique. No one has painted the light, breezes, women, and children of the Malva-rosa beach like him. He was a "light-filled barbarian," in Valle-Inclán's phrase. He meant it as criticism. I'd take it as a compliment.

14: The Defeat of Revolutionary Hope

"A revolution is really taking place, not an odd shuffle or two in cabinet appointments"

W.H. Auden

Several chapters have touched on the 1936–39 Spanish Civil War: the bombing of the steel plant at Sagunt; the storing of the Prado's art treasures in Valencia's Torres dels Serrans; the bombing of Valencia and Alacant; the rescue from Gandia of fleeing Republicans. This chapter deals more fully with the Civil War in the *país valencià*. Though it ended eighty years ago, it still defines Spanish politics.

THE MAP OF HORROR

Paterna, a town of some 60,000 people, is on a hill just inland from the city of Valencia. Its center consists of tranquil streets of low-rise housing, an Arab tower with a view to the sea and ancient caves where some twenty families still live, "peacefully and in comfort," as one resident told me. I have arranged to meet Javier Parra, Esquerra Unida (Left Unity) councillor in Paterna. Javier drives us under the highway that connects Paterna to Valencia. We stop by a scruffy wood beside the road. A few wreaths of flowers lie against a low wall. They had been placed there by the Socialist Party on April 14, anniversary of the 1931 declaration of the Second Republic, in commemoration of the 2,237 people known to have been shot against this wall after the Civil War. The wall has crumbled on top and earth has accumulated below it. This ordinary piece of rubbishy scrubland on the outskirts of a city is a desolate place. There is a project to reconstruct the wall and place 2,237 names on it, but this has not yet come to fruition.

The 2,237 people are buried in mass graves in Paterna cemetery. Since mid-2017 excavations have been under way to identify the bodies. I had known of the executions at Paterna for many years, but wrongly imagined the *fossa comuna* (mass grave) as one big pit. In fact, there are dozens of small pits, corresponding to the dates of execution. On the day in early May when we visited the cemetery, ArqueoAntro, the company in charge of exhuming the victims' remains on behalf of their descendants, was excavating *fossa* 128, where 130 people were thought to be buried. I asked how they knew who was where. The photojournalist Santi Donaire, responsible for recording the progress of the excavations, explained:

> "You have to understand that all these executions were legal. Of course they were completely illegitimate fascist reprisals against workers and peasants who were only guilty of defending the Republic, but they were people condemned after arrest, trial with judge and prosecutor, sentence of death and the Civil Guard carrying out the sentence. This means that all their names and mass graves are recorded in the cemetery archives."

The half-dozen archaeologists painstakingly brushing reddish earth from a cranium are working under a beige tent. So far only fourteen families have requested the opening of this grave. As news of an exhumation emerges, more family members contact ArqueoAntro. In the other graves already excavated, some 70 percent of the dead have their family members involved.

In the 1980s, when the Socialist Party governed in Valencia, there was no call for exhumation. From 1995, with the PP in power, it was impossible. Since 2015, under the Botànic government, recovery of bodies has been permitted and encouraged. Rosa Pérez, vice-president of the Diputació of Valencia, is committed to honoring the dictatorship's victims: "Over forty years since Franco died, and we still have our roadsides and cemeteries full of unmarked graves." All over the Spanish state, there are at least 120,000 victims of the Franco dictatorship in unmarked graves.

Excavating with great care grave 128 at Paterna

It is the Association of Family Members of Victims of Francoism who have pushed for the reopening of the *fosses*. This is a movement of grandchildren. The sons and daughters, brought up under the dictatorship, acquired the habit of silence. The first grave to be opened at Paterna, *fossa* 113, in mid-2017 contained forty-nine bodies heaped on top of each other and with bullet holes splintering bone. The president of the Association, Santi Vallès, describes Paterna cemetery as a "map of horror."

The members of the Association want to identify their relatives and take the bodies home for proper, marked burial. Javier told me:

> There's a debate that is not taking place. Of course the desires of the families have to come first. Most of the people shot in Paterna were from other parts and you understand that their families should want to take the remains back to their villages. But in a few decades their bones will be emptied into a common grave anyway. However, if they remain here, collective memory can be kept alive.

Paterna cemetery imposes silence and seriousness. There is a tall bronze monument to one side commemorating the victims. Relatives have placed plaques (often flowers, too) on the various common graves. These are intensely moving. The nameless of history, laborers, and clerks who dared rise up for justice and were beaten down, are given names. There is even a fifty-year-old Civil Guard. One can imagine a scenario: someone perhaps disgusted by the executions, who refused to take part and was himself condemned for rebellion. The Paterna cemetery is a collective place of homage, where the argument can be made to successive generations that fascism must be crushed. One understands

Javier's desire for a collective memorial; and one understands, too, the relatives who want to take the bodies to their village cemeteries.

For obvious reasons—it was a time of terror—there are no, or very few, eye-witness accounts of the executions and burials. Javier tells me that, as sadistic punishment, a communist was appointed one of the burial squad. This man, Leoncio, placed papers identifying victims in bottles. Santi Donaire tells of another gravedigger who found someone alive after the firing squad. He asked the priest for advice. The priest took out a revolver, held it to the gravedigger's forehead and said: "You know what you have to do or you will be next." When the gravedigger returned to the execution wall, he found that the Civil Guards were finishing off anyone still alive. The story may not be strictly true, but underlines the close connection of the Church and dictatorship.

Mass grave of executed Republicans at Paterna

Valencia was a Republican stronghold. At the start of the war, a powerful revolutionary movement took control of the area. Many bosses and fascists who did not flee were killed. Factories and workshops were collectivized. The city then became capital of Republican Spain from November 1936, when the government fled besieged Madrid, to October 1937. It was also the last area to fall to Franco's troops, with thousands trapped in ports such as Gandia and Alacant. There was no frontier for them to flee across and the ports were blockaded by Mussolini's navy.

Until recently the city's year as state capital has been little commemorated. Recently means when the three-party, left-wing coalition led by Joan Ribó finally replaced the Partido Popular in the City Council in June 2015. A Civil War route has now been set up, including a visit to three buildings in the Carrer Cavallers that housed Republican ministries and an air raid shelter in the Carrer Serrans. Another shelter, for 700 people, can be visited in the basement of the city hall. During the war, Valencia city suffered over 400 bombing raids, mainly by Italian planes from nearby Mallorca, which killed several hundred civilians.

Poignantly, some eighty-five revolutionary changes to street names have been recalled: not renamed, but recalled: Avinguda del Port was briefly Lenin Avenue, Carrer Trinquete Caballeros was Pancho Villa, and Corona was La Pasionaria Street. Logically, nobles fared badly: Marques de Turia became Buenaventura Durruti Street. My favorite: Isabel la Católica was (the socialist) Margarita Nelken street. And one can imagine Blasco Ibáñez's posthumous fury: the avenue named after him became Avinguda de la Unió Soviètica. I say "poignantly" because those changes in names in 1936 represented a hope for a better future that was wiped out by the victory of fascism. In 1939, the streets were renamed again, mostly in honor of Franco's generals.

SOCIAL REVOLUTION

When the military rose up against the Republic on July 17–18, 1936, it was defeated rapidly in Barcelona and Madrid. In Valencia, then as now Spain's third city, the result hung in the balance for a good ten days. The two main trade unions, the CNT (National Labor Federation) led by anarchists and the Socialist UGT (General Workers Union), called a general strike as soon as they heard the news of the military rebellion. The CNT, strong among dockworkers, agreed to join the Popular Front committee, which controlled the city after deposing the civil governor because he had refused to arm the workers. Some churches were burned, including the Sants Joans (Holy Johns) in central Valencia.

The army stayed in barracks, with commanding General Martínez Monje insisting he was no rebel. Shaken by the failure of General Goded to take Barcelona (and his execution), Martínez Monje sat on the fence, waiting to see whether the uprising was successful. Finally, even the more conservative elements in the Popular Front committee agreed that the position was unsustainable. A rebellion of rank-and-file soldiers in Paterna against the coup forced their hand. The committee dropped its arguments that an assault on the barracks would drive middle elements into the enemy camp and supported the storming and taking of the barracks on the night of August 1–2. Rage at the slaughter of several hundred militiamen by the supposedly loyal Civil Guard at La Puebla de Valverde on July 29 (see next chapter) also drove the decision. Valencia defeated the military uprising a good week later than any other major city in Spain. The rest of the *país valencià* followed the same pattern.

Within the Republic a battle between revolutionaries and reformists erupted. While the Socialists and Left Republicans wanted to carry on with Republican order, defending capitalist democracy, the anarchists, particularly strong in Catalonia and Valencia, saw the defeat of the military as the decisive moment to fight for the abolition of private property and full social revolution. They rapidly occupied all strategic buildings, such as the radio station and telephone exchange. They pushed forward at once with collectivization of society: factories, docks, transport, and the *horta*.

Strange as it might seem to people with little interest in politics, the anarchists' severest opponents on the Republican side were communists. The Communist Party, much weaker than the anarchists at the start of the war, was a more disciplined force. Within a year, because of its appeal to the middle classes and the Republic's dependence on Soviet arms, it had grown to become the dominant political party. The communist strategy in Spain was to form a broad Popular Front, with a centralized government and army. The Communist International, controlled from Moscow, even denied that a revolution was taking place in the Spanish state. It argued that revolution would alienate both "democratic" governments such as the USA, France, and Britain and middle-class sectors in Spain.

The argument was surely right in that revolution did alienate these governments and sectors—how could it not? Any radical change at all is always opposed by those affected negatively. However, the chances of winning the war were reduced by the Communist Party's rolling back of the social revolution actually taking place. Millions were disoriented and demoralized. War is not just a military, but a political question. The debate is still alive today between historians who support the Popular Front alliance of workers and middle-class anti-Franco parties that crushed the revolution and others who argue that the revolution of the anarchists and the anti-Stalinist Partit Obrer d'Unificació Marxista (POUM) suggested a lost path to victory.

Where the CNT was strong, as in the main factories in Valencia city, Sagunt, or Alcoi, collectivization was rapid. This was nothing like the forced collectivization practiced by Stalin in the Soviet Union in the 1930s. It was direct expropriation by the workers, who organized themselves through assemblies. Contrary to the owners' belief, chaos did not ensue. Workers were quite capable of managing a factory without senior management and owners.

Gaston Leval, in his classic *Collectives in the Spanish Revolution*, considers the city of Alcoi the best example in the whole of Spain of collective organization of production. The rapid collectivization was fruit of the city's long tradition of struggle and libertarian democracy, which meant that there were already 4,500 members of the anarchist-led CNT on the outbreak of war in 1936. Leval explains:

> In Alcoy 20,000 workers administered production through their Syndicates and proved that industry functions more economically without capitalists or shareholders and without employers fighting among themselves and thereby preventing the use of technical plant…
>
> The government could only bow before these achievements and order arms from the syndicalised engineering workshops in Alcoy, just as it ordered cloth from the socialised textile industry to clothe the army, and ankle-boots from the factories in Elda in the same province of Alicante which were also in the hands of the libertarians.[145]

---

145   Leval, p.231.

"The government could only bow before these achievements": in other words, they had to accept as a *fait accompli* the abolition of capitalist ownership of the means of production.

The *horta* was more complex. The anarchist columns that left the cities to collectivize the villages and smaller towns consisted mainly of industrial workers. They met a peasant mentality that was quite different from their way of thinking. While the anarchists wanted to collectivize all farms, the Communist Party won support among small landowners in the *horta* by defending private property. The historian Antony Beevor quotes Communist International statements:

> "We respect those who want to work their land as a collective, but we also request respect for those who want to cultivate their land individually."

And the appeal to patriotic sentiment:

> "To oppress the interests of small farmers means oppressing the fathers of our soldiers."[146]

Despite this opposition from the communists and small landowners (the expropriation of large landowners was not controversial: these supporters of the rebellion had left or been killed) and the huge logistical problems involved, the CNT managed to organize a network of about 270 local committees throughout the *horta* that purchased, packed,l and exported the orange crop, successfully replacing several thousand middlemen. Citrus fruits grown in Valencia were the Spanish state's main foreign currency earner at the time.

---

146   Quoted in *The Battle for Spain*, p.122 (Chapter 11).

The historian Burnett Bolloten explained the impact of the revolution:

> ...the labor unions impinged upon the interests of the middle classes in almost every field. Retailers and wholesalers, hotel, café, and bar owners, opticians and doctors, barbers and bakers, shoemakers and cabinetmakers, dressmakers and tailors, brickmakers and building contractors, to cite but a few examples, were caught up relentlessly by the collectivization movement in numberless towns and villages.[147]

Bolloten's words underline how many proprietors and intermediaries had their livelihoods affected. Most of these would ultimately favor the victory of Franco and the return of their privileges. Meanwhile, they supported the Communist Party's discipline and appeals to order.

Normal life carried on after the revolution erupted: people still went to work, shopped and chatted to the neighbors. At the same time, normal life was turned upside down. Here is an anecdote that Wilebaldo Solano liked to tell. A Valencian medical student in Barcelona, Solano was sent back to Valencia in the first days of the war to help organize the POUM. A middle-aged woman came into the office and said: "My husband beats me. What are you going to do about it?" Taken aback, twenty-year-old Wile stuttered his sympathy and said: "We'll send someone round to see him."[148] Revolutionary upheaval transformed personal life.

---

147   Bolloten, p.63.
148   Story told by POUM leader Wilebaldo Solano (1916-2010) to historian Andy Durgan.

IRON COLUMN

In the entire state, there was no formation more consistent in its commitment to revolutionary anarchism than Valencia's Iron Column. Its rise and fall is the story of how the revolution that flowered in July and August 1936 had been uprooted a year later. Valencia saw a large number of big landowners and factory bosses killed in the first weeks of the war. They would be taken for a "ride" and their bodies left by the side of the road in the *horta*. The Column was responsible for many of these extrajudicial killings.

The Column recruited mainly from Valencia building workers and dockers, and steelworkers from Sagunt. Of its eventual 3,000 members, several hundred were prisoners freed from the prison of Sant Miquel dels Reis in the north Valencia neighborhood of Els Orriols.[149] These ex-prisoners caused problems. Some had been jailed for political offenses and were easily integrated into the Iron Column. However, in Bolloten's words, "the immense majority were hardened criminals, who...had entered the column for what they could get out of it, adopting the anarchist label as a camouflage."[150] The Iron Column maintained idealistically that all prisoners were victims of capitalist society and could be reformed. They did not accept that some had been brutalized beyond reform.

Criminal activity (theft, personal revenge killings, etc.) by members of the Column caused such tension between the regional committee of the CNT and the Column that,

---

149   Sant Miquel dels Reis is a huge Renaissance building, formerly a monastery, at that time a prison, and now the city's main library, just outside the ring road and facing the *horta*. It is known, with some exaggeration, as the Valencian Escorial.
150   Bolloten, p.315.

Monastery, prison, and library. Sant Miquel dels Reis, the "Valencian Escorial"

for a time, the former cut off supplies to the latter. Just as important a source of tension was the Column's political line. It openly attacked the anarchist ministers in the central government, based in Valencia from November 1936. How could leaders of anti-state anarchism become members of the state's government? These traitors to anarchism, in the Iron Column's view, were helping to recompose a capitalist state that had been powerless in the revolutionary days of August 1936.

Even more serious than this political conflict with its own CNT leadership, the Column had armed clashes with the communists. Iron Column members probably murdered prominent members of the Communist Party and the UGT (including Josep Pardo, the latter's secretary in Valencia, on September 23). They took part in bank robberies and stole from shops. They also committed actions that were "crimes" for the government and communists, but were justified in terms of the revolution. For example, they sacked the Bank of Spain, police headquarters, and government offices, burning criminal records and tax and property documents.

Though their criminality was exaggerated for political reasons, there is little doubt that released criminals and, quite possibly, Falangist provocateurs took advantage of the Iron Column's open-door policy and radicalism. On October 2, 1936, the Column assaulted Castelló prison and killed fifty-three right-wingers held there. Max Aub has a character, Rivadavia, who catches the near-nihilist tone of extreme-radical anarchism: "If this world is a load of shit, I don't see why it needs to be reformed. Finish it off and start again."[151]

In late October a Column member, Tiburcio Ariza, was shot dead by the police when he supposedly resisted arrest on suspicion of killing Pardo. At Ariza's mass funeral on October 30, the cortége marched past the Communist Party headquarters (the expropriated Palau Cerveró, now Bancaixa) in the Plaça Tetuan. Machine guns opened fire from the party building. The anarchists, caught in a trap, returned fire before being forced to flee, leaving Ariza's coffin and about thirty new corpses.[152]

In the following days, armed skirmishes were common in the streets of the city, as the Iron Column and its allies sought vengeance. The police was reinforced, preparatory to

---

151   *Campo abierto*, p.260 (Part III, Chapter III). My translation. With characteristic irony, Aub then has this same ultra-left Rivadavia flee Madrid with the anarchist minister Garcia Oliver in November 1936.
152   For the slaughter in the Plaça Tetuan, I have relied on Chapter VII of Paul Preston's deeply moving *Spanish Holocaust*.

the central government's arrival in Valencia, and the Iron Column was cajoled back to the Teruel front, some hundred kilometers inland. In the following months it resisted the attempts to suppress the autonomous militia and to organize all fighters into regular army units, which the government was pushing for in early 1937 with the acquiescence of the "anarchist" ministers.

Despondent at the move toward a regular army and the non-revolutionary drift of the government, Iron Column members started deserting from the front. Things came to a head in March 1937 when the Column was integrated into the regular army as the 83rd Brigade, though not before several members were killed and arrested in further clashes with the police. The fate of the Iron Column and the fighting in Barcelona at the start of May 1937 heralded the end of anarchist power and the fall of the Left Socialist Largo Caballero as prime minister in May. The revolution was over: the POUM was suppressed, collectives were decollectivized, all militias became regular army units.

When the war started, all lights in Valencia had to be left on at night so that fascist snipers could not shoot from dark windows. When the Italian air force started bombing the city from Mallorca in late 1937, all windows had to be blacked out. The city moved from light-filled optimism to the darkness of impending defeat. Along the way, it settled into bureaucratic routine as the seat of government. The anarchist revolution had been crushed, to be replaced by the discipline of the communists, who were not threatening the lives of the old bosses, as the revolutionaries had done, but were imprisoning and silencing political dissidents to their left.

THE PROPAGANDA WAR

The Spanish Civil War had a huge impact on the British left. Massive solidarity with the Spanish Republic was an underlying factor in the Labour landslide of 1945. The Tories had sabotaged the Republic. Solidarity committees were organized in every city and many small towns. About 2,800 British people volunteered to fight in the International Brigades. Enormous sums were raised for Medical Aid. British nurses and doctors were active in caring for the wounded.

The Republic also won overwhelming support from artists and writers. The propaganda war was won internationally, even while the real war was being lost. Spain became the great cause for a generation of left-wing intellectuals. However, the military rebels, despite being openly supported by Mussolini and Hitler, were able to neutralize the main western governments, through both the Non-Intervention Pact and the likes of Joseph Kennedy, who led the Catholic lobby in the USA that prevented the Roosevelt government from lifting Congress' embargo on supplying arms to the Republic.

In July 1937 the second Anti-Fascist Writers' Congress brought together 200 writers from thirty countries for two weeks in Valencia (held in what is now the city hall) and Madrid. Organization of this successful Communist Party front was a logistical nightmare. For example, the British poet Stephen Spender, refused a visa by the British government, crossed the Pyrenees with a false passport supplied to him by André Malraux in the unlikely name Ramos Ramos.

The congress had the positive aim of rallying writers behind the Republic and the negative one of pushing the Communist Parties' own political line. André Gide, a defender of the Republic, was repeatedly attacked for his critique of the Soviet Union. George Orwell was scathing about "the 'Anti-Fascist Writers' who held their congress in Madrid and ate banquets against a background of starvation."[153]

W.H. Auden, the most famous British poet of the 1930s, did not take part in the Writers' Congress. Yet he did support the Republic and visited Spain earlier— for seven weeks from January to March 1937—with the aim of driving an ambulance, but ended up assigned to broadcasting. He wrote his poem-pamphlet *Spain* on returning. Though later attacked by Orwell for its phrase "necessary murder" and then withdrawn by Auden from his Collected Works, at the time it was widely praised and often read at meetings to collect money for Medical Aid for Spain.

Auden also wrote an article "Impressions of Valencia," in which he talks about poster artists, the large amount of food available (despite the war, the *horta* had not disappeared) and the hotels full of journalists ("conspicuous as actresses"), officials, and soldiers.

> And everywhere there are the people…They are here, driving fast cars on business, running the trains and the trams, keeping the streets clean, doing all those things that the gentry cannot believe will be properly done unless they are there to keep an eye on them…For a revolution is really taking place, not an odd shuffle or two in cabinet appointments.[154]

---

153   A 1946 review, reprinted in *Orwell in Spain*, p. 372.
154   Auden, *Spanish Civil War Verse*, p.100.

His view that a revolution was taking place is worth quoting because Auden was on the conservative wing of those who supported the Republic.

Auden's friend Stephen Spender (Ramos Ramos) has often been criticized for his liberal ambivalence. He joined the Communist Party, then rapidly left it. In retrospect, however, Spender seems much clearer and braver in expressing openly his doubts and fear in poems and articles than many of the writers of heroic couplets. He hears machine-gun fire:

> I assure myself the shooting is only for practice
> But I am the coward of cowards. The machine-gun
>   stitches
> My intestines with a needle, back and forth;[155]

Of course, this liberalism, however truthful, and self-absorption, however honest, was no way to win a revolutionary war. For that, you need organization and heroic commitment.

DEAD IN CUSTODY

Bob Smillie was someone with heroic commitment and clear ideas. Grandson of a Scottish miners' leader, he volunteered with the small Independent Labour Party (ILP) battalion that fought with the POUM on the Aragon front.[156] ILP leader James Maxton explained:

---

155   Spender, *Port Bou, Spanish Civil War Verse*, p.354.
156   The ILP Battalion had only forty members, though its propaganda impact was greater than its size suggests.

Bob Smillie viewed the Spanish struggle not as one between capitalist democracy and fascism, but rather as the struggle of the Spanish working class against the forces of fascism and international capitalism.[157]

On trying to leave Spain to return to Scotland for a speaking tour in June 1937, the twenty-year-old Smillie was arrested and sent to Valencia's Model prison (see Chapter 9). He was charged with rebellion. Maxton visited Smillie in prison and found him in good health. Then, in mysterious circumstances, Bob Smillie died, officially of peritonitis, but many believe he was murdered, either directly or indirectly by neglect of his appendicitis. He was buried rapidly and anonymously. George Orwell, who fought with Smillie in Aragon, wrote:

> Bob Smillie…was physically one of the toughest people I have met…People so tough as that do not usually die of appendicitis if they are properly looked after. But when you saw what the Spanish jails were like—the makeshift jails used for political prisoners—you realized how much chance there was of a sick man getting proper attention.[158]

He died at the height of the communist witch-hunt against the POUM, when the party was banned, its leaders arrested, and Andreu Nin murdered. Despite his youth, Smillie was no ordinary rank-and-file volunteer,

---

157   (Consulted May 7, 2018) www.spartacus-educational.com/Spsmillie.htm.
158   Orwell, *Homage to Catalonia*, Chapter 14.

but a member of the executive of the International Revolutionary Youth Bureau and thus a political target for the Communist Party.

Mariado Hinojosa, herself a descendant of victims of the dictatorship and an anti-fascist activist, took us to the huge Valencia cemetery, on the southern outskirts of the city. It has a somber beauty. With their family tombs, more luxurious than the living poor's houses in the neighboring quarter of Sant Marcellí, the rich seek to perpetuate power and privilege after death. Mariado told us she had gained permission to consult the cemetery archive, found the record of Robert Smillie's burial and, from the coordinates in the records, worked out the exact spot among the tombs where he was interred. She has placed a small rhododendron by the gray cement wall of a mausoleum.

I asked Mariado what she thought had happened to Bob Smillie:

> No one knows for sure, but I believe he was arrested because he had spoken too explicitly of politics in his letters home. Given the contradictions about dates between the official version at the time and records unearthed now, I think that he was taken from the Model prison to the Russian-controlled *xeca* (secret prison) in the Santa Úrsula Convent, beside the Torres de Quart. If he can be exhumed, we may find out whether he died violently.

As well as the flowering plant commemorating Bob Smillie, Mariado showed us the huge lawn covering the various mass graves of Franco's victims. A monument was put up by Rita Barberá's City Council to commemorate the dead on both sides of the Civil War. Putting an explicit = sign between the two sides is a formula used by the right in Spain to conceal that the war was caused by military rebellion and that the Franco side was responsible for the great majority of executions. Since the PP's 2015 exit from power, Barberá's message has been covered over. On top, descendants of the dictatorship's victims can now place comments and memorials.

THE REARGUARD

Angela Jackson, in her definitive *British Women and the Spanish Civil War*, quoted the Quaker refugee worker, Francesca Wilson, who was told by a driver: "in Valencia people have too easy a life—too much to eat, too much time sitting in cafés. They get depressed."[159] It was the rearguard, far from the front line.

In the first months many women fought in the anarchist and POUM militia, but as the militia were disbanded and their members integrated into the regular army, women returned to support tasks such as cooking and nursing. British women in Spain, many of them freethinkers, whether communists or Quakers, found Spanish left-wing society frustratingly sexist. Nan Green described an anarchist meal where the women served the male revolutionaries, then stood behind them and only sat down to eat when the men had finished. Nan Green was a communist with no love for the anarchists, but there is no reason to doubt her story.

Not just the Spanish feared free women. *The Times* correspondent in Valencia wrote of "women, armed and aggressive...All that womanhood traditionally stands for

---

159   Angela Jackson, p.177.

is rapidly disappearing."[160] This enthused the communist aristocrat, Jessica Mitford:

> I cut pictures of women guerrillas out of the papers, determined, steady-looking women, wiry, bright-eyed, gaunt-faced, some middle aged, some almost little girls. How to take my place at their side?[161]

The many British women volunteers in Spain were not guerrillas, alas, but mainly engaged in a more traditional job: nursing.

The *país valencià* was a place of refuge for the wounded. Arturo Barea wrote of Calp, where he was resting from the stress of besieged Madrid:

> Men of the International Brigades, sent to the hospital of Benisa to recover from wounds and exhaustion, came every day in lorries to bathe in one of the three shallow, scalloped little bays at the foot of the rock...Some had their arms and legs in plaster, some had half-healed scars which they exposed to the wind and sun, lying in the wet sand by the pale, over-scented sand-lilies.[162]

Sylvia Townsend Warner wrote a poem about wounded soldiers at Benicàssim, contrasting their suffering with the idyllic landscape:

---

160   *Ibid*, p.190.
161   *Ibid*, p.192.
162   Barea, pp. 687 and 688-9.

The air is heavy with sun and salt and colour.
On palm and lemon-tree, on cactus and oleander
A dust of dust and salt and pollen lies …

… along the strand
in bleached cotton pyjamas, on rope-soled tread,
wander the risen-from-the-dead,
the wounded, the maimed, the halt.[163]

Valencia was a place of refuge for children and the homeless, too. Barea sent his four children from Madrid to the relative safety of Vila-real, near Castelló. Francesca Wilson set up sewing workshops for refugee girls in Alacant and Murcia, a colony for fifty older refugee boys at Crevillent, near Elx, and a summer camp at Benidorm.

However, the war was moving closer. After the recapture of Teruel at New Year 1938, Franco's troops moved toward Valencia city. They took most of Castelló province in spring 1938, which cut off Catalonia from the rest of the Republic, but were then stopped by grim, consistent resistance along the XYZ line of deep defenses between Almenara, near Sagunt, and Segorbe. Here, to Franco's generals' surprise, their armies were halted, suffering 20,000 deaths in a month. Then the Republic's June 1938 counterattack that became the Battle of the Ebro forced Franco to withdraw his troops from the Valencia front.

When defeat did come in March 1939, the *país valencià* saw fleeing soldiers gather in the ports of Valencia, Gandia, and Alacant. Few got out. The *Stanbrook* departed Alacant on March 28 for Oran with over 3,000 people on board, the crew anxious that it might sink at any moment. No other ships escaped. Some 15,000 Republican soldiers

---

163   Jackson, p.209.

were captured by Italian troops at Alacant on March 30. Some committed suicide, trapped on the quay. Most ended up in makeshift, overcrowded prisons: cinemas, bullrings, a sports stadium. The political leaders, most of whom had urged resistance to the end, had already got out by plane.

15: No One Gets out of Here, Even in Dreams

"Spain is not Spain, it is an immense trench,
a vast cemetery red and bombarded:
the barbarians have willed it thus"

Miguel Hernández[164]

This chapter discusses Miguel Hernández and Max Aub, the two great Valencian writers of the Civil War.

THE WANDERER

Max Aub Mohrenwitz (1903–72)[165] was born in Paris to a German father and French mother. His father was a traveling salesman of jewelery. World War I, with the family's relatives on opposite sides, brought them to settle in Valencia when Max was eleven. His story makes him one of the archetypes of a twentieth-century wanderer, uprooted from countries by three wars and imprisoned by fascism. He had four nationalities in his life: German, French, Spanish, and Mexican (land of his thirty-year exile), and he spoke four languages: German, French, Spanish (the language of his writing), and Valencian.

---

164   *Spanish Civil War Verse*, p. 282. Translated by Inez and Stephen Spender.
165   Much of my information on Aub comes from *Retorno a Max Aub*, the catalogue of the 2017 Exhibition put on by the Instituto Cervantes in Madrid, then Valencia.

Max attended the Lycée français in Valencia, one of the city's few lay schools. Arriving in this strange town, he at once loved and adopted it: the smell of oranges, the beach, the dusty river, the decaying monuments. He became a traveling rep like his father rather than go to university. He came to know intimately the towns and villages of Spain. This helped make him later a committed, realist writer, republican, and socialist. He was fascinated by the real ferocity of how people lived. This is not to say he was uninterested in ideas. In his travels he sought contact with literary vanguards. He became a modernist and experimental writer, quite unlike Blasco Ibáñez. Lyrical, sarcastic, passionate in turns, Max Aub is a singular writer, with a vast number of published works: novels, diaries, poetry, short stories, micro-fiction, collage, theater, and essay. He experimented in book design and layout. Often he combined his texts with drawings or photos:

In 1926 he married the Valencian Perpetua Barjau, "Peua" (1902–91), his intimate and support for the rest of his life. Member of the Socialist Party since 1929, in the Civil War Aub became cultural attaché at the Spanish Embassy in Paris and was responsible for organizing the Spanish Pavilion at Paris' 1937 World Fair. He negotiated with Picasso for his famous Guernica painted for the Pavilion. He defended the picture against complaints that it was too abstract to be a weapon of struggle: "If Picasso's picture has any defect it is that it is too real, too terribly true, atrociously true." To Aub, it could be said, Madrid's Reina Sofía Museum owes its greatest tourist attraction. Picasso wanted to donate his masterpiece to the Republic, but Aub insisted on payment, which eventually gave the Spanish state right of ownership of the painting.

Back in Spain toward the end of the war, Aub co-wrote and assisted André Malraux in the powerful short film *Sierra de Teruel*. It was filmed in Valdelinares, now a ski resort and, though in Aragon, close to the Valencian village full of mountain streams and ponds where Aub used to spend summer vacations, Viver de las Aguas. In the 1990s a Max Aub Foundation was set up near Viver, in Segorbe, a large inland town on the Mudéjar highway from Sagunt to Teruel. Like Aub himself, *Sierra de Teruel* barely survived the war. It was thought that all copies had been destroyed in Nazi-occupied France, but in 1945 one copy was found in a wrongly marked case.

After the Civil War defeat in March 1939, Aub was buffeted all around France. His life was in danger, not just as a Spanish exile denounced as a communist (though he wasn't), but as a Jew (his father was Jewish). Denounced anonymously in May 1940 as a "German Jew, naturalized Spaniard during the Civil War, a notorious communist and active revolutionary," he was held in Paris' Roland Garros internment camp (the tennis was suspended). Then he was sent to the Vernet concentration camp, near Pamiers in the Pyrenean foothills. Released after six months, he was denounced again, re-arrested, and transferred to Nice prison in June 1941. Released, he was again arrested in September 1941 and sent back to Vernet. Transferred in November to the Djelfa prison camp in Algeria, he was forced to labor on a railroad before release in May 1942. Then he missed the boat to Mexico assigned to him with a safe-conduct and had to hide in a nursery. Finally, in September 1942, he reached Mexico, where he lived in exile till his death. In 1945 he was reunited with Peua and their two daughters. He had survived.

CROW MANUSCRIPT

Max Aub was both a jokey character and an entirely serious witness to war and exile. In Mexican exile he wrote *Jusup Torres Campalans*, a false biography of a non-existent painter with paintings included. So good was the imposture that, it is said, David Siqueiros, the Stalinist muralist notorious for leading an attack on Trotsky's house in Mexico City, boasted: "Oh yes, I knew Campalans, but he was no good."

Aub was author, too, of surreal stories such as *Manuscrito Cuervo* (Crow Manuscript), a history of the Vernet prison camp told by a crow called Jacobo, who could of course fly over the barbed wire as the prisoners could only dream of doing.

> [One prisoner] told a guard that the night before he had dreamed he escaped. They gave him a thrashing.
> - No one gets out of here, even in dreams.[166]

His most famous short story, published in 1960 in Mexico, fifteen years before the actual biological event, was *La verdadera historia de la muerte de Francisco Franco* (The True Story of the Death of Francisco Franco). This bitter comedy (Aub wrapped up disaster with jokes) tells of a group of Spanish exiles whose shouting and ugly European pronunciation embitter the life of Ignacio, a waiter in the Café Español in downtown Mexico City. The exiles loudly proclaim their prowess in the Civil War. Obsessively, though the years pass and their hair whitens, their sentences start, "When Franco falls…" "The day we go back…"

---

166   *Manuscrito Cuervo*, p.132.

After twenty years suffering the Spanish customers who are ruining his life ("If men go deaf, it's because of them"), Ignacio decides to act. But how? Simple. He obtains a false passport and takes a vacation in Madrid. He shoots General Franco at the July 18 military parade and escapes in the chaos. He travels around Europe at leisurely speed to give the Spanish exiles time to go home. When he returns to work, to his shock and horror, he finds the Spaniards still dominating his café. They haven't gone home. They still say the same things. What's worse, still more exiles have arrived due to the repression following Franco's assassination.

As one can imagine, this sad parable of exiles' impotence, like most of Aub's work, was not published in Spain during Franco's lifetime.

His greatest literary achievement was a series of six novels, composed over thirty years, entitled *El laberinto mágico* (*The Magic Labyrinth*). Ronald Fraser explained their titles:

> The "labyrinth" was to him Spain itself. More pertinently than the generic title, each of the novels has a title beginning with the word campo, "countryside," "field," or "camp" with its ironic ambiguities: the suggestion of nature's free and open spaces; the field of battle or the enclosed prison-world of labor camps.[167]

The first two, *Campo cerrado* (Closed Field, translated as *Field of Honour*) and *Campo abierto* (Open Field) were written in

---

167   Ronald Fraser, Introduction to *Field of Honour*, p. x. The great oral historian Ronald Fraser (1930-2012) lived in Valencia for the last twenty-five years of his life.

1939 in the very first months of Aub's exile back in France after the Civil War defeat, in the passion of wanting to record what had happened. They were not completed and published, though, until 1943 and 1951, when he had reached Mexico. *Campo cerrado*'s English translation, *Field of Honour*, was not published till 2009, way too late. Such was the destiny of the exiled writers of the Civil War generation. Most were not re-integrated into Spanish literature after the dictatorship.

What shines through Max Aub's life story is his absolute commitment to literature, though he was not at all indifferent to politics. In his years in and out of French prison camps, he wrote. If he had no paper, he wrote in his head. He believed in his own writing: whenever, in Mexico, he found no publisher, he self-published. He had published before the war, but his writing expanded in scope and fluency after 1939. The story goes that at Vernet he had only one book, a Spanish dictionary. His constant reading of it increased and refined his vocabulary.

WATCHING THE ANARCHISTS

Max Aub believed in the power of literature to combat the forgetting of history's victims. He became Valencia's finest twentieth-century fiction writer—if we take the liberties of placing Blasco Ibáñez in the nineteenth century that he looked back to and Rafael Chirbes in the twenty-first.

Field of Honour shows the best and the weakest of Aub. The best lies in its masterly opening chapters, when the young Rafael leaves his mountain village, Viver de las Aguas, in the 1920s for the provincial capital, Castellón, "...a broad, flat town, with no other character than the lack of it." Aub had imbibed Valencia city's more exuberant style of color and a touch of fantasy in the adornment. For him Castellón was white-walled, unimaginative, and ordinary.

Field of Honour is rapid, full of unusual vocabulary. Aub adores the sound of words: even native speakers are irritated at times by having to resort to the dictionary. It has sharp descriptions of Rafael's family in Viver, the people of Castellón, and then 1930s Barcelona. As well as this ability to express succinctly what he sees, Aub is not scared to comment. His commentaries are often caustic:

> …the traders live for business; all of them sons of the red earth, rich by inheritance, embezzlement, or obstinacy. They know no god but their oranges.[168]

The weakest parts in novelistic terms, though very interesting politically, lie in the middle of the book, where Aub has Falangist, anarchist, Catalan nationalist, and communist characters each hold forth in lengthy conversations. It is somewhat schematic, but at Aub's frequent best, the characters spout their monologues, while the narrator balances and punctures their pretensions with terse description. Thus, Aub explores the balance between revolutionary words, so easy, and action, so difficult to get right and, if wrong, dire in its consequences.

Field of Honour is a fine, uneven novel, with an ending that matches the brilliance of its start. As the 1936 revolution erupts, events force the observer Rafael to decide which side he is on. Here the prose is again snappy and rich in imagery, dozens of characters drawn in a few phrases. Pleasurably, some of these are real historical people, such as the anarchists Durruti and Garcia Oliver or the Barcelona coup leader, General Goded. In this finale, the lonely village boy is swept into a great historical movement. Aub, though,

---

168   *Field of Honour*, p.13 (Chapter 2).

is no cheerleader for revolution. His sarcastic, skeptical mind and his way of looking sideways at events, just as Rafael leans on a Ramblas wall and watches the anarchists firing, impede any glorious ending.

Aub's range is broad: from the unheated flop-houses and heated café debates on the Parallel to discussions in the Palau de la Generalitat. He shows revolutionary Barcelona through the eyes of Rafael, an anonymous immigrant more interested in sex, bull-fighting, and his own mysterious and frightening identity, than the moments of history he is living through.

Aub was a social democrat, not a revolutionary or communist. Indeed, after the war he spent some time writing to French ministries to demand that "communist" be removed from his prison documents—successfully. Unlike many left-wing, anti-communists of the 1930s, he did not become a Cold War warrior in the 1950s. He maintained a reformist belief in social justice within a liberal capitalist state throughout his life. In his writings he was on the side of the oppressed. The richly drawn Romualda in *Campo abierto* is an example. She is enraged by injustice: "What's the reason why the children of the poor are poor and the children of the rich are born among silks? There's no God can justify this ..."[169]

A humorous book about a concentration camp like *Manuscrito Cuervo*[170] would be in extremely bad taste if the author had not been there. But he had. After all the magnificent jokes, Aub ends with sixteen pages naming, to ensure they are not forgotten, some of his unfortunate

---

169   *Campo abierto*, p.246 (Part III, Chapter II). Translation by Gareth Thomas in *The Novel of the Spanish Civil War*.
170   The full title is *Manuscrito Cuervo, Historia de Jacobo*, (Crow Manuscript, Jacob's Story). It was published in Mexico in the mid-1950s and rescued from obscurity in Spain in 2011.

fellow prisoners. Humor was a way of handling suffering. Aub uses a flat, factual prose, suitable for both jokes and serious historical record:

> There must be about 6,000 internees in the camp. Most don't know why they are here. (In this there is absolute equality between internees and guards).
>
> I list as follows the details of a few, chosen at random. To be more precise, give date and place: 22 June 1940, Vernet camp, Ariège Department. France. Platform 38, Area C.[171]

DAILY LIFE IN THE REVOLUTION

The six novels of *The Magic Labyrinth* form a choral chronicle that seeks to record, so that the victors' version should not be the only one, the stories of the defeated. Literature against fascism, to remember what had happened so that fascism's version could be rebutted in a future.

While *Field of Honour* is the story of a Valencian country boy, wide-eyed, lost, and searching in Barcelona, capital of the 1936 revolution, *Campo abierto* tells ferocious stories of the first weeks of the war. It is an even better novel. It starts with 200 pages set in the city of Valencia. Six chapters discuss the experiences of six characters, surrounded by a cast of dozens. They cover student actors, foreign revolutionaries, a tramway conductor, shopkeepers, footballers, and an "anarchist" crook.

---

171   *Ibid*, p.121.

In *Campo abierto*, as in the entire *Laberinto mágico*, there is no one-dimensional exaltation of heroism, so often the weak point of Civil War writing. This said, at the novel's climax, Aub's rapid, understated prose does achieve epic qualities, as he records a bombing, names the dead and dying, and lists the "Figaro" battalion of barbers defending Madrid on November 7, 1936, the night that its people, supported by the International Brigades, halted Franco's armies in the outer suburbs of the city.

Aub seeks to portray contradictory characters with flaws and virtues trying to find their way through a chaotic labyrinth. One can see that Aub was no revolutionary militant, for he does not believe that a correct political line can avert chaos. He does not resort to the unreality of monolithic heroes or to the caricature of reality that is propaganda. He is not a revolutionary militant, but he is a revolutionary writer—the Picasso of the Spanish novel.

Campo abierto is divided into three parts: the first in Valencia, the third in Madrid, with a brief second part in Franco's Burgos. Communists, Catholics, socialists, anarchists discuss endlessly. A socialist admires the communists for their discipline, but disagrees with their communism. A right-winger may be a decent person; a left-winger may not be. Critic Gareth Thomas wrote that: "Aub's characters engage in extensive monologues and dialogues during which his novels' action comes to a halt."[172] This does happen, but usually the sharp dialogue carries the books forward. Dialogue to reveal action and character is a strength of Aub: not for nothing was he also a playwright. His detailed descriptions are terse and vivid, like a series of notes. His is the world of ordinary workers caught up in revolution. People at war are not just defined as CNT or

---

172   Thomas, p.99.

party militants, but through their daily lives, their jobs, and commitments at home.

Campo cerrado and *Campo abierto* share their shifting scenes and fragmented style with other novels of the Civil War, influenced by the new art, cinema. His friend André Malraux's *Days of Hope* and Arturo Barea's *The Clash* come to mind. A large fresco with scenes of revolution, war and sudden death cannot be painted so sharply through conventional, sequential narrative. *Campo abierto* has some 500 characters in 400 pages, rushing on and off the page, to death, betrayal, or lucky survival. Aub, as an experimental writer in the 1930s, was particularly well placed to dominate this style.

The magnificent first section of *Campo abierto*, set in Valencia, deserves a closer look. "Gabriel Rojas, 24-7-36" tells the story of a typesetter whose wife is giving birth. He runs through the streets to find a doctor. On the way back he is shot dead by a rooftop sniper. A brutal, simple story.

The second chapter, "Vicente Dalmases," explains, in the context of a group of young actors taking over a theater, how Alfredo Meliá, an amiable socialist tram conductor, is denounced by his wife's lover as a fascist. The anarchists search Alfredo's apartment. They find a Falange card in his name. He is taken away and shot. Then it emerges that his wife and her lover have forged the card.

The third chapter, "Manuel Rivelles," features a young man in the theater company, "who in a spirit of contradiction joins the anarchist youth." He shows off by volunteering for the front. He is betrayed and killed before firing a shot against fascism. The brief chapter is integrated into a notorious real event. The CNT had insisted on Civil Guards loyal to the Republic being distributed among other militia groups, to prevent them going over to the enemy. In Manuel Rivelles' column, everyone gets out of the trucks for a final weapons inspection at La Puebla de Valverde, the last big village between Valencia and the Franco-held city of Teruel. The Civil Guards surprise the anarchists and slaughter them. In the real event, on July 29, 1936, between 250 and 400 anarchists were killed. The Civil Guards then joined the Francoists at Teruel.

Betrayal is a theme through all Aub's work. "Vicente Farnals" in Chapter 4 helps an old football friend to flee abroad. Farnals is a socialist; his friend has become a fascist. He refuses to hand over his friend to certain execution. He refuses to betray his friend, but has he betrayed the revolution by putting personal loyalty first?

In the longest chapter, "Jorge Mustieles" votes for his father's execution. His father is a hardline village boss, arrested for storing arms. To prove himself a real revolutionary, Jorge betrays him. Then his father is released. Jorge, dominated by his father, follows him to the Francoist side. There Jorge himself is executed for his revolutionary activities in Valencia.

A bitter story, made especially powerful because it is told from Jorge's point of view. Aub makes the reader understand, probably sympathize with, Jorge's mistakes and weakness.

If there is a moral anywhere, it is in "El Uruguayo," the sixth and final chapter of the Valencia section. A leader of an anarchist gang accumulates stolen cash and jewels while rounding up and killing fascists. He buys a forged passport to flee the country, dreaming of a life of idle luxury in France. He is arrested, taken for a ride, and, with a bullet in the back of the neck, dumped in the *horta* by the side of the road to Sagunto, where he had left so many others in the preceding weeks.

It is only now, through the movement to recover historical memory in Spain, the breakdown of the two-party system, and the work of his Foundation at Segorbe, that Aub is being published and evaluated in Spain. Lucid as always, Aub himself explained his fate:

> The Republican exile, above all if he is a writer, lives and works in a void, silenced in his country of origin and only half integrated in his country of adoption. We rot, we disappear.[173]

"I AWAIT DEATH WHILE SINGING"

Miguel Hernández did not survive. He was not as lucky as Max Aub. Born in 1910 in Oriola (or Orihuela), in the deep south of Alacant province, he died in prison aged thirty-one. He left school at fifteen to care for his large family's goats, but he already had the habit of reading. Soon he was writing poetry, associating with the city's young intellectuals and haunting the public library. He traveled to Madrid, where his poetry won him recognition by the great poets of the day, such as Neruda and Lorca, and the friendship of Vicente Aleixandre (the 1977 Nobel Prize winner) to whom he dedicated his 1937 book *Vientos del pueblo* (Winds of the People). He joined the Communist Party in the Civil War.

Pablo Neruda, who visited Oriola, insisted that Hernández had to get out of this city with its *tufo sotánico y satánico* ("soutanic and satanic stench"). Neruda's play on words was prescient: sixty years later the ultra-religious, rubbish magnate Ángel Fenoll would turn Oriola into a cesspit of corruption (see Chapter 10).

---

173   Aub, in a story *El remate (The Outcome)*, quoted in Kamen, p.421.

Oriola is indeed full of churches and convents. It nestles under a bare, dusty hill. Its old center is beautiful, monumental, like many of the inland towns of the *país valencià* adorned with castles: Xàtiva, Elda, Villena, Jérica, Cofrentes, Morella, as they mark the frontier between Valencia and Castile. Today many of these towns have their old Arab-based centers carefully restored. Oriola is one such. It has a series of linked squares, with ecclesiastical buildings, museums, and palaces, including a cathedral with three doors, like Valencia's, and a cloister outside the cathedral, as it (the cloister) was brought here from a destroyed church in 1942. What has changed since Neruda's time are two things: the careful polishing of stone to make the old center a tourist attraction and the presence of Miguel Hernández. Hernández is everywhere: a university campus named after him, a square, his birthplace, a school, paintings in an exhibition, posters. Oriola may have been run by the communist-hating PP for decades, but they know that a big-name poet brings tourists in.

The juxtaposition of the communist poet and the Franco-loving Church is startling. Right beside the Centro Cultural Hernández, a statue of the Virgin has a plaque:

First Centenary
of the Dogmatic Definition
of the Immaculate Conception.
1854-1954
Orihuela

If the tourist authorities think about it at all, it must be hard to build a tourist identity on the basis of two such contradictory themes: fundamentalist Christian shrines and communist poet.

The other remarkable thing about Oriola is revealed by the town's map. One side details the city with its monuments, working-class blocks, slums, and middle-class expansion. The other side shows the coast. Though Oriola is fifteen kilometers inland, like Elx it has an extension of nine kilometers of coastline, completely covered by vulgar villa developments including what thirty years ago was the wild promontory of Cap Roig. Some green remains: five eighteen-hole golf courses. Oriola-by-the-sea, just like neighboring Torrevieja, is a popular second home for north Europeans.

Miguel Hernández became well-known for reciting his poems to soldiers in the trenches. They responded to him, for he identified with them:

> I am open, look, like a wound
> I am sunk, look, I am sunk
> In the middle of my people and their ills.
> I'm wounded, wounded and evilly wounded,
> Bleeding through the trenches and hospitals.[174]

Being a goatherd-poet had opened doors for him when he arrived in Madrid in the early 1930s, but later he came to dislike the term and the paternalism it conveyed. In the chaos at the end of the war, Hernández was disoriented and ignored. He was not invited to escape with the Republic's cultural elite.[175] No longer of use in the Communist Party's propaganda, he was returned, one could say, to the status of goatherd/common soldier. He walked 300 kilometers home to his wife and son, who were living in Cox, a village near

---

174   From "Recoged esta voz" ("Hear this Voice", my translation).
175   Rafael Alberti said Hernández was invited to flee with them, but didn't want to leave.

Oriola. Warned of the danger he was in, he then fled through Andalusia and was finally arrested in Portugal by the dictator Salazar's border guards, who handed him over to the Spanish police. He was condemned to death for having been a political commissar in the communist Fifth Regiment. His sentence was commuted to life imprisonment. Little use it did him.

No indignation is too great for the treatment of Miguel Hernández and the hundreds of thousands of prisoners in damp overcrowded prisons, with little food, few washing facilities, and no medical treatment. Antony Beevor puts it starkly: "The poet Miguel Hernández suffered from pneumonia in the prison of Palencia, bronchitis in the prison of Ocaña, and typhus and tuberculosis, of which he died, in Alicante prison."[176]

When he was dying, the authorities refused to transfer him to a sanatorium. He was murdered as surely as Lorca.

Hernández's poetry is hard to separate from his desperately sad life. He was the man of the people that Republican Spain desired, the goatherd talking in the authentic tones of the poor. His eyes in the photos are large and stare intensely: none of Aub's irony and playfulness. His myth was consolidated by his terrible death.

Though the heartbreaking facts of Miguel Hernández's life are reasons why he is respected, this should not conceal the quality and weight of his poetry. He stands alongside Lorca as the great Spanish poet of his very talented generation. Why? It is not easy to put into words without cliché. He expressed the experience of the poor working the land. He spoke directly of love and death. His language and images could be easily grasped. He knew what it was to work under an implacable sun:

---

176   Beevor, p.451.

When farm-workers in the early morning
steer the plough handle stirring the quiet,
they wear a silent, golden blouse
of silent sweat.[177]

It is harsh poetry, not the lyrics of green and gentle lands,
but strong words of hard lives:

Flesh for the yoke, he was born
humiliated not handsome,
with his neck persecuted
by the yoke for the neck.[178]

He identifies with the earth in his famous lines:

Me llamo barro...
My name is earth though I'm called Miguel.
Earth is my job and my destiny,
staining with its tongue whatever it licks.[179]

Hernández is not a *naif* poet, despite his class origins
and his tough directness. Well-read in the classics, the
autodidact controls his material. His powerful lines of
war, love, and nature may appear simple, but they express
complex emotions. Direct is the word, rather than simple,
for the echo they leave in the mind is not simplistic:

I await death while singing,
for there are nightingales who sing

---

177   "El sudor" ("Sweat", my translation).
178   "El niño yuntero" ("The Ploughboy", my translation).
179   "Me llamo barro" ("My Name is Earth", my translation).

above rifles
and in the midst of battles.[180]

He compares himself to the nightingale who continues singing
despite the noises of war. While the soldier sings, he knows
that he shall die; whereas the nightingale, Keats' "immortal
bird," will carry on singing after the battle has quieted.

Hernández lived the war intensely, with death all
around him. Open-hearted, he is one of those people who
seem to lack a protective outer skin. And he lived a love
story. He wrote to his wife and son from prison. As Max
Aub's crow soars over the barbed wire, so Hernández's
family's laughter lifts him over the prison wall:

Your laughter makes me free,
It gives me wings.
It takes away my loneliness,
It tears prison off me.[181]

Paco Ibáñez, raised in Valencia in those terrible post-war
years of hunger and fear, set several of Hernández's poems to
music and made them anthems of the 1970s "transition," the
fight to defeat the dictatorship that had killed Hernández.
The best-known must be "Andaluces de Jaén," now the
official hymn of Jaén province, a song denouncing class
oppression:

Andalusians from Jaén,
proud olive-pickers…
Who, who raised the olive trees?

---

180   The last verse of "Vientos del pueblo me llevan" ("Winds
of the People Carry Me", my translation).
181   "Nanas de la cebolla" ("Onion Lullabies", my translation).

They weren't raised by nothing,
nor by cash nor the boss,
but by the silent earth
work and sweat.

Hernández is direct in his language and frank in his emotions. His words are torrential and powerful, but his verse is well-worked in order to transmit emotion, not just express it:

I wrote in the sand
Life's three names:
Life, death, love.

A sudden wave,
So often going away,
Came and rubbed them out.[182]

Aub and Hernández are such different writers: one who lived all over the world, the other who never left Spain except for a night in a Portuguese police cell; one who wrote an enormous body of work in different styles, the other, a poet of soaring emotion sunk in the Spanish earth. Aub tackled the nightmare of fascism with inventive, humorous sophistication. Hernández was the sort of writer who delves deep, very deep, in one particular patch: "We poets are wind of the people. We are born to blow through their pores and lead their eyes and feelings to more beautiful peaks."[183]

---

182   "Escribí en el arenal" ("I Wrote in the Sand", my translation).
183   Hernández, Introduction to *Vientos del pueblo, Antologia popular*, p.41.

In 2018, the Botànic government declared March 28, the day of Miguel Hernández's death in 1942, the Day of Valencian Democratic Memory, when the victims of Francoism are remembered.

16: Empty Beauty

"A kind of fairyland that history had forgot"

James A. Michener, *Iberia*[184]

M ost of the population of the Comunitat Valenciana lives on the coastal strip: 518 kilometers of coastline running back ten, fifteen, or twenty kilometers from the Mediterranean to the AP7 highway and the hills. The density of coastal population is true of the whole Mediterranean shore, whether in Algeria, Lebanon, Greece, or Spain. Villages and towns grew into cities where trade routes across the sea prospered. In today's Comunitat Valenciana, the three provincial capitals, Castelló, Valencia, and Alacant are on the coast. Most of the population and most of its tourist, agricultural, and industrial wealth are densely packed onto the coastal strip. Yet the greater part of the Comunitat's surface area is mountainous and sparsely populated. These mountains are traditionally neglected areas, though now they are valued more, at least in theory, as global warming, combined with the covering of the coast with cement, has made the coast a more humid and harsh environment in summer. Rafael Chirbes writes:

> Even in summer's hottest days, when I am in bed
> I can hear the night dew dripping from the roof
> to the pavement, especially these nights, when the
> air becomes more tropical than Mediterranean,

---

184   Michener, p.678.

> sticky nights in which you turn and toss sleepless, endless even though they are the shortest in the year.[185]

It is a good argument for the clean, fresh mountain air of the Rincón de Ademuz.

BARE ROCK

Chapter 5 discussed the Maestrat and Morella, Ramon Cabrera's mountain fortress. This chapter looks at the Rincón de Ademuz enclave (the "Ademuz Corner"), the highest and most mountainous part of the Comunitat Valenciana. In Spain there are a dozen "enclaves," sections of land that belong administratively to one province, but are totally surrounded by other provinces. The strangest of all is Llívia (in the Pyrenees), belonging to the Spanish state, but surrounded by France.

The Rincón de Ademuz is the biggest of these enclaves (at 370 square kilometers). It belongs to the Comunitat Valenciana, but is surrounded by the provinces of Cuenca and Teruel. Here no Valencian is spoken. The Moors were defeated by armies from Aragon under Pedro (Pere) II in 1210, before Jaume I's conquest. Despite its proximity to Aragon, for complex historical reasons it remained part of the Kingdom of Valencia and now of the Comunitat Valenciana.

The most spectacular way to approach this remotest county of the Valencian Community is from the capital. Large yellow signs in the city announce ADEMUZ and if you follow these, you drive easily along the Ademuz road the thirty kilometers to Llíria, but after Llíria you enter a

---

185   Chirbes, *En la orilla*, p.378.

winding mountain road that is little changed from Franco times. There are no *quitamiedos* (fear-removers), the term for fencing between the road and fear-filling drops to deep gorges where the River Túria trickles or rages, depending on the season and its proximity to a reservoir. Finally, the car limps into Casas Bajas, the first village in the Rincón. A trip of fifty kilometers has taken two hours.

This route from the capital shows how isolated the Rincón was, but few drive this way anymore. Now you can drive from Valencia along the A3 highway to Madrid, past Bunyol and Requena and turn off toward Landete at Utiel. This is wine country and the tranquil road rolls through row on row of low-cut vines. Occasional *bodegas*, looking more like mansions than industrial enterprises, illustrate the wealth in wine. They say of Utiel it is a "hollow" city because of all the underground wine cellars.

This newer route leaves Valencia province after Sinarcas for the province of Cuenca and enters Valencia again—now, the Rincón de Ademuz—after Landete. The road begins a descent through a deep cutting, bare rugged rock on either side. Brown cliffs rise to the right, with pines that cling to the cliff wherever it is less than vertical. Their roots seem to penetrate the rock itself and their trunks to defy gravity. To the left, the town of Ademuz on its hillside comes into view, a pattern of brown and white dots up to the great table mountain that overlooks it (not unlike the slab of rock that dominates and protects Morella). The first glimpse inspires doubt. The buildings seem to grow out of the rock: are they really houses or are they just rock formations? The second impression finds it primitive and ancient. It could be a town in the Atlas or a carless medieval village.

All the hills here are flat-topped: soft, conglomerated rocks. James G. Ballard, analyst of Spain among his more famous qualities, said in a 1995 talk: "Spain is a dramatic landscape, arid, very elemental, as if created by the central nervous system, something that the English landscape of meadows and rolling hills isn't."[186] Here you can see and feel that landscape of bare rock, near to the nerves and undisguised by green fields. Mountains are sheer and naked, not rolling, and dressed in green.

Down the sunken spine of the Rincón, between the cliffs, runs the River Ebrón, which joins the Turia (the river that fails to reach the sea in Valencia city) at Torrebaja. There are seven villages along the river valley: El Cuervo (in Aragon), Castielfabib, Los Santos, Torrebaja, Ademuz, Casas Altas, and Casas Bajas. A fertile plain between the brown or red cliffs, narrow at Castielfabib and opening out at Torrebaja and Ademuz, accompanies the river. The green of the valley highlights the ferocity of naked rock and the stony harshness of the land away from the river. Vultures and eagles glide overhead.

In his epic *Iberia* (1969), the American James A. Michener (1907–97) tells how, traveling to Teruel from Cuenca by car in the late 1960s, he got lost one autumn afternoon. He found himself in a desolate, stony landscape. Then he spotted "a high solitary peak on whose top perched a little town." The road took him through a tunnel under the village, which led him to a glimpse of a beautiful, fruit-filled valley, where "a bubbling river was coaxed into irrigation ditches." Looking up, he saw on the seemingly unscalable rock "a remarkable church whose slab-sided, unbroken walls dropped from a great height precipitously into deep gullies."

On the main square, Michener found the village's only bar (now the Bar Martínez). The friendly, energetic woman

---

186   My notes from Ballard's talk at the British Institute, Barcelona, April 1995.

who irrupted into the bar dispelled the sad first impression caused by the village's poor housing, lack of inhabitants, and empty bar run by a man of few words. She dispatched the quiet man, her husband, to fetch a folder of photos from a neighbor. With the same vitality as her mother, her ten-year-old daughter (now Rosita, the proprietor) took Michener up to the roof and from there he looked down on the valley enclosed between vertical cliffs:

> Lush fields of wheat and corn glistened in the sunlight, forming a golden checkerboard in which the darker squares were fields of apple trees and pear and apricot and cherry, with here and there areas of low-growing grapevines.[187]

Michener reflected that in a country known for its *machismo* it was the women who were in charge. He writes of Rosita's mother: "a woman of enormous vitality…Like many Spanish women in their late thirties, she was dressed in black, but her face was so animated that she made the dark clothes seem a party dress."[188]

Michener was in Castielfabib, the jewel of the Rincón. The bare rock serves as foundations and walls of houses that hang over cliffs. Its twisting streets are more daunting and steeper than the alleys on the rock of Peníscola. Most of Castielfabib's population is elderly and it is not a place old people can easily move around. If it were in France or Tuscany, it would be a town with polished wooden beams and restored cobblestones, full of guesthouses, restaurants, and gift shops. As it is, it has escaped that fate, the fate of Altea or Peníscola.

---

187   *Ibid*, p.681.
188   *Ibid*, p.680.

If you're fit, visit Castielfabib in Easter week and follow the Via Crucis through the town. In 2017 some eighty people followed the wooden cross, the drummer, and the Virgin borne on her float through the thirteen stations, all struggling up and down the streets. These are so steep that some houses seem improbable, with entries on different floors, vertical drops, and sudden views.

On Easter Saturday, in a more pagan rite of spring, young men chop down two poplars, carry them up to the main square, peel off the bark, cover them with grease, dig holes to plant them, and haul them upright with ropes. On top is a pine branch and the young men compete in trying to climb the tree trunks. On Easter Sunday morning the most original feature of the village's Holy Week celebrations takes place. It does not occur every year. If there is a young man prepared to do it, he clings onto the church's great bell, called Guillermina, at the top of the tower and hangs on for his life as the bell turns right over and around and around as it is rung, the clanger striking the cast bronze beneath him. If in fright he raised his head he would be killed by the bell's thick beam. If he loosens his grip he would fall the sixty feet from the bell tower. The neighbors boast that there have been no casualties in the several centuries of the ceremony. "More people fling themselves off the cliffs," an old woman told me cryptically. Evidently the bell ceremony was common in the Middle Ages, but no one has clarified its connection to Easter religious ceremonies.

The bell tower is part of the old church-fortress of Castielfabib (originally the Moorish castle, Castell-al-fabib), now partially restored. It is a special monument, because it is clearly both a church and a fortress and because of its position. Walk through the tunnel leading to the church entrance and look out from the balcony of bare rock beyond. You can see how the fortress dominates upstream

Castielfabib's church-fortress dominating the gorge

and downstream the fertile lands of the Ebrón gorge. The bare cliffs where vultures nest frame the kitchen gardens and the apple and plum orchards of the gorge. The light at dusk in this unpolluted spot brings all the rocks in the dying sun into sharp relief.

LAND OF EMIGRATION

The Ebrón/Turia valley's orchards are home to very special apples: the *espériega*, which looks inside as if it has been frozen or crystallized, *reineta*, *miguela*, *garcía*, *ricarda*, and *normanda*, all sought after in past times in the markets of Barcelona and Madrid. In a 1955 census, 73,761 apple trees were counted in the Rincón. In the spring their white blossom floods the river valley. The writer Francisco Candel smelled in autumn 1964 a tang of apple hanging over the town of Torrebaja and watched mules loaded high with boxes carrying apples from the trees to the warehouses.

The Rincón's apples are now returning to fashion, as they have the fresh taste of mountain air, defying the blandness of supermarkets' mass-produced, fluffy-fleshed fruit. They are crunchy apples, throwing a sharp juice around your mouth as you bite them.

Castielfabib's fortress-church is not the only reminder of the Rincón's Moorish past. The narrow streets of both Castiel and Ademuz twisting up and down hills follow their original Moorish layout. Their houses perch cunningly in unorthodox spaces and shapes. In Ademuz, too, there is a hermitage, now part of a school playground, with writing over the door in Hebrew. Part of this mistreated building dates back to fourteenth-century Gothic: "mistreated" because, while it awaits funding for restoration, modern graffiti compete with the Hebrew inscription.

Nowadays nearly all the shops in Ademuz, the Rincón's capital and by far its biggest town with some 1,100 inhabitants, are on the main road parallel to the *vega*, the river's green valley. From the hermitage a narrow road climbs the steep hill. This was the Royal Road from Aragon, now fully built-up. Here you can still see ancient houses constructed by flat slabs of stone set vertically on top of each other and held in place by plaster. It seems impossible, but the plaster, originally fixed by wooden frames, sets so firmly and rapidly that the walls of vertical slabs like coins standing on end stay in place for centuries.

At the top you come to the great church, with startling cracks. People say they date back to the earthquake of 1656, but they look wide, recent, and dangerous to a lay eye. Until 2017, the church had a large plaque commemorating the Civil

Apple trees and Ademuz

War dead on the Franco side, with the Roman fasces. These remnants of the Franco dictatorship on Church property are common in conservative, rural Spain, and in some cities, too. Cuenca still boasts a cross on its cathedral commemorating the founder of the Spanish Falange, José Antonio.

The huge church and the square in front of it are not the center of the town that they appear to be. In fact a nearby gate, the only remaining gate in the old city wall, leads into the original town, with a number of wealthy houses and the very pretty town hall square of wooden balconies and flowers.

One might think that the villages so close together, the Turia valley's apples and pears and Ademuz's big houses mean that the Rincón is wealthy. Michener saw the abundant fruit trees and thought so. But the reverse is true. Clearly some landowners or shopkeepers lived well, but this has been a land of emigration, of the poor leaving the land to fill Spain's big cities, a phenomenon of the twentieth century throughout the Spanish state. It was particularly accelerated under the Franco regime.

The Rincón is a depopulated area. Emigration, mainly to Barcelona and Tarragona, but also to Valencia city and Sagunt, have left it now with only some 2,700 permanent residents, and most of these elderly. This triples or quadruples at Easter and in August, as emigrants return for their vacations. They kept their village houses when they left, for there were no buyers. The population of the Rincón reached a peak in the census of 1920, with 11,194 inhabitants. The biggest drop occurred from 1950 (9,362 inhabitants) to 1981 (3,866).[189]

The move from country to city is part of a tendency all over Spain, indeed all over the world. Industrialization meant better wages, or wages, when the pre-war Rincón subsisted on a mainly barter economy. In the city you wash clothes in a machine not a stream. There is electric light and running water. In the country there is now light through cables and water piped to taps, but this was not the case sixty years ago when emigration was at its peak.

In recent years such depopulation has led to the foundation of the Serranía Celtibérica Association, which has delineated an area of the Spanish central highlands covering some 65,000 square kilometers (twice the size of Belgium) that includes the Rincón. It claims to be the least populated area in Europe, with eight inhabitants per square kilometer, fewer than in Lapland. The Association's aim is to demand assistance in repopulation from the EU, with investments such as those made in Lapland. This area of the Spanish state is worse off than Lapland, where there are

---

189   Rodrigo Alonso, p.54.

many young people; in Celtiberia most of the population is over sixty-five. The birth of a child is as rare as the sighting of a wolf. Here in hundreds of villages at risk of extinction, the few old people sit around and wonder out loud, "which of us will be the last one?"

The EU defines as "remote" any place more than forty-five minutes by car from the services of a city, and by that criterion 76 percent of the Serranía Celtibérica is remote. It contains only three cities with over 25,000 people: the provincial capitals Teruel, Soria, and Cuenca.

Of course, these are high-mountain areas, cold and infertile, with few resources: that is why their populations migrated. I sought out Concha Tormo, president of the Serranía Celtibérica Association, to tell me what can be done to reverse the declining population. She lives in a beautiful, small house overlooking the ravine in Arroyo Cerezo, a village belonging to Castielfabib. Arroyo Cerezo at 1,320 meters (almost the height of Ben Nevis, Britain's highest mountain at 1,345 meters) is the highest village in the Rincón. "I can't see what can be done to save these dying villages," I told her. Concha answered indignantly:

> Of course there are solutions. The problem is, there's no political will to reverse depopulation. The most important task is to create "dignified" work to retain the few young people who remain and attract new inhabitants. I'll give you an example. What "resources" do we have in rural areas? Elderly people. And what don't we have? Young people. If sheltered housing was created for old people who are alone but can look after themselves, skilled work would be created and the elderly wouldn't have to abandon their villages to go and live with their children in the city.

That's just one example. Overall, communications have to be improved, especially internet. Tax reductions for entrepreneurs and micro-companies are needed. We have to give value to the natural resources of rural areas. For example, in the mountains redcurrants, blackcurrants, or gooseberries can be grown easily. If no value is given to the rural world, depopulation will never be stopped, as rural has always been a synonym of yokel.

I could go on. Up here we have primitive cave paintings, but nothing's done to protect them. People will pay to see reproductions in a city museum, but they aren't shown where the original ones are.

Concha has plenty of viable ideas. Yet there is no political will. Who wins seats in the Valencian Parliament with the votes of the 2,700 inhabitants of the Rincón?

No Young Women

A large number (twenty-one at the latest count) of *parcs naturals* (nature parks), with a level of ecological protection, have been created in the Comunitat Valenciana. Several of these are on the coast, such as the Albufera lagoon, the Santa Pola salt pans or the Serra d'Irta at Peníscola, but most are in the hills, where coastal dwellers who can afford it flee the humid coastal summer. The level of protection is not high and a park has often been designated after the horse has bolted: for example, the Serra Gelada Park includes the city of Benidorm. Yet even this park serves its purpose: protection of the city's surrounds makes it more attractive to visitors.

The parks are not designed with an ecological intention, but to serve as state-subsidized pleasure areas for the clients of hotels and nearby residential estates. Nevertheless, they do have some ecological impact. In the Rincón de Ademuz, there is one such park.

The Ebrón-Turia river valley drops from some 1,000 to 700 meters within the Rincón. It is surrounded by still higher country, a rough mountainous landscape. Four of the six highest mountains in the Comunitat Valenciana are here, including the highest, the Cerro Calderón at 1,839 meters. The Calderón is the central feature of the nature park of Puebla de San Miguel, a compact, red-roofed village at 1,100 meters' height, a hair-raising drive of seventeen kilometers from Ademuz. The Puebla suffers from the same depopulation as the rest of the Rincón, but the new (since 2007) nature park offices bring some life to the village. Even so, the only bar has closed. No one can earn a living here except the park employees and the forest ranger brigades, public employees who clean the mountains and fight fires. To date, despite the dry summers and the spread of the processionary caterpillar that attacks pine trees, turning their green needles brown and leaving them more vulnerable to disease, there has been no major forest fire in the Rincón. Outdoor barbecues and smoking are strictly forbidden.

The writer Francisco Candel and two friends walked into Puebla de San Miguel in 1964, when its population was still 250 and not the forty of today. He found a village buried deep in poverty and ignorance: "Sad atmosphere. People evasive. It's one of the villages we've encountered that arouses the most pity."[190] Enormous yellow squashes for pig food were piled before the doors. Kids playing in

---

190   Candel, p.125.

the streets ran away on spotting the strangers. It was an extremely isolated village, four hours walk from Ademuz and connected only by a difficult track to the other side of the mountains toward Valencia city. Candel emphasizes its poverty. People may write of the mountains' lyrical beauty, but who can live there? The priest tells him there are no young women. They have gone as servants to the city: no wages for these girls, but food and lodging and a mouth less to feed in the village. There are thirty or forty young men aged twenty-five or thirty. They have no entertainment: they are thinking only of leaving. "They're demoralized," the priest says. Emigration is not just an economic question, but also one of quality of life. The eighty-year-old Aurelio told me in Arroyo Cerezo twenty-five years ago: "Myself, I liked it in the village. I preferred working on the land to working in a Barcelona factory. But there was no future for our children here."

Candel finds an inn. In every village there was an inn, for the tinkers and salesmen, traveling by mule to sell pots, cooking oil, leather goods, baskets, or anything not produced in the village. Candel writes a brilliant paragraph on the innkeeper:

> She is a poem. Fat, foul-mouthed. She had her husband under her thumb, a shrunken, feeble man who didn't open his mouth the whole time. She doesn't stop shouting at her two daughters. She has a strange sort of snort and spits on the floor...With her foot—she wears espadrilles— she scrubs the spittle into the floor. She does this continually while we are having supper.[191]

---

191   *Ibid*, p.130.

Candel is an excellent source on how the Rincón was, just over fifty years ago, well within living memory. Villages without electricity or running water. Sadness in the air because people were living through a change—emigration, depopulation—that was destroying an impoverished, but stable way of life. Here is more of his description of the inn, where the three travelers sleep in one long room with rows of beds.

> At the end is the toilet. It's a bench with a hole, a hole that emerges in the stables. When you sit on it and evacuate your bowels, you feel you're bombarding some strange more or less military target from a great height. At the same time it's like a chimney that draws well and from time to time powerful currents of air freeze your bottom. The large room containing the toilet is also a granary, as there are sacks of maize and other cereals.[192]

The straw in the stables, human and animal excrement mixed, would be shovelled out every now and again into outdoor piles to ferment before being spread on the fields as rich manure. Fertilizer didn't come in plastic bags.

Today, the only possibility of survival in these remote villages is by combinations, *multi-trabajo*, "several jobs": a small pension perhaps plus some land to cultivate, some sheep and chickens, bees, perhaps a rural bed-and-breakfast if you have the money to do up your house. There is a ring of fields around Puebla de San Miguel, but the people who work this land are nearly all pensioners. Eighty year-olds driving tractors is a common sight. In ten or twenty years, they will be dead. And the village?

---

192 *Ibid*, p.132.

The people there love it. This is high-mountain health and tranquillity. In the village there are several beautiful houses. They have been restored with love and care, the great wooden *sabina* (savin: *Juniperus sabina*) beams treated and stained bright brown, the stone facades cleaned and repointed. But hardly anyone lives there: these are houses of emigrants' children or grandchildren who now spend vacations in the village. Maybe they come most weekends if Valencia city was the destination of their emigration. There are incomers, too, people fleeing the cities, but again they face the same problems of survival.

Of course, the *multi-trabajo* is no different from most jobs in the cities nowadays. In Spain in 2008 at the start of the economic crisis, people complained indignantly that they were *mileuristas*: people earning as little as 1,000 euros a month. Now young people aspire to be *mileuristas*. They are nearly all on short-term contracts, too, so cannot plan to buy a house or have children. But will they move to a village: better climate, better health, cheaper accommodation, less stress? Unlikely. There are no bars, no shops, only intermittent internet under the shadows of the mountains. No bustle and no "life." As yet, people have not been able to break with the powerful pull of consumerism. The "dignified" jobs Concha talks of barely exist.

Puebla de San Miguel, the beautiful yet doomed village, lies in a bowl. Circling it are the fields where cereals—corn, barley, rye, or oats—are grown. In a second ring, beginning to ascend the mountains, are *carrascas* (holm oaks); a third ring, higher still, consists of *sabinas*, now protected by law. As well as scattered specimens, there are two large forests of *sabinas* in the park. These very special trees are gnarled, scarred, and misshapen. The cracked bark is coated with moss and lichens, sign of the health of this high-mountain air. They are not tall trees like poplars or thick-spreading like walnuts or English oaks, but squat with wide trunks. Some need half a dozen people with arms outstretched and holding hands to embrace them.

Some of these special, slow-growing trees are 900 years old: the park staff know because they drill into the center and count the rings. Many trees are hollow and provide homes for owls and squirrels. Or bees: a skilled apiarist will hear the buzz and lure out the swarm to his/her hive.

For many years I have had a chunk of reddish *sabina* wood on a shelf in a room. Still, each time I open the door, I can smell its aroma, something like sandalwood. The other day, someone was cutting an old beam for firewood in a garage some fifty meters away. The fierce smell dominated the air. *Sabina* logs burn long and slow, throwing out their scent from a winter night's fire. Their wood is so hard and strong that most of the roofs of the Rincón's houses are supported by *sabina* beams, which are almost immune to woodworm.

Harsh Beauty

On the other side of the Rincón from Puebla de San Miguel, we return to Arroyo Cerezo, the most distant village from Valencia city in Valencia province. Though remote, Arroyo Cerezo is only a few kilometers off the main Cuenca-Teruel road. Today there are only eight permanent residents, mostly over seventy and only one under fifty. As in Puebla de San Miguel, at vacation times the population swells. At the annual open-air supper in the church square in mid-August, over a hundred people sit down to eat at long tables on the pews carried out from the church.

The village is not beautiful, but it is open. It does not squat at the bottom of a narrow, steep valley, like villages in the Pyrenees where the sun in winter barely reaches down.

Arroyo has long views that rest your eyes across the cereal fields to the hills and distant mountains. If you like space, solitude and walking, it is a great place.

Arroyo Cerezo (it translates as Cherry Tree Gulch) has a particular style of architecture, with thick stone walls that keep out the heat in summer and exclude the extreme cold in winter. Houses are low, like the trees and bushes beaten by the wind. Traditionally the ground floor was for animals: mules, horses, donkeys, among which in the straw the family did their necessities, with above a floor for living, warmed through the snowy winters by the animals—a kind of underfloor central heating.

The low, traditional houses have deep south-facing porches, for even in mid-January, though it may freeze at night and the wind howl like a tortured bear, at midday the temperature can rise to over 68°F (20°C) and you can eat lunch in your porch in short sleeves.

The flattish, high country is split by deep ravines. This is where the high plain of central Spain clashed in prehistoric times with the Mediterranean coast. At Arroyo a coral reef visible on one side of the main ravine (the one that flows seawards from Concha's house) and frequent fossils of oysters and sea urchins show the marine origins of the high mountains.

You can climb the hill to the Cruz de los Tres Reinos (Cross of the Three Kingdoms), at 1,555 meters the fifth highest peak in Valencia. There is no cross, just a white concrete survey point marker; and no real peak, just a slightly rising slope. The three kingdoms were Castile, Aragon, and Valencia and it is said that the three kings could meet here, each seated in his own territory. The walk up to the Cross from Arroyo is best attempted in summer, when poplars and walnut trees shade the path beside the stream. Cracked limestone cliffs point at the sky like irregular teeth. The effects of emigration and mechanization are evident on this track. The old paths have been widened for tractors; the dry-stone walls are nearly all fallen. The ancient skills of anonymous wall-builders are seen in the walls that remain standing. The many-sized stones selected fit together sweetly without cement. Now, the boundaries between the small plots of wheat or barley are covered with thistle and bramble. Cultivated plots, in past generations at barely accessible points, have given way to the occasional flock of sheep and goats. Fallen branches sprawl untidily. Sixty years ago, when the village had a population of 300, every last bit of firewood was collected and every path and boundary line between fields scythed neatly. Now, everywhere, the land wears an air of abandonment.

We walk across the flat mountain top among colonies of repopulated pines (easier to repopulate than people) and bushes of spiky gorse, wild roses, lavender, and thyme. Everywhere shrubs of savory (used in earlier times to flavor the village's cherries) release a strong fragrance as you brush through them. These are all low-lying bushes, twisted by the capricious action of the winds. In their beauty the mountains are harsh lands, quite unlike the coast's fruitful, warm plenty. Up here, there are no soft leaves for wiping a baby's bottom: bring tissues, but take them away again. The unpopulated hills need people, but no litter.

Or instead of climbing, you can walk through the flat country, bordering the ravines. May is the best month. The thyme bushes are in flower, pinkish stamens on white flowers. Red poppies, blue flax on slim stalks, snapdragons, rosemary, and dozens of flowers whose names I do not know surround the paths. If you step off the path, the cliché of a "carpet of flowers" is literal. Bluish rye and barley with plumes grow in the cultivated fields. Every way you look, gorse's flowers turn the ugly, spiky bush into a yellow flag.

Trees bend close to the ground, scourged by winter winds. These trees are savins, ash, or junipers, whose black berries flavor stews as well as gin.

You can see the flash of white that marks the ski slope of Valdelinares some fifty kilometers away. As you walk, small brown grasshoppers leap away, a flash of blue under their wings. And if you look close, you see wild-boar and deer droppings and the ground full of holes. Ants pile discarded husks around their nests and their chain gangs patter out and back hauling giant pieces of food. Some round holes in the ground belong to spiders. You can sometimes spot the shine of the spider's still eye watching from the bottom of its hole. If you poke with a stick, the black, hairy spider will often jump out vertically. A game to give friendly frights to children and visitors peering closely.

The Rincón de Ademuz is a land of harsh beauty. The corn does not grow tall. Most of its people had to leave.

17: Valencia's Market Garden and Great Lake

"Orange blossom, like sweet-smelling snow, covered the gardens and sprinkled its perfume through the narrow streets of the city"

Vicente Blasco Ibáñez, *Entre naranjos*

HORTA AND CENTRAL MARKET

The Mercat Central, Central Market, in Valencia city lays claim to being Europe's largest food market. Like the Boqueria in Barcelona, it is both a tourist attraction and where local people do their shopping. The colors and range of vegetables and fruits piled high on some 300 stalls bring home visually the richness and size of Valencia's *horta*, the basis, over ten centuries, of the city's wealth. This huge market garden around Valencia city extends roughly from the River Xúquer to the south to the hills behind Sagunt in the north.

Three points to make about the *horta*. In both Valencia city-dwellers' and outsiders' imagination, the *horta* is a cornucopia of extravagant fertility. The tiles in the Estació del Nord (Chapter 7) feed this vision. The *horta* is imagined to reflect the loud, exaggerated festivals and fanciful architecture of the country.

This is myth. It is true that the water from the many rivers racing off the mountains to the coast is channeled carefully to every plot through a series of gates and ditches and the sunny climate means that more than one crop a year can be cultivated. The *horta*, though, is not a wild, jungle-like place where anything grows. Many places around the Mediterranean are as fertile. In Valencia, decades and centuries of hard work have composted the land. There are few trees: the mulberries of previous centuries along the paths have ceded to oranges. Joan Mira describes the *horta* like this:

> A carefully drawn landscape, regular, squared, with such flat surfaces they look as if they have been smoothed out with a spatula. A landscape much easier to understand if, instead of imagining it in terms of the baroque and exuberant, we conceive it in terms of rational practice and productivity.[193]

It is a different kind of beauty. It is true that one may find startling, exuberant houses in the *horta*, reflecting the fantasy of some farmer and reminding the wanderer on foot or by car that wealth has come from here, out of the ground. Hard work and maximum exploitation of the land are the essential factors, though. It is another view of Valencians. Farmers do not live idly in a benevolent climate, but have worked hard, and still do, for prosperity.

Secondly, the *horta* is suffering and is no longer sustainable. Prior to mechanization, animal and human excrement was left in piles to ferment before being spread on the land. Now, fertilizers are chemical. Exploitation of the land requires respect for it: a balance in the soil that chemical fertilizers destroy. Add to this the increased use of herbicides and pesticides and the *horta* is being poisoned. Evidence of use of chemicals to boost production is that the towns of the *horta* and Valencia city itself are constantly swallowing agricultural land, yet the *horta*'s production remains the same.

---

193   Mira, p.159.

The movement Per l'Horta calculates that in the last fifty years 70 percent of the *horta* has been lost to roads, housing and industrial estates. Even so, it is a strange step back in time to drive out north beyond the city ring-road and enter narrow lanes to small villages among fields of tiger-nut plants and orange groves irrigated by ancient water channels. Look back and you can still see the tower-blocks of Valencia's outer suburbs. However, abandoned smallholdings and the detritus of the modern world puncture quickly any dream of a rural idyll.[194]

The difficulty of being able to make a living out of the land nowadays, with supermarkets driving down prices, has led to many uncultivated plots. The Botànic government passed protective legislation in February 2018 to encourage the renting of abandoned plots and the reform into housing of empty industrial premises. It is too soon to know if this will be effective.

Chemical fertilizers' effects are also seen—or not seen by the human eye—in the leaching of pollution into the Albufera and the extremely high concentration of glyphosate in Valencia city's drinking water. Not just the *horta* is being poisoned, but its and the city's residents.

Water is the third factor. The water that feeds Valencia and its *horta* has always poured down the Xúquer and Túria rivers from the Cuenca mountain ranges, where Atlantic storms from the west deposit their rain. The sources of these two rivers and the Tagus (Tajo) that runs the other way, to Lisbon, are very close. In 2017, in a sign of things to come, the Tagus was at a historic low and the Cabriel (a lesser river from the same range) was dry for the first time in living

---

194   Chapter 11 of Jason Webster's *A Body in Barcelona* catches very well both the attractive beauty and the decadence of the *horta* today.

memory. The canal that transfers water from the Tagus to the Segura can no longer guarantee water to the southern part of Alacant and Murcia.

Nevertheless, one would not imagine such problems at the Mercat Central, whose color, noise, and bustle is unequalled anywhere in the Valencia morning. Its fruit and vegetables are seductive in their colors and quantities for any northerner, reduced to buying in supermarkets or an occasional lingering fruit shop among the High Street's charity outlets. There are still vendors selling just one product: potatoes, spices, or offal (here you can find out what sheep's lungs look like) or sacks of snails (common in paella).

Central Market

There has been a market since medieval times on this noble site, right opposite the Silk Exchange. Photos show that it used to be a higgledy-piggledy jumble of canvas-covered stalls at the mercy of the weather. The market was the childhood playground and education of Vicente Blasco Ibáñez, who was brought up in his parents' flat above their grocery shop in a neighboring street. His parents' rise from impoverished immigrants from Aragon to prosperous shopkeepers was the backbone of his first Valencian novel, *Arroz y tartana* (1894). In a famous passage he recalled the market's vitality:

> …with its open-air stalls, their ancient awnings that trembled in the least breath of wind, bathed by a red sun of sweetened transparency, the shouting of the stall-holders, the blue cloudless sky, the excess of light that toasted everything to gold, from the walls of the *Lonja* to the huge baskets of the vegetable sellers, and its vapor of trampled vegetables and fruit prematurely ripened by the always-warm temperature.[195]

The market was the "belly and lungs" of the city, where people met, had a drink, struck deals, offered and found jobs, as well as buying and selling food and, in the surrounding streets, all kinds of merchandise. The square was also more sinister. For centuries it was a place of execution. It was here that the parents of Joan Lluís Vives, along with so many other victims of the Inquisition, were burned. A recent plaque by an LGTB collective commemorates Margarida Borràs, executed in 1460. Another plaque recalls a happier, though short-lived, fire: in 1937 the *falles* of the Market Square proclaimed Freedom.

---

195   Blasco Ibáñez, *Arroz y tartana*, Chapter 1.

The present light-filled building dates from the 1920s. Mosaics and colored glass adorn the outside. Built like the railway station and the Colom market in an *art nouveau* style, its wrought-iron structure, ceramics, glass, and brick make it worth looking upwards if you can tear your eyes from the raw food. Its height allows the light to pour in through the glass. There used to be some 900 stalls, low marble slabs separated by iron railings, but now the passages are wider and the stalls have been combined into today's 300, mostly new, spotlessly clean and brightly lit. No trampled vegetables or rotting fruit.

Despite tradition and their beauty, markets in Spain are in decline, losing the fight against supermarket dominance: the Valencian chain Mercadona is discussed below. Some, like the Colom market in Valencia, have already closed. The Colom has been converted to an upmarket mall of bars and restaurants with the occasional fancy fruit stall. At least the beautiful building has been conserved (see Chapter 10).

Nonetheless, most neighborhoods and all towns still have their markets, where you can buy all the fresh ingredients from the sea or *horta*. What do you do with fresh food? You cook it. It takes more time than the pre-prepared meals heated in the microwave. But you will get your time back, as you're likely to live fitter for longer.

PAELLA

Paella is Valencia's best-known dish. Not just Valencia's: in the last fifty years it has become Spain's most representative cooked food. Like tagine or casserole, "paella" is both the food and the utensil that the food is cooked in. The paella utensil is a wide, round, shallow-sided metal pan.

Earlier chapters have commented on the marshy land and lagoons all along the near-tideless shore. The Albufera lake, just south of the city, is the most extensive such area on Spain's Mediterranean coast. In the wetlands around the Albufera, especially on its southern side, toward Sueca, rice is cultivated. It is rice that is the basis of paella.

There is as much paella mystique as there is around wines. You hear people protest that "this is not a proper paella" because fish is combined with chicken or because the dish lacks or contains snails. The basic dish has no mystery: you fry vegetables and meat and then you add water (or stock: rice cooked in rich stock will improve a paella) and rice, cooking the rice in the fried contents, i.e., you don't cook the rice apart then add it.

There may not be a proper paella, but there is certainly an improper one. Colman Andrews found this monster: "I have a recipe, clipped from a Los Angeles newspaper a few years back, for a 'paella' made with leftover turkey, canned chopped clams, sliced pepperoni, and Spanish rice mix—in a microwave!"[196]

Back to Valencia, here's Jason Webster's description of one:

> Cámara looked down at the dark yellow mixture of rice, chicken, rabbit, and green beans and was pleased to see there were plenty of specks of brown socarraet in there as well—the crispy, gooey bits from the bottom of the paella dish where the rice was more toasted, and the flavours more concentrated …
>
> The first mouthful was delicious: enough oil as a vehicle for the myriad tastes, but the rice was still a little chalky and not overdone. Paella, he often thought, was best regarded as a combination of pan-frying and boiling: both were needed to create this unique dish.[197]

---

196   *Catalan Cuisine*, p.211.
197   Webster, *A Death in Valencia*, p. 117.

Paella's origins lie in the big, open dish cooked by laborers on a wood fire during the rice harvest, most probably using eels that used to be common around the Albufera. The round, flat pan lends itself to communal eating. Even today you cannot find a paella for one person in any half-decent restaurant.

A paella is as easy to cook as a fried egg, but like any simple food it needs skill and practice to get it just right. The wide metal pan has to be level, with the heat evenly spread. The rice has to be cooked in just enough water (or stock), so that it comes out neither too mushy (overcooked) nor hard. When the rice has absorbed nearly all the liquid, the pan is taken off the heat and left to stand for a few minutes. A gourmet touch is to burn lightly the bottom of the pan, forming a crust that has to be scraped off, the *socarraet* that Max Cámara refers to above.

You can put what you like into a paella, but the characteristic Valencia paella today uses green beans, *garrofons* (large white beans), and sometimes artichokes, rosemary, and saffron to flavor and color, and chicken and rabbit. Curiously, given the long Mediterranean coast, there is no fish or shellfish in the standard Valencian paella. In other parts of the Spanish state (Catalonia, for example), seafood is a basic ingredient. Saffron, too, is unlikely outside upscale restaurants. Artificial coloring is used, as saffron costs 3,000 euros per kilogram, for the petals are tiny and need long patient labor to pick and separate.

If you are going to eat paella as a main course, you can find it advertised in most Valencian restaurants, but you need to wait twenty minutes or half-an-hour. Beware instant paellas. Forswear take-away paellas. It should be cooked to order and served straight from the bubbling pan. It is a midday meal, too, designed for long family or friendly lunches. The problem for many of us northerners unfamiliar with small breakfasts and suppers is that the big, long lunch sends us to sleep. That is where lengthy after-lunch conversation fuelled by coffee, the *sobremesa*, comes into play. If not, if you are dull or in dull company, you submit to a siesta on a sticky afternoon, then stay up late and enjoy the cooler evening.

Another option is a great pleasure. Visit Valencia in winter and sit out for the paella on the Malva-rosa beach or at one of the restaurants on the "island" of El Palmar, on the ten-kilometer spit called La Dehesa, sand dunes anchored by pine forest between the sea and the Albufera. To spend December in Valencia is to cheat winter. Then walk off the full lunch through the trees and sand.

VENETIAN MIRROR

El Palmar is a very special village. It used to make its living from the lake's produce (duck, eels, fish) and now survives from paella restaurants (some twenty-five) and tourist trips by boat around the polluted lake. Here, Blasco Ibáñez set his last Valencian novel, *Cañas y barro* (Reeds and Mud). This is, if possible, an even more ferocious tale than *La barraca*, discussed in Chapter 13. The reeds and mud of the title are the building materials of the *barraques* (cabins) of El Palmar. They are also the habitat of those who live around the lake, who, in the rice fields, "work all day with mud and water to their waists, their legs chewed by leeches and back toasted in the sun."[198] The cabins were black with lung-destroying smoke from the cooking fire. Everyone shuddered with malaria. On the mail-boat carrying passengers with which Blasco opens his novel,

---

198   Blasco Ibáñez, *Cañas y barro*, p.32.

An insupportable stench rose from the boat. Its boards were impregnated with the odor of the baskets of eels and the dirtiness of hundreds of passengers: a sickening mixture of slimy skin, scales of fish bred in mud, dirty feet and clothes whose grime had polished and shined the seats of the boat.[199]

It is understandable that today's residents of El Palmar are not too enamored of the novel. In his Valencian novels Blasco Ibáñez, in the tradition of Dickens or Victor Hugo, pushed realism up a notch, exaggerating for effect the terrible destinies of his characters, though there is little exaggeration in the descriptions of the Albufera's people. He is there also as a politician, to record and denounce.

The Albufera ("the little sea" in Arabic) looms large in the imagination of Valencians and visitors: an inland lake beside the city that brings birds, eels, and fish to the tables of the well-off. Today the Albufera is half the size it was in the fifteenth century, when Ausiàs March hunted duck with the king's falcons. With great labor, described in *Cañas y barro*, the residents of El Palmar and other lakeside villages have over the centuries filled in land around its shores to plant rice.

Not just the lake's size, but its quality has declined. It has suffered brutally from the waste of neighboring industries and from fertilizers on the fields that have encroached on its area. Nature park though it is, the poisons have reduced the frogs, eels, and fish. Otters are long gone. On a visit to El Palmar only a few years ago, we found a stench of decay floating through the village air: heaps of dead fish lapped gently against the sides of the narrow canals behind the houses.

---

199   *Ibid*, p.6.

Despite its decline, the Albufera is still Spain's biggest lake, home to some ninety nesting species of bird and a resting site for many more migrating species. Teal, pochard, egret, and several kinds of duck are common. The lake is little more than one meter deep and the traditional flat-bottomed boat is propelled by a pole (like Oxbridge students' punts) and a sail. The boats glide silent through the dense islands of reeds, where water-fowl and rats find sanctuary. Go at dawn or dusk, when the rays of the rising or setting sun give a metallic dazzle to the water. The lake is "blue and sharp as a Venetian mirror."[200]

The view from a boat on the lake is quite different from the view from the shore. There are still a few *barraques*, the characteristic steep-roofed houses of the *horta*, like an upside-down V, some with a little cross on top, though they are conserved mainly for tourist purposes. The Albufera is a place of optical illusion. In morning mist or evening haze, clouds and people walking on the shore seem to walk in the water upside down. Other boats appear to float above the water, slightly distorted. The lagoon is an "immense green metal plate, reflecting upside down the red and bluish hills cutting across the horizon."[201] The Arabs believed that the sun reflected in the mirror of the Albufera increased the brightness of the sky over Valencia city.

As well as becoming smaller over the centuries, the Albufera swells and shrinks according to the season. It is linked to the sea through three channels, the Perelló, Perellonet, and Pujol. From November 1 to January 1 the channels' lock gates are closed so that the waters of the lagoon rise and flood the rice fields around its shores. This is the season to imagine the Albufera in its past glory. The

---

200   *Ibid*, p 14.
201   *Ibid*, p.195.

water rises to cover some fifteen kilometers from north to south, from the edge of Valencia city to Sueca.

Rice

To return to paella, not just a national dish, but a meal for festivals and family events. At weekends, extended families pour out of the city to their second home, often little more than a hut in the *horta*, and spend the day in the country around a paella. It is a dish best cooked outside on a wood fire. Women may rest, too. Like barbecues in US suburbia, paellas are the domain of men (though these outdoor experts may well not scrub the dishes).

Paella is not the only rice dish. Over the last 200 years rice with whatever vegetables are available has been the staple midday meal of the poor. Often this is cooked in the oven with any kind of fish or with chicken or rabbit; or as stews, cooked in *cassoles*, baked clay pots. In the highland areas, the stews will have mutton or pork, perhaps game rather than fish, potatoes instead of rice. This said, the poverty of centuries in the highlands means that until recently pigs or sheep were eaten only on high days or holidays. Around Xàtiva, inland but not in the highlands, *arròs al forn* (rice in the oven) is a heavy stew, using rice but otherwise nothing coastal: chickpeas, pork, and sausages make it similar to the hearty stews served all over Spain under different names.

From this popular food culture, a number of dishes have been standardized into restaurant delights. *Arròs negre*, black rice, is striking, the color derived from squid ink. Chewy finely-cut squid is dotted through the rice. In *arròs del senyoret*, gentleman's/toff's rice, the prawns are peeled, the cuttlefish is chopped into small pieces, and the mussel shells removed, so there is no need for toffs to dirty their fingers. It's quite my favorite. *Arròs a banda* (rice apart) is rice cooked in fish stock. Its name comes from the custom of cooking the rice separately from the vegetables and fish. Often the two plates are served apart, too. In the fishing villages, it was and is a way of using the various small bony fishes caught in nets by accident.

Arròs amb crosta, rice with an egg crust, is typical of Elx and Oriola. Unlike any other rice dishes, this pork and chicken dish is finished off in the oven to give it a crust. *Arròs en fesols i naps* (rice in beans and turnips) is the most popular of the "wet" rice dishes, i.e., those with ample sauce. With pork, bacon, and black pudding, it is a heavy stew for a cold day.

Not everything is rice, though rice's fame rings louder. All along the coast fish stews, fried fish, dishes with shellfish (prawns, lobsters), with or without rice, can be found. Gandia is the home of *fideuà*, where vermicelli replaces rice. In the most luxurious versions, giant prawns, cuttlefish, and monkfish (*rap*), a large-eyed big-headed fish much prized in Spain, adorn the dish. The origin of *fideuà* is unclear, but may well come from the post-Civil War period when rice was expensive and from the Italian influence, always present through trade across the Mediterranean and especially so when Mussolini was a key ally of Franco.

White Blossom

Roughly, in terms of Mediterranean climates, Valencia is like Los Angeles; Barcelona, slightly cooler, like San Francisco. Valencia is hot and sticky in summer, and this is when people drink *horchata/orxata*.

It is to Jaume I the Conqueror that is attributed the story of a servant-woman who brought him an ice-cold drink. The king drank it down, allaying the humid heat of his first Valencian summer, and said *és d'or, xata* ("This is

Orxata bar, central Valencia

gold, girl.") And so *orxata* was named, the milky-looking
drink that is not based on milk, as it might seem, but on
crushed tiger nuts (*xufes* or *chufas*) and water. The tiger nuts
are cultivated mainly at Alboraia, just to the north of the
city. *Orxata* is not a drink to be consumed with food, but
a refreshment at any time of day. Buy your *orxata* not in a
supermarket carton, but freshly made at one of the *orxata*
bars or stalls scattered through Valencia that still survive the
onslaught of prepacked sugary drinks. It is served often with
fartons, slim glazed pastries.

Valencia's steamy heat means that, as well as cold drinks,
cold food is welcome. The most popular "strong salad" (not
just lettuce and tomato) is *esgarra(d)et*, similar to *esqueixada*
in Catalonia, consisting of strips of salted cod, black olives,
and roasted red peppers, soaked of course in olive oil.

Here's a Valencian three-word menu that will leave you faint with pleasure:

Esgarradet
Paella
Arnadí

Arnadí, a cake of sweet potato or pumpkin with almonds, is one of the many desserts with their origins in Arab times. Desserts vary according to area: almond cakes and tarts in the mountains, sweet potato cakes in the hills behind Sagunt, "gypsy's arm" at Llíria, the use of dates in Elx and Alacant. I have chosen Arnadí partly because it is a pretty word for the short menu, but also to write some paragraphs on almonds.

Almond trees are the first to flower on the hills in late winter. Their white blossom lights up the barren-looking slopes of stone and red earth. Jason Webster, in his beautiful book *Sacred Sierra* about a year on an isolated hill-farm (*mas*) inland from Castelló, explains:

> The first plant to come fully into bloom after midwinter, the almond is seen as a symbol of hope and the coming of spring. After the phylloxera disaster of the end of the nineteenth century, many local farmers moved from grapes to almonds as their staple produce, so that nowadays in February and March the hillsides south of the Penyagolosa are awash with delicate white and pink blossom, glistening in the low winter sun.[202]

---

202   *Sacred Sierra*, p.327.

Bitter almonds

When you stare up at the mountainside on a bright late-winter day, the almond flowers are not at first distinguished from the powdering of snow just 200 meters higher up the slope. Sometimes, so delicate a sight, the snow falls on the ground over the primroses and on the almond blossom itself.

Almonds certainly bring hope in this story. A tourist asked an elderly woman in a Valencian mountain village: "Is there anything special to see here?" The woman replied: "There are no wife-beaters here." Oh yes? We've heard this before, a typical *machista* denial of an all-too-common social blight in Spain (as elsewhere). The elderly woman went on to explain: "One day a woman went to the doctor with a purple swelling all round her eye. 'Whatever's happened to you, señora?' 'My husband beat me up.' The doctor told her:

'Listen, go to my almond grove, pick a kilogram of fruit, peel them, grind them, and make a special pudding for your husband with lots of sugar. I guarantee you: he won't beat you again.' Three days later they buried the husband." Bitter almonds contain cyanide. Sugar shrouds the taste. There are no wife-beaters in that village. A bittersweet story.

The almond theme leads onto Valencia's most famous sweet, *turrón* (*turró*), a post-dessert sweet for scoffing with coffee or liqueurs. Nougat or fudge are the closest translations. This is sold in the Christmas/January 6 season all over Spain. *Turró* is associated with Xixona, a small town half-way between Alacant and Alcoi. Here there is a *Turró* Museum, all the *turró* firms of Spain have their headquarters and turró manufacturers are the main employers.

There are two basic kinds of *turró*: *Turró de Xixona* uses crushed almonds and is soft, like fudge, and *Turró d'Alacant*, made of whole almonds, is crisp and crunchy, more like nougat but denture-destroying, not suitable for gifts to elderly relatives. The industry dates back to the seventeenth century and was popular among Europe's upper classes. Queen Victoria is said to have been a devotee.

Often on the table with *turró* are *neules*, another ancient dessert. *Neula* is a word with its root in the Latin *nebula* or mist, which gives an idea of the subtlety of this layered tube of brittle biscuit.

Mercadona

Fresh food markets are in life-or-death competition with the Valencian firm Mercadona. Changes in habits of consumption are encouraged so fast that even while supermarket success is closing the markets, a further change, internet-purchasing (e-commerce), is threatening the supermarkets. For now, Mercadona is still predominant.

Founded in the 1980s, taking off in the 1990s, in 2018 it had 24 percent of Spain's supermarket share, but the figure is higher in the *país valencià*. Throughout the state it employs about 75,000 people. It survived spectacularly well the economic crisis that started in 2008, and in 2017 it was Spain's most profitable company. Like Inditex, it is so successful that it spends no money on advertising.

What is Mercadona's secret? Its relationships with its workers and with its suppliers. In its internal culture, Mercadona refracts reality through a distorting lens[203]: its customers are *jefes* (bosses—Juan Roig, the real boss, is called the president); its workers are *gerentes* (managers). It selects young *gerentes* with a starting salary of 1,100 euros net a month, rising to 1,400 after four years (2016 figures). One should add that in Spain there are fourteen not twelve monthly payments a year. In these years of recession, when to be a *mileurista* (earn 1,000 euros a month) is an unattainable ambition for millions of young people, this is a good wage.

It is a "self-insuring company," meaning that it does not pay the Social Security for time off sick, but pays its *gerentes* directly. It compensates for this "privatization" of Social Security by paying the state system some 700 million euros a year. This means it can control the workforce with its own doctors, only giving time off for illness in the most obvious cases. Mercadona's absenteeism indices are no more than 1.5 percent. It also has a profit-sharing scheme and gives a sizeable Christmas bonus to workers who have behaved well through the year, i.e., hard workers who have not been sick or absent.

---

203   Much of my information on Mercadona comes from Jordi Évole's program on the chain, *El fenómeno Mercadona*, broadcast on La Sexta TV channel on November 27, 2016.

The work contract stipulates that you have to inform the company if you are going to meet with other Mercadona employees outside working hours and that you cannot criticize the company publicly. It is, of course, fiercely anti-union. No union organizer lasts long. Unlike most companies, which took advantage of the economic crisis to worsen conditions and lower wages, so that now most new jobs in Spain are precarious, Mercadona acted with a longer-term view. It has molded a loyal, better-paid workforce with job security. This security, however, depends on remaining docile, dependent, and controlled. Mercadona's success is based on erosion of the rights of its workers (sorry, "managers").

The company has also been in the vanguard in its relationships with its suppliers. It has 125 suppliers working solely for the company. This is big business: just its bread (tastier than that of most bakers) amounts to 110,000 kilograms a day. It demands "open books" of its suppliers, i.e., Mercadona can examine the books at any time. This situation of dependence allows the company to drive prices down. Prices may even fall to the cost of production, which happens in the case of fruit crops bought in advance.

Mercadona's supermarkets have cheerful staff (friendliness is mandatory) and cheap quality produce for the customer (the "boss"), no matter if the supplier goes broke, and no one is inclined to criticize them.

One Great Orange Garden

When James A. Michener was studying in Glasgow in the late 1920s, he took a summer job on a tramp steamer taking coal to Italy, then returning from Valencia with oranges for the marmalade factories in Dundee. At dawn on the boat's return trip, the young Michener was on deck, excited by the prospect of setting foot for the first time on Spanish soil. Before the coast came into view, "the offshore breeze carried to our dirty little freighter the odor of orange blossoms, heavy and pungent."[204]

When the boat halted off Burriana/Borriana, Michener noticed that there was neither harbor nor quay. How were they going to load the fruit? Soon he saw in the water enormous heads of oxen dragging barges laden with steel barrels full of oranges. A man swam beside each ox, one hand on a horn guiding it to the ship.

Once on board, the oranges were cut in half inside the barrels, which were filled with salt water. On the way back to Glasgow, the motion of the ship would prepare the oranges for bitter marmalade. I have not seen this method of soaking oranges in salt water validated in any history or recipe book, but Michener is quite definite about what he saw.

Michener himself went ashore on one of the barges pulled by swimming oxen. He was told this was a way of loading and unloading ships that went back to Roman times. Of the multiple foreign writers on the Spanish state, none has arrived so romantically, drawn by oxen. We have mentioned Joaquín Sorolla's paintings of oxen hauling fishing boats in and out of the water on Valencia's Malva-rosa beach. Their use was nothing unique to Burriana/Borriana. And framed on the wall of Blasco Ibáñez's house on that same beach is further confirmation of the use of oxen: this quote from *Flor de mayo*, his novel of the Cabanyal fishing families:

> To get the boats out, the oxen of the fishing community waded into the waves, beautiful blonde and white animals, huge as mastodons,

---

204   Michener, *Iberia*, p.7.

moving with weighty majesty and shaking their
large double chin with the supreme haughtiness
of a Roman senator.

To the south of the Xúquer, beyond the Valencian *horta*,
oranges are dominant. And when you enter the *país valencià*
from Catalonia in the north, you notice almost at once a
change: orange fields begin. As around Gandia to the
south, by Vila-real and Castelló oranges are the dominant
crop. New fields with new irrigation climb the stony, dry
hillsides. Even in 1949, oranges were everywhere. Rose
Macaulay wrote of the country between Vila-real and
Burriana/Borriana: "The country was now one great orange
garden ... Oranges, even in high summer, are piled on every
market stall in the towns, and in the panniers of the small
donkeys that smaller boys ride about streets and roads."[205]

Oranges are heaped high in the Mercat Central,
stacked in lorry after lorry for the long haul to northern
Europe (no boats or oxen now) and sold off stalls by the
side of the road. Local, fresh, a bargain, one thinks, and
sometimes they are awful cast-offs; but at other times these
mesh bags contain fruit of all different sizes, rejected by
the supermarkets because of their mottled skin, but tasting
wonderful. The best oranges stay in Valencia, a local saying
goes, true when it is true.

The sensual, intoxicating fragrance of orange blossom
reached Michener out at sea and fed the wild dreams of
Rafael at Alcira in Blasco Ibáñez's *Entre naranjo*s. Blasco
Ibáñez imbues the orange groves surrounding the small city
with Rafael's passion for Leonora, a bohemian opera singer.
He is listening to Leonora playing Schubert:

---

205   Macaulay, p.85.

> …through the open windows entered the breathing of the murmuring garden under the golden light of autumn, the spiced perfume of ripe oranges, whose faces peered out between the garlands of leaves.[206]

It is a sweet and intoxicating fruit, closely identified with Valencia, but the industry is relatively recent. This book has referred to two great booms in Valencia's Christian history: the Golden fifteenth Century and the building spree of the 1990s and 2000s. There is a third, less known and less obvious: the second half of the nineteenth century. This was when oranges took over from silk as Valencia's most profitable product. The opulent municipal buildings, the tree-filled squares and great bourgeois palaces, now mainly banks, on Carrers Barques or Pintor Sorolla and the fashionable shopping street Colom, are all products of the orange boom. Much of the money for the Eixample, with its *art nouveau* buildings, came from this wealth. Orange money was invested in industry, too, turning Valencia into a modern industrial town.

Between 1870 and 1936, orange production multiplied tenfold, especially in the plain around Castelló, where oranges replaced other crops, and around the River Xúquer, where dry land was irrigated. By 1910, orange exports ran at over half a million tons, mostly to Britain. They became Spain's principal foreign currency earner, important both in the Civil War and in the early years of the dictatorship. Citric fruit exports today are still a massive earner. The German supermarket chain Lidl dominates the market: in 2016 it bought 1,200 million euros worth of oranges, 87 percent of which was for export to Europe. The difference now is

---

206   Both quotes are from *Entre naranjos*, pp.139 and 228.

that the big chains that dominate the market, whether Lidl, Mercadona, or Carrefour, are driving production prices down. Today orange producers are in crisis. The supermarket chains, now distributors, intermediaries and vendors all in one, are raking it in. For example, in 2016/17 Navelina oranges were bought from the producer at 19 cents a kilogram and sold to the customer at 1.71 euros.[207]

In *Entre naranjos* there is a character Don Matías who exports oranges to England, which brings to mind Vicente Cañada Blanch (1900–93). Born in Burriana/ Borriana, where Michener came ashore, Cañada Blanch moved to London aged twenty to work in the Covent Garden fruit market. He became the main exporter of Valencian vegetables and oranges to the United Kingdom. Not just a businessman, in 1977 he founded in Greenwich the Spanish School (Instituto Español), now named after him. Cañada Blanch wanted the school to offer education "so that emigrants' children are not compelled to be waiters in London." In 1993, the school, property of the Spanish government, moved to the more central 317 Portobello Road, Notting Hill, where it thrives still, teaching in Spanish and English. This is not, though, free, universal education. Matriculation costs between £3,000 and £4,000 per pupil a year.

The Cañada Blanch Foundation also funds exchange scholarships between Spain and the United Kingdom and, in 1994, set up the Príncipe de Asturias Chair of Contemporary Spanish History (held by Paul Preston) and a Centre for Contemporary Spanish Studies at the London School of Economics. The Centre's seminars, library, and publications have become the main driving force in Britain for research into Spain.

---

207   *El Temps*, April 10, 2018, pp.25-7.

Thus, the Valencian orange trader became the principal Maecenas for both the education of Spanish children in London and the academic study of contemporary Spain.

The Friar's Kitchen

The Serra Calderona divides the provinces of Castelló and Valencia. Marked by rough escarpments and peaceful valleys, it is home to several religious communities. The Carthusian Porta Coeli, founded in 1412, is the most spectacular. As so often in the Spanish landscape, its intensely green trees and crops are set off against hills of bare rock. An aqueduct with eleven arches bears water to Porta Coeli's walled grounds. The notice before the huge silent buildings is severe: "The monastery cannot be visited. Respect its silence. Thank you."

What concerns us here, though, is the Franciscan Sant Esperit Monastery, very much of the world unlike nearby Porta Coeli. Sant Esperit lies in a pine forest in a secluded valley outside Gilet, where the mountain range stretches hilly fingers toward the coast. Gilet is a small town only eight kilometers by road from Sagunt and about thirty kilometers north of Valencia.

The Serra Calderona Nature Park feels the pressure of vacation homes and weekend outings from the city. Close to this hum but apart, both physically and philosophically, Friar Ángel runs a kitchen and dining room at Sant Esperit. He is a militant follower of the cooking revolution of Juan Altamiras, an Aragonese Franciscan who lived in the eighteenth century. Altamiras wrote a cookery book, famous in its time and rescued from obscurity in 2017 by a British food historian, Vicky Hayward, *New Art of Cookery, A Spanish Friar's Kitchen Notebook*. Friar Ángel explains: "The simple can be exquisite. Altamiras takes ordinary people's food and makes it delicious. He creates wealth from poverty and something spectacular from what is simple." He is eloquent, too, with a dig at modern Michelin-starred sophistication:

> Altamiras' cooking is an essential counterweight to the complexity of the cuisine that is so fashionable today, with highly complicated techniques and ingredients that are hard to get and expensive, out of most people's reach.[208]

Friar Juan Altamiras' cookbook was first published in 1745 and went through numerous editions over the following 150 years. Its 200 recipes, which he cooked for friars, travelers, and the destitute alike, were tasty and economic, as they used simple ingredients and local produce. As Friar Ángel puts it: "Simple cooking and few ingredients: great meals."

Altamiras' cooking revolution suggests a possible solution to the corruption of the earth and seas by pesticides and the ruining of people's health with fast food. The Mediterranean diet is famous today for its use of olive oil and fresh vegetables; but even as the diet becomes famous, fewer people eat it, as the *horta* shrinks and the supermarkets impose a ready-meal model.

Vicky Hayward summarizes Altamiras' importance for today:

> ...you can see how the patterns of what we call the Mediterranean diet took shape. For example, olive oil, replacing fresh or cured lard, runs right through the meatless recipes and one begins to see why there are so many Spanish techniques for cooking with it. The salt cod chapter also suggests

---

208   The quotes from Friar Ángel are from the newspaper *Levante*, November 5, 2017.

how Mediterranean classics came about when cooks played with humble, cheap ingredients on meat-free days. Onion, garlic, and tomato come into their own then.[209]

Anyone is welcome to eat Saturday or Sunday lunch at Sant Esperit, cooked by Friar Ángel in the style of Altamiras. This is not a guidebook, but I've recommended one hotel in Sagunt and warned against one bar in Calp. Why not end up praising a monastery meal, the eighteenth-century menu of the future?

---

209   *Ibid.*

Bibliography

I have biased this bibliography toward books in English, though several in both Catalan/Valencian and Castilian are included.

I have quoted often Rose Macaulay's acute, warm-hearted, and liberal *Fabled Shore*. Richard Ford's classic *Handbook* is erudite, witty, and releasingly ruder than I would dare to be. For modern Valencian politics, I have relied on the books by the journalists Víctor Maceda and Sergio Castillo Prats and, in general, on the daily paper *Levante* and the weekly *El Temps*.

Jason Webster's well-written detective novels featuring Max Cámara are a very accessible path into modern Valencia for the English-language reader. Rafael Chirbes' two late novels, *Crematorio* and *On the Edge*, the latter now available in English, are the best fiction on the building boom, the economic crisis, the destruction of the environment, and political corruption in Valencia.

GENERAL BOOKS

Edith A. Browne, *Spain*, A & C Black, London 1929 (originally 1910)

Jimmy Burns, *Spain, A Literary Companion*, John Murray, London 1994

Núria Cadenes, *Vine al sud! Guia lúdica del País Valencià*, Columna, Barcelona 2008

Sergi Castillo Prats, *Tierra de saqueo*, Cuadrilátero de libros, Barcelona 2013

Rafael Chirbes, *Crematorio*, Anagrama, Barcelona 2007 (A TV series based on the book is available in DVD)

Rafael Chirbes, *On the Edge*, New Directions, New York 2016

Havelock Ellis, *The Soul of Spain*, Constable, London 1929 (originally 1908)

Richard Ford, *Handbook for Spain*, Vol. 2, Centaur Press, London 1966 (originally 1845)

Antoni Furió, *Història del país valencià*, Tres i Quatre, València 2015

Joan Fuster, *Nosaltres, els valencians*, Edicions 62, Barcelona 2016 (originally 1962)

Théophile Gautier, *A Romantic in Spain*, Signal Books, Oxford 2001

Adam Hopkins, *Spanish Journeys*, Penguin, London 1993

Rose Macaulay, *Fabled Shore*, Hamish Hamilton, London 1949

Víctor Maceda, *El despertar valencià*, Pòrtic, Barcelona 2016

David Mitchell, *Here in Spain*, Lookout, Fuengirola 1988

Jan Morris, *Spain*, Faber & Faber, London 2008 (originally 1964)

John Payne, *Catalans and Others*, Five Leaves, Nottingham 2016

Sacheverell Sitwell, *Spain*, Batsford, London 1975 (originally 1950)

Ted Walker, *In Spain*, Corgi, London 1987

Jude Webber and Miquel Strubell, *The Catalan Language*, The Anglo-Catalan Society, Sheffield 1991

THE FOLLOWING BOOKS INFORM A PARTICULAR CHAPTER

Chapter 2

Eduardo Galeano, *Conversaciones con Raimon*, Gedisa, Barcelona 1987

Cees Nooteboom, *Roads to Santiago*, Harvill, London 1997

Chapter 3

Gerald Brenan, *The Literature of the Spanish People*, Penguin, London 1963 (originally 1951)

Ausiàs March, *A Key Anthology* (ed. Robert Archer), The Anglo-Catalan Society, Sheffield 1992

Ausiàs March, *Verse translations of thirty poems* (text & translation by Robert Archer), Barcino/Tamesis, Barcelona/Woodbridge 2006

Joanot Martorell, *Tirant lo Blanc*, Macmillan, London 1984. Translated & introduced by David H. Rosenthal

Arthur Terry, *Catalan Literature*, Ernest Benn, London 1972

Chapter 4

Marion Johnson, *The Borgias*, Macdonald, London 1981

Manuel Vázquez Montalbán, *O César o nada*, Planeta, Barcelona 1998

Chapter 5

Elena Moya, *La maestra republicana*, Suma de Letras, Barcelona 2013

Javier Urcelay Alonso, *Cabrera, el Tigre del Maestrazgo*, Ariel, Barcelona 2006

Jason Webster, *Sacred Sierra*, Chatto & Windus, London 2009

Chapter 6

James G. Ballard, *The Kindness of Women*, HarperCollins, London 1991

Arturo Barea, *The Forging of a Rebel*, Granta, London 2001 (and Chapters 13 & 14)

Karen O'Reilly, *The British on the Costa del Sol*, Routledge, London 2000

Sylvia Plath, *Letters Home*, Harper and Row, New York 1975

Anne Stevenson, *Bitter Fame*, Penguin, London 1990

Giles Tremlett, *Ghosts of Spain*, Faber, London 2007

Chapters 7-9 (Valencia city)

Vicente Blasco Ibáñez, *Arroz y tartana*, Plaza y Janés, Barcelona 1996

Henry Kamen, *The Disinherited*, Penguin, London 2008

Joan F. Mira, *València. Guia particular*, Barcanova, Barcelona 1992

Alicia Palazón & Artur Ahuir, *Valencia. History of the City. Walks and Routes*, Valencia City Council, Valencia 2007

Miles Roddis, *Valencia Encounter*, Lonely Planet, London 2010

Manuel Vicent, *Tranvía a la Malvarrosa*, Alfaguara, Madrid 1994

Jason Webster, *Or the Bull Kills You*, Chatto & Windus, London 2011

Jason Webster, *A Death in Valencia*, Chatto & Windus, London 2012

Jason Webster, *Blood Med*, Chatto & Windus, London 2014

Chapter 11

Jordi Garcia-Soler, *Crònica apassionada de la nova cançó*, Flor del vent, Barcelona 1996

Jean Genet, *The Thief's Journal*, Penguin, London 1976

Marià Sànchez Soler, *Alacant a sarpades*, Denes, Alacant 2003

Mariano Sánchez Soler, *Cuarteto de Alacant*, Denes, Alacant 2017

Isabel-Clara Simó, *Júlia*, La Magrana, Barcelona 1983

Chapter 13

Vicente Blasco Ibáñez, *La barraca*, Prometeo, Valencia 1919

Vicente Blasco Ibáñez, *Entre naranjos*, Circulo de Lectores, Barcelona 1998 (Introduction by Manuel Vicent)

Joan F. Mira, *La Prodigiosa Història de Vicent Blasco Ibáñez*, Bromera, Alzira 2004

Begoña Torres González, *Sorolla*, Libsa, Madrid 2018

Chapter 14

Antony Beevor, *The Battle for Spain*, Phoenix, London 2007

Burnett Bolloten, *The Spanish Revolution*, University of North Carolina, Chapel Hill 1979

Ed. Valentine Cunningham, *The Penguin Book of Spanish Civil War Verse*, Penguin, London 1980 (and Ch. 15)

Andy Durgan, *The Spanish Civil War*, Palgrave, London 2007

Angela Jackson, *British Women and the Spanish Civil War*, Warren and Pell, Barcelona 2009

Gaston Leval, *Collectives in the Spanish Revolution*, Freedom Press, London 1975

George Orwell, *Orwell in Spain*, Penguin, London 2001

Abel Paz, *Crònica de la Columna de Ferro*, Hacer, Barcelona 1984

Paul Preston, *The Spanish Holocaust*, Harper, London 2011

Chapter 15

Max Aub, *Field of Honour (Campo cerrado)*, Verso, London 2009 (originally 1943)

Max Aub, *Campo abierto*, Cuadernos del Vigía, Granada 2017 (originally 1951)

Max Aub, *Manuscrito cuervo*, Cuadernos del Vigía, Granada 2011 (originally 1955)

Miguel Hernández, *Poesías*, Taurus, Madrid 1975

Miguel Hernández, *Antología popular*, Col·legi Oficial de Llicenciats de Catalunya i Balears, Barcelona 1976

Instituto Cervantes, *Retorno a Max Aub* (catalogue), Madrid 2017

Gareth Thomas, *The Novel of the Spanish Civil War*, C.U.P., Cambridge 1990

Chapter 16

Francisco Candel, *Viaje al Rincón de Ademuz*, Nova Terra, Barcelona 1968

James A. Michener, *Iberia*, Corgi, London 1971 (and Ch. 17)

Carles Rodrigo Alonso, *El Rincón de Ademuz*, ADIRA, Ademuz 1998

Chapter 17

Colman Andrews, *Catalan Cuisine*, Atheneum, New York 1988

Vicente Blasco Ibáñez, *Cañas y barro*, Plaza y Janés, Barcelona 1977

Vicky Hayward, *New Art of Cookery, A Spanish Friar's Kitchen Notebook*, Rowman & Littlefield, Lanham (Maryland) 2017

Marion Trutter, *Culinaria Spain*, Könemann, London 2004

Jason Webster, *A Body in Barcelona*, Chatto & Windus, London 2015

Glossary

(words in Valencian unless specified cast.
for Castilian Spanish)

POLITICAL

Blaver (blavero, cast.) = "Bluey" (right-wing Valencian nationalist)

Compromís = (literally "Commitment") Coalition of Valencian nationalists, Greens, and some ex-Communists

Conseller = Councillor or Minister in the Generalitat

Conselleria = Department or Ministry in the Generalitat

Corts (Cortes, cast.) = Parliament

Diputació = Provincial Council

Furs (Fueros, cast.) = Charter

Generalitat = Government of the Autonomous Community of Valencia

ILP = Independent Labour Party

PP: Partido popular (cast.) = People's Party (Spain's main Conservative party from 1989 to 2018)

País valencià = Valencian lands

Països catalans = Catalan-speaking lands

Podemos (cast.)/ Podem = "We can" (new left-reformist party)

POUM: Partit obrer d'unificació marxista = Workers' Party of Marxist Unification

RTVV = Valencian Radio & Television

València en Comú = Valencia Together, Podemos/Podem's electoral front in Valencia city

Xeca (checa, cast.) = Stalinist secret prison during Spanish Civil War

GENERAL

Alacantí = A man from Alacant (feminine: alicantina)

Autobombo (cast.) = Blowing one's own trumpet, self-aggrandisement

Barraca = Typical high-peaked thatched cabin (plural: barraques)

Botànic = Botanical (as in Botanical Garden and the left-wing, post-2015 Botanical government)

Carrasca = Holm-oak

Carrer = Street

Cassola = Baked-clay cooking pot

Convers = A Jew converted to Christianity (usually by obligation or force)

És d'or, xata = This is gold, girl

Fossa comuna = Mass grave

Garrafons = Large white beans

Horta (huerta, cast.) = Market-garden (cultivated land around Valencia city)

Gerente (cast.) = Manager

Infanta (cast.) = Princess

Jefe (cast.) = Boss

Jueria = Jewish quarter

Kellys (cast.) = "Las que limpian," hotel cleaners, "chamber-maids"

Llotja (lonja, cast.) = Exchange market, auction-house

Lluna = Moon

Machista (cast.) = Male-chauvinist

Mas = Hill-farm

Mascletà = String of fireworks

Mercat central = Central market

Mileurista = Someone who earns a thousand euros a month

Neula/es = Wafer

País = Country, land

Polacos (cast.) = Poles (contemptuous word for Catalans and Valencians)

Serra = Mountain range

Sobremesa (cast.) = Talk at table after eating

Socarraet = Slightly burned bottom of a paella

Tallat (cortado, cast.) = Espresso coffee with a dash of milk

Trencadís = *art nouveau* mosaic

Trileros (cast.) = Pea-men (tricksters asking punters to find the pea under three cups)

Turró = Nougat

Xufes (chufas, cast.) = Tiger-nuts (for making *orxata*)

Index of Places and People

Ademuz (town), 321, 322, 326, 327, 331, 332

Ademuz, Rincón de (county), xiv, 220, 320-338

Agulló, Guillem (killed by fascists), 149

Al-Azraq, 30, 239

Alacant (Alicante), xi, xiii, xiv, 25, 26, 32, 63, 79, 80, 96, 112, 124, 129, 130, 177, 199, 200, 215, 221-233, 234, 238, 244, 245, 250, 251, 252, 254, 260, 275, 280, 283, 297, 298, 311, 314, 319, 342, 353, 355

Albacete, 159

Albaida, 25

Alberti, Rafael (poet), 313

Alboraia, 25, 220, 255, 352

Albors, Agustí, 236

d'Albret, Juan (King of Navarre), 72

Albufera (lagoon), 29, 45, 63, 109, 139, 220, 259, 330, 341, 344-349

Alcira, 25, 177, 220, 259, 359

Alcoi, xiii, 25, 30, 79, 220, 233-241, 244, 283, 355

Alcossebre, 93, 94

Aleixandre, Vicente (poet), 311

Alexander VI (Roderic de Borja), 38, 45, 64-69, 71, 72, 74-77, 90, 163

L'Alfàs del Pi, 114

Alfons "the Benign" (reigned 1327-36), 50, 51

Alfonso "the Magnaminous" (reigned 1416-58), 45, 46, 58, 67, 92, 167

Alfonso XI of Castile, (reigned 1312-50), 51

Alfonso XII (reigned 1874-85), 105

Algemesí, 25

Algeria, 63, 224, 232, 233, 301, 319

Almansa, 36, 37, 39, 220

Almenara, 297

Almería, 244

Almussafes, 25

Alonso, Dámaso (poet), 57, 58

Altamiras, Juan (cook), 362-364

Altea, 110-112, 114, 323

America, 37, 41, 50, 64, 72, 76, 78, 101, 171, 201, 206-208, 231, 232, 270

Amsterdam, 71

Andalusia, 21, 25, 218, 219, 314, 316

Andorra, xiv, 132

Andrews, Colman (cook), 135, 243, 345

Aragon, 16, 18, 21-23, 25, 29, 31, 36, 37, 45, 49-51, 58, 64, 74, 90-92, 101-103, 138, 171, 172, 292, 293, 301, 320, 322, 326, 336, 343, 362

Archer, Robert, 43, 44, 46, 48

Arroyo Cerezo, 329, 332, 335, 336

Arse, 4, 5, 11, 207

Asturias, 11, 361

Aub, Max, xiii, 172, 223, 288, 299-311, 314, 316, 317

Auden, W.H. (poet), 275, 291, 292

Avignon, 90-92

Aznar, José María, 129

Azorín (José Martínez Ruiz), 260

Bacardí, Facundo & Amàlia, 30

Balearic Islands, xiv, 202, 269

Ballard, James G., 109, 114, 321, 322

Balzac, Honoré de, 58

Barberá, Rita, 130, 158, 202, 207, 210-212, 266, 294, 295

Barcelona, xi, 23, 31, 35, 38, 40, 49, 52, 54, 64, 85, 91, 102, 120, 130, 135, 139, 144, 149, 169, 175, 181, 189, 192, 193, 218, 228, 240, 269, 281, 285, 289, 305-307, 322, 325, 328, 332, 339, 341, 351

Barea, Arturo, 110, 111, 261, 262, 296, 297, 309

Barjau, Perpetua, 300, 301

Baudelaire, Charles (poet), 49

Beaumont, Luis de, 72

Becket, Thomas, 74

Beethoven, Ludwig van, 101

Beevor, Antony, 284, 314

Beijing, 95

Bembo, Pietro, 63

Benavent, Marcos, 212, 213

Benedict XIII (Papa Luna), xii, 17, 67, 87, 90-93, 204

Benedict XVI (pope), 204

Beniarjó, 25, 44

Benicarló, 25, 89, 109, 155

Benicàssim, 25, 94, 109, 296

Benidorm, xiii, 25, 33, 95, 96, 109-111, 113-133, 163, 220, 230, 245, 250, 330

Benifairó, 25

Benimàmet, 192

Benissa, 25, 26, 232, 296

Benlliure, Josep (painter), 134, 178-181, 186, 187, 264, 271, 274

Benlliure, Marià (sculptor), 181, 186, 264, 271

Benlloch, 98

Bentham, Jeremy, 183

Berlanga, Luis García, 89

Berwick, Duke of, 36, 37, 39

Bilbao, 188, 189, 191, 249

Blair, Cherie & Tony, 200

Blasco, Rafael, 216, 217

Blasco Ibáñez, Vicente, xiii, xiv, 18, 22, 27, 62, 64, 145, 169, 178, 186, 257-271, 274, 280, 300, 304, 339, 343, 347, 348, 358, 359

Blasco-Ibáñez Blasco, Libertad, 267

Blasco-Ibáñez Blasco, Sigfrid, 269

Bolívar, Simón, 101

Bonet, Maria del Mar (singer), 240

Borja, Cèsar (Cesare Borgia), 64-66, 68-73, 75-77

Borja, Francesc (saint Francis Borja), 45, 73-78, 162, 163

Borja, Joan, 70, 72

Borja, Lucrècia (Lucrezia Borgia), 64, 66-70, 75-77, 156, 163

Borràs, Margarida, 343

Borrell, Frederic, 237

Borriana (Burriana), 220, 358, 359, 361

Borrow, George, 99, 100

Brassens, Georges (singer), 240

Brenan, Gerald, 43, 46, 47, 49, 53, 82

Bristol, 95

Brontë, Emily (poet), 140

Browne, Edith, 247

Bruges, 171, 172

Buenos Aires, 262

Bunyol, 34, 321

Burchard, Johann, 65, 66

Burgos, 24, 152, 308

Burns, Jimmy, 19, 136

Byron, Lord (poet), 101

Cabrera, Ramon (Count of Morella), xii, 99, 101-106, 320

Cadenes, Núria, 66, 222, 227, 237

Calatrava, Santiago, 64, 182, 186, 191-198

Calderón (mountain), 220, 331

Calderón de la Barca, Pedro, 52

Callixtus III (Alfons de Borja), xii, 17, 64, 66, 67, 76, 91

Callosa d'en Sarrià, 126

Calp, 109, 110, 112-115, 220, 250, 296, 364

Camps, Francisco, xii, 197, 200-208, 210, 212, 214-216, 219

Candel, Francisco (Paco), 89, 326, 331-333

Candela, Félix, 192

Canterbury, 74

Cañada Blanch, Vicente, 361, 362

Cañizares, Cardinal (Archbishop of Valencia), 160

Capa, Robert, 237

Capella, Ester, 201, 202

Capone, Al, 96

Caravaggio (painter), 173, 185

Carlet, 162

Carlos III (reigned 1759-88), 137

Carlos V (emperor, reigned in Spain 1516-58), 75

Don Carlos (pretender to the Spanish throne, nineteenth century), 99, 100-103, 105

Cartagena, Luis Fernando, 216

Casado, Colonel Segismundo, 80

Casanova, Giacomo, 136-138

Casas Altas, 321

Casas Bajas, 321, 322

Casas, Ramon (painter), 187

Castalla, 231

Castañer, Ramón (painter), 236

Castelló (Castellón), xi, xv, 50, 78, 89, 95-98, 104, 208, 220, 268, 288, 297, 304, 305, 319, 353, 359, 360, 362

Castielfabib, 322, 326, 329

Castile, 3, 13, 50, 51, 152, 231, 274, 312, 336

Castillo Prats, Sergi, 129, 130, 195, 200, 207, 208, 212, 218, 365

Catalonia, xii, xiv, 21, 25, 29, 31, 36, 45, 50, 75, 89, 101, 124, 131, 149, 162, 174, 180, 182, 203-205, 218-220, 231, 240, 241, 269, 282, 293, 297, 346, 352, 359

Catanei, Vanozza, 68

Catherine of Aragon, 171, 172

Cavanilles, Antonio, 182

Cervantes, Miguel de, 8, 52, 53, 58

Cervantes (town), 262

China, 122, 146

Chipperfield, David, 206, 207
Chirbes, Rafael, 78, 79, 82, 83, 117, 118, 218, 304, 319, 320, 365
Christie, Agatha, 64
Churchill, Arabella, 39
El Cid (Rodrigo Díaz), 23-25, 89, 99
Clement V (pope), 90
Clement VIII (pope), 90
Cofrentes, 36, 112, 220, 312
Colalucci, Gianluigi, 150
Columbus (Cristòfor Colom), 64, 72
Compte, Pere, 154
Conesa, Vicente, 132
Conrad, Joseph, 101
Constantinople, 56, 146
Coppola, Francis Ford, 200
Córdoba, 146, 237
Correa, Francisco, 214
Corsica, 45
Costa, Ricardo, 213, 214
Cox, 313
Cruz de los Tres Reinos (mountain), 336, 337
Cuenca, 320-322, 327, 329, 335, 341
Cuesta, Esteban, 216
Cuevas, Pedro (murderer), 149
Cullera, 93, 109, 111, 112, 220

Davis, Miles, 9
Dènia, 21, 78, 109, 112, 220
D'Este, Alfonso (husband of Lucrècia Borja), 69
Dickens, Charles, 58, 262, 348
Djerba, 45
Dostoyevsky, Fyodor, 262
Dumas, Alexandre, 262

Dunant, Sarah, 70
Dundee, 357
Durruti, Buenaventura, 280, 305

Ebro (Ebre), River, 3, 88, 101, 201, 297
Ebrón (River), 322, 325, 331
Ecclestone, Bernie, 205
El Cuervo, 322
El Palmar, 347, 348
Elda, 127, 231, 283, 312
Eleanor of Castile (Queen of Aragon, 1329-36), 50
Elx (Elche), xiii, xiv, 220, 243-251, 266, 297, 313, 351, 353
England, 37, 39, 52, 55, 101, 361
Erasmus, 171, 172
Escorna, Joana, 45, 48
Espartero, General, 90, 104
Espriu, Salvador (poet), 241
Évole, Jordi, 204, 356

Fabra, Albert, 205
Fabra, Carlos, 96, 268
Faulkner, William, 58
Felipe V (reigned 1700-46), 31, 32, 35-39, 101, 156
Felipe VI (king, 2014-), 31, 188, 190, 191
Fenoll, Ángel, 215, 311
Fernando VII (reigned 1813-33), 100, 140
Ferran I of Aragon (reigned 1412-16), 31
Ferran of Aragon (reigned 1479-1516, Ferdinand, Fernando, King of Spain), 13, 16, 64, 72, 73, 174
Ferrater, Carlos, 125

Ferré, Leo (singer), 240

Ferrer, Vicent (saint), 16-19, 61, 66, 92, 93, 161, 162, 185

Fielding, Henry, 58

Fitzgerald, John, 132

Florence, 67, 71, 231

Ford, Richard, 7, 136-138, 166, 185, 233, 247, 365

Fortuny, Marià (painter), 180

France, 11, 37, 78, 83, 102, 104, 120, 140, 181, 233, 282, 301, 304, 307, 310, 320, 323

Franco, Francisco (dictator), 8, 24, 32, 40, 41, 45, 72, 79, 80, 85, 96, 102, 121, 122, 137, 148, 158, 202, 213, 218, 221, 223, 225, 228, 232, 240, 241, 249, 250, 269, 277, 278, 280, 282, 285, 294, 295, 297, 302, 303, 308, 310, 312, 318, 321, 327, 328, 351

Fraser, Ronald, 303

Freud, Lucian (painter), 193

Friar Ángel (cook), 362-364

Fuster, Joan, 49, 92, 149, 202, 203, 268

Galdós, Benito Pérez, 15

Galeano, Eduardo, 41, 47

Gandia, xii, 27, 35, 44, 45, 52, 63, 64, 71-86, 93, 109, 111, 156, 220, 235, 275, 280, 297, 351, 359

Garbo, Greta, 261

Garcia Oliver, Joan, 288, 305

García, Sergio, 104

García, Yolanda (kelly), 230

Garcilaso de la Vega (poet), 52

Gaspar of Verona, 67, 68

Gaudí, Antoni, 139, 175

Gauguin, Paul (painter), 179

Gautier, Théophile, 151

Gehry, Frank, 188, 250

Genet, Jean, 221, 225

Genoa, 146

Gibraltar, 83, 108, 109, 113

Gide, André, 290

Gilet, 362

Glasgow, 357, 358

Glastonbury, 162

Goded, General, 305

Godella, 186, 187

van Gogh, Vincent (painter), 179

Góngora, Luis de (poet), 52

González Pons, Esteban, 214

González, Felipe, 11

González, Julio, 181, 182

Goya, Francisco de (painter), 142, 162, 163, 179, 184, 249, 271

Granada, 26, 33, 76, 77

El Greco (painter), 142, 173, 184, 193, 249

Greece, 101, 131, 319

Green, Nan, 295

Gregory XI (pope), 90

Griñó, María, 103

Guadalest, 126, 127, 220

Gualba, Martí Joan de, 57

Guardamar de Segura, 220, 249-252

Guernica, 221, 250, 300

Hannibal, 3-5, 8, 11, 14, 103, 207

Havelock Ellis, Henry, 35, 185

Hayward, Vicky, 362, 363

Hayworth, Rita, 261

Henderson, Gavin (Lord Faringdon), 80

Henry VIII, 171

Hernández, Miguel (poet), xiii, 241, 299, 311-318

Herrero, Hortensia, 150

Heston, Charlton, 23, 24, 89

Hewson, Sherrie, 123, 126

Hiddink, Guus, 148, 149

Himes, Chester, 26, 232

Himmler, Heinrich, 162

Hinojosa, Mariado, 293, 294

Huesca, 162

Hughes, Ted (poet), 115, 121

Hugo, Victor, 69, 70, 262, 348

Huntington, Archer Milton, 270, 271

Ibáñez, Paco (singer), 241, 316

Ibi, 127, 231, 233, 241, 244

Ibiza (Eivissa), 63, 112, 138

Ibn-al-Abbar (poet), 22

Iglesias, Julio (singer), 213

Illueca, 90, 93

Iribas, José Miguel, 122

Isabel I (Isabella, reigned 1469-1504), 3, 13, 14, 72, 172, 174

Isabel of Portugal (empress, 1526-39), 75

Isabel (queen of Spain, reigned 1833-68), 100-103, 105

Isabel de Villena (writer and nun, "Sor Isabel"), 45, 50, 58-61, 184

Italy, 36, 46, 63, 71, 74, 148, 180, 184, 357

Jackson, Angela, 295, 297

Jacques, Hattie, 123

Jaén, 316

James II (King of England), 39

Jaume I "the Conqueror" (king, Count of Barcelona, reigned 1213-76), xii, 4, 15, 21, 25, 29-31, 35-37, 50, 90, 99, 127, 161, 167-169, 173, 174, 321, 351

Jaume II "the Just" (reigned 1291-1327), 90

Jérica, 36, 311

Jimena (ruler Valencia, 1099-1102), 23, 24

Joan I (reigned, 1388-96), 92

John, Elton (singer), 213

Johnson, Marion, 70

José Antonio, 223, 327

Joyce, James, 58

Juana, *la Pastora*, 103

Juanes, Juan de (painter), 184

Juliana, Enric, xi, 202

Julius Caesar, 77

Kamen, Henry, 172, 311

Keats, John (poet), 316

La Núcia, 126

La Puebla de Valverde, 281, 310

Landete, 321

Lapland, 328

Largo Caballero, Francisco, 289

La Vila Joiosa, 127, 238, 239, 245

Las Vegas, 95

Le Pen, Jean-Marie, 233

Lebanon, 319

Led Zeppelin (band), 9

Lerroux, Alejandro, 269

Lisbon, 341

Livy, 3, 5

Lleida, 66, 161

Llíria, 96, 320, 353

Llorca, Fernando, 261

Lloret, 124

London, 71, 79, 104, 144, 171, 198, 200, 237, 273, 361, 362

Lope de Vega, 52

Lorca, Federico García (poet), 311, 314

Loren, Sophia, 23

Los Angeles, 351

Los Santos, 322

Lucía, Paco de, 9, 261

Macaulay, Rose, 4, 5, 7, 24, 28, 87, 89, 91, 92, 117, 161, 166, 167, 222, 223, 226, 238, 239, 245, 359, 365

Maceda, Víctor, 130, 202, 205, 208, 213, 215, 216, 242, 365

Machiavelli, Niccolò, 67, 70, 71, 73, 77

Macià, Antoni, 249

Madrid, xi, 11, 50, 52, 80, 101, 103-105, 119, 121, 124, 135, 137-140, 142, 149, 163, 181, 182, 187, 189, 201, 204, 210, 214, 218, 219, 222, 231, 250, 258, 260, 261, 267, 268, 270, 271, 274, 280, 281, 288, 290, 291, 296, 297, 299, 300, 303, 308, 311, 313, 321, 325

Malmö, 194

Malraux, André, 290, 301, 309

Manises, 27, 141, 166

Mann, Anthony, 89

March, Ausiàs (poet), xiii, 41, 43-53, 57, 58, 67, 75, 86, 207, 241, 259, 348

María Cristina (Queen Regent, 1833-40), 140

Maria de Castella (Regent, Crown of Aragon, 1432-58), 45, 48, 59

Marseille, 80

Martínez, Eva, 212

Martínez Monje, General, 281

Martorell, Isabel, 45, 52

Martorell, Joanot, 50, 52, 54-58, 60, 75, 135

Marx, Karl, 100

Mary Tudor, 171

Maxton, James, 292, 293

Mediterranean Sea, xi, 5, 15, 27, 34, 49, 50, 63, 78, 82, 83, 88, 91, 94, 103, 109, 111, 112, 120, 122, 125, 135, 140, 153, 167, 178, 182, 220, 224, 245, 253, 258, 272, 319, 336, 340, 345, 346, 351, 363, 364

Meliá, José ("Don Pepe"), 228, 229

Mendizábal, Juan, 100, 101

Merenciano, Marco, 148

Mexico, 301, 302, 304, 306

Michener, James A, 318, 319, 322, 323, 327, 357-359, 361

Milan, 67, 69, 195, 231

Milans del Bosch, Jaime (general), 142

Mira, Francisco, 252

Mira, Joan, 144, 155, 174, 267, 340

Miró, Gabriel, 224-226

Mislata, 22, 166, 183

Mitford, Jessica, 295

Montllor, Ovidi (singer), 15, 233, 235, 240-242

Montpellier, 31, 90

Montserrat, 162

Moore, Rowan, 192

Moraira, 112, 114, 232

More, Thomas, 171, 174

Morella, 36, 87, 98-100, 102, 104, 105, 220, 312, 321

Morocco, 14, 176

Morris, Jan, 245, 248-250
Morris, Sarah-Jane, 254
Moya, Elena, 98
Murcia, 11, 140, 200, 215, 244, 297, 342
Murillo, Bartolomeo (painter), 184, 185
Mussolini, Benito, 351

Naples, 46, 49, 52, 58, 67, 184, 186
Naseiro, Rosendo, 129
Navarra, 72, 102, 103
Nelken, Margarita, 280
Neruda, Pablo (poet), 311, 312
New York, 95, 148, 186, 194, 237, 270, 271
Nin, Andreu, 293
Nooteboom, Cees, 14, 23, 24
Novelda, 231
Numantia, 3

Ocaña, 314
Ojos Negros, 10
Oltra, Mónica, 211, 212, 218
Onil, 127
Oran, 80, 224, 232, 297
Oriola (Orihuela), xiii, 36, 50, 209, 215, 216, 220, 245, 253, 311-314, 351
Orpesa, 94, 109, 220
Ortega, Amancio, 150
Ortiz, Enrique, 215
Orwell, George, 291, 293
Oviedo, 197
Oxford, 80, 171, 349

Palencia, 314
Palestine, 15
Pamplona, 72

Papa Luna (see Benedict XIII)
Paris, 89, 186, 199, 240, 258, 271, 274, 299, 300, 301
Paris, Pierre, 249
Parra, Javier, 275, 278, 279
Parra, Mayte, 241, 242
Paterna, 27, 148, 166, 220, 275-279, 281
Payne, John, 16, 24, 34
Peníscola, xii, 67, 87-94, 99, 109, 111, 220, 323, 330
Penyagolosa (mountain), 220, 353
Penyal d'Ifach (mountain), 109, 112-115, 232
Perpinyà (Perpignan), 90
Pérez, Álvaro, *el Bigotes*, 214, 215
Pérez, Rosa, 277
Peset, Dr, 148
Picasso, Pablo (painter), 179, 182, 250, 271, 300, 308
Pinazo, Ignacio (painter), 186, 187, 198, 271
Plath, Sylvia (poet), 115-118, 121, 133
Polo, Carmen, 121
Polop, 120, 126
Port de Sagunt, 10-12
Portugal, 52, 72, 78, 314
Power, Tyrone, 261
Preston, Paul, 288, 361
Puebla de San Miguel, 331, 333-335
Puig Campana (mountain), 125, 126, 220
Puig, Ximo, 42, 99, 212
Pujol, Jordi, 218
Puzo, Mario, 64
Pyrenees, 335

Quevedo, Francisco de (poet), 52

Raimon (singer), 39-42, 45, 47, 213, 240, 241

Rajoy, Mariano, 201, 214

Ramón y Cajal, Santiago, 138

Real Madrid, 149

Requena, 32, 140, 321

Reyna, María Consuelo, 203

Rhodes, 55

Ribalta, Francisco (painter), 173, 179, 184

Ribera, Josep, *Il Spagnoletto* (painter), 36, 179, 184-186

Ribera, Juan de (the Patriarch of Antioch), 173, 174, 179, 241

Ribó, Joan, 146, 280

Richards, Marianne, 104

Ripoll, José Joaquín, 215

Ripollés, Juan, 98

Roddis, Miles, 4, 5, 139, 151, 191

Rodrigo, Joaquín, 9

Roig, Jaume (poet), 60, 61

Roig, Juan, 150, 356

Rome, 3, 5, 65, 67, 69, 73, 90, 91, 103, 131, 161, 180, 181, 186, 187, 271

Rosenthal, David, 52-54, 58

Roussos, Demis (singer), 9

Rouvigny, Marquis de, 39

Rus, Alfonso, 39, 213

Rusiñol, Santiago (painter), 178, 187

Ruzafa (Russafa), 22, 26, 175, 176

Sabiñán, 92

Sagunt (Saguntum, Morvedre), xii, 2-11, 13-17, 19, 21, 63, 115, 177, 220, 275, 283, 286, 297, 300, 310, 328, 339, 353, 363, 364

Salonika, 14

San Francisco, 207, 351

Sánchez Soler, Mariano, 221, 222, 227, 228, 244

Sant Jordi, Jordi de (poet), 46, 67

Santa Pola, 250, 251, 330

Sanz, Vicente, 199

Saragossa, 11, 23, 92, 142

Sardinia, 45

Savonarola, 64

Scipio Africanus, 4

Scott, Ridley, 200

Segorb, 220, 297, 301, 311

Segura (River), 220, 252, 342

Serpis (River), 44, 63, 80, 81

Serra d'Irta (hills), 93, 94, 220, 330

Seville (Sevilla), 50, 52, 64, 130

Sforza, Giovanni, 69, 77

Sicily, 55

Simó, Isabel-Clara, 237

Siqueiros, David (painter), 302

Sissi (Empress Elisabeth of Austria), 248

Sitges, 120

Sitwell, Sacheverell (poet), 243, 249

Smillie, Bob, 292-294

Solano, Wilebaldo, 285

Soria, 4, 329

Sorolla, Joaquín (painter), xiii, 179, 180, 186, 187, 257, 266, 270-274, 358, 360

Spain, xii, xiv, 4, 5, 7-11, 13-16, 24-26, 31-33, 35-37, 39, 41, 50, 52, 53, 57, 64, 70, 72, 76, 78, 79, 88, 96, 100-102, 105, 119-124, 128, 130, 136-138, 140, 142, 147-150, 162, 167, 171, 172, 174, 179, 181, 182, 184, 185, 188, 195, 197, 201,

203, 207, 208, 212, 214, 218, 221, 225, 227, 229, 231-236, 239, 244-246, 250, 253, 254, 257, 258, 260, 261, 269-271, 274, 280-284, 288, 290, 291, 293, 295, 296, 299, 301, 303, 306, 310, 311, 314, 317, 319-321, 327, 328, 334, 336, 344, 345, 349-351, 354-357, 360-362

Spencer, Diana, 39
Spender, Stephen (poet), 290, 292, 299
Stone, Sharon, 261
Strauss & Perlowitz, 269
Suchet, Marshal, 5-7, 38, 182, 187
Sueca, 63, 149, 202, 345, 350
Swift, Jonathan, 188
Switzerland, 132, 196, 206

Tabarca (island), 220, 224, 251
Tajo (Tagus), River, 341, 342
Tarragona, 7, 327
Tauroni, Augusto, 217
Tenerife, 194
Teresa de Ávila (saint), 59
Terry, Arthur, 44, 60, 61
Teruel, 9, 11, 31, 289, 297, 301, 310, 320, 322, 329, 335
Thatcher, Margaret, 11
Thomas, Gareth, 306, 308
Tirso de Molina, 52
Toledo, 19, 76, 152, 185
Tolstoy, Leo, 58, 262
Tormo, Concha, 329, 330, 334, 336
Torrebaja, 322, 326
Torreblanca, 98
Torres, Begoña, 257, 273
Torrevella (Torrevieja), 220, 253, 254, 313

Tortosa, 101-104
Townsend Warner, Sylvia (poet), 296
Tremlett, Giles, 119, 120
Trotsky, Leon, 302
Tunis, 22, 251
Túria, River, 26, 138, 141, 145, 164, 178, 204, 211, 220, 280, 321, 322, 325, 327, 331, 341
Turkey, 14

Unamuno, Miguel de, 260
Urban VI (pope), 90
Urban VIII (pope), 244
Urdangarín, Iñaki, 217
Utiel, 32, 140, 321

Valdelinares, 301, 338
València (Valencia) city, xi, xii, xiii, 5, 11, 15, 17, 21-26, 28-31, 33, 35, 37, 43, 45, 49, 50-52, 58, 59, 63, 64, 67, 78, 96, 105, 109, 121, 130, 134-198, 204-207, 209-211, 217, 220, 222, 224, 226, 229, 231, 241, 245, 259, 262, 265, 269, 273, 275, 280, 281, 283, 285, 286, 287, 289, 290, 291, 293, 294, 295, 297, 299, 300, 303, 304, 307-310, 312, 316, 319, 321, 322, 328, 332, 334, 335, 339, 340-342, 344, 345, 347, 349-351, 358, 360, 362
València (Valencia), Autonomous Community, Kingdom of Valencia, *país valencià*, xi-xv, 3, 4, 6, 15-18, 21, 22, 25, 26, 30-38, 40, 42, 45, 49-52, 62, 65, 75, 78-80, 83, 84, 87, 89, 92, 93, 96, 99, 100, 111, 113, 120, 137,

140, 149, 150, 156, 160, 167, 174, 179, 182-186, 188, 192, 198-203, 207-215, 217, 218-221, 223, 227, 233, 242, 244, 253, 254, 258, 259, 268, 270, 275, 277, 280-282, 284, 286, 296, 299, 304, 312, 319-321, 330, 331, 336, 339, 344-347, 352, 355-357, 359, 360

Valentino, Rudolph, 261

Valldaura, Margarida, 171

Valle-Inclán, Ramón del, 260, 261, 265, 274

Valverde, Justo, 132

Vargas Llosa, Mario, 43, 54, 58

Vázquez Montalbán, Manuel (poet), 70, 71, 73

Velázquez, Diego (painter), 52, 143, 179, 184, 185, 249, 271, 273

Veneto, Bartolomeo (painter), 76

Venice, 67, 80, 85

Vernet, 301, 302, 304, 307

Viana, 72, 73

Vicent, Manuel, 71, 258, 260, 264

Vila-real, 359

Villar de los Navarros, 103

Villena, 32, 36, 220, 231, 312

Vinalopó, River, 245

Vincent the Deacon (saint), 162

Violant of Hungary (queen, 1235-51), 30

Viver de las Aguas, 301, 304, 305

Vives, Joan Lluís (Ludovicus), 13, 169-172, 174, 343

Walker, Ted (poet), 25, 26, 245, 249

Webster, Jason, 102, 144, 158, 159, 176, 211, 341, 345, 353, 365

Wentworth, 104, 105

Wilde, Oscar, 262

Williams, Kenneth, 123

Williamson, Sid, 254

Wilson, Francesca, 295, 297

Wincanton, 58

Xàbia (Jávea), xv, 63, 109, 112, 253, 273

Xàtiva, 28, 32, 35, 36-40, 64, 66, 99, 184, 213, 217, 220, 311, 350

Xeraco, 82

Xixona, 127, 220, 230, 233, 234, 244, 355

Xúquer (Júcar), River, 111, 112, 259, 339, 341, 359, 360

Yahya al-Ghazal, 146

Zaplana, Eduardo, xii, 129-132, 199-202, 210, 212, 216

Zaragoza Orts, Pedro, 119-122, 124, 127, 128, 129

Zola, Émile, 257-259, 262, 264

Zurbarán, Francisco de (painter), 142